May 2007

First edition, vol. #1

Presented to ROBERT TRICE, one
of the great men of the aerospace
industry of his generation, with
respect and best wishes from
the author.

Wes Green

D1565895

MARKETING IN THE INTERNATIONAL AEROSPACE INDUSTRY

This book is dedicated with admiration and respect to my brothers and sisters in the aerospace industry around the world

Marketing in the International Aerospace Industry

WESLEY E. SPREEN

ASHGATE

Published by
Ashgate Publishing Limited
Gower House
Croft Road
Aldershot
Hampshire GU11 3HR
England

Ashgate Publishing Company
Suite 420
101 Cherry Street
Burlington, VT 05401-4405
USA

Ashgate website: http://www.ashgate.com

British Library Cataloguing in Publication Data
Spreen, Wesley E.
    Marketing in the international aerospace industry
    1. Aeronautics - Equipment and supplies - Marketing
    2. Aerospace industries
    I. Title
    629.1'0688

Library of Congress Cataloging-in-Publication Data
Spreen, Wesley E.
    Marketing in the international aerospace industry / by Wesley E. Spreen.
        p. cm.
    Includes index.
    ISBN 978-0-7546-4975-5
    1. Aerospace industries--Marketing. I. Title.

    HD9711.5.A2S68 2007
    629.1068'8--dc22

                                                                    2006033053
ISBN 978-0-7546-4975-5

Printed and bound in Great Britain by MPG Books Ltd, Bodmin, Cornwall.

Contents

List of Figures

List of Tables

Introduction

Aerospace is an industry like no other.

The product, the ultimate technological symbol of our age, has immeasurable impact upon culture, lifestyle, human relations, and international military and political events. Its manufacturing occurs in structures that are literally the world's largest buildings. Its employees, numbering in the millions, are among the best and the brightest. Its major companies are national metaphors of economic hegemony and industrial prowess.

The marketplace is implacably international. Aerospace is the largest industrial exporter of the United States, locked in a perennial struggle with Europe for dominance, as Asian participation grows remarkably.

Originally born as archetypical twentieth century capitalistic undertakings, the companies have become a fixation of national governments, which have promulgated laws and economic policies for their specific benefit or constraint, occasionally going so far as to acquire ownership.

Why Do We Need a Textbook on Aerospace Marketing?

Time-honored general principles of marketing apply to the aerospace industry. Venturing beyond these generalities, aerospace marketers need guidance that relates directly to the unique business practices of their specific industry. The industry is characterized by peculiar traditions, laws, government regulations, technology, financial practices, contracting practices, safety requirements, export controls, and international collaboration. The civil and military segments of the market co-exist, sometimes symbiotically, sometimes at cross-purposes, but with distinctly different marketing practices.

In spite of the diversity of the marketplace, the acquisition processes of major customers are highly structured and share many common characteristics. Airlines are all different, but their ways of evaluating, financing, and buying aircraft have fundamental similarities. Sovereign national governments are also different, but their ministries of defense tend to follow similar purchasing procedures.

The purpose of this book is to define aerospace marketing as a distinct subsidiary discipline, to consolidate knowledge and insight of this discipline in a single volume, and to impart useful information that can be utilized by current or future aerospace professionals in the pursuit of their careers.

Our approach to this study will take an inveterately international perspective. Whenever possible, we will compare and contrast practices in the major aerospace markets, the USA, the UK, France, Germany, and Japan. The industry has a distinctly international personality that will be reflected in our view.

As a reflection of its many unique characteristics, the practice of marketing in the aerospace industry is sometimes given names to differentiate it. Often called

Business Development or *Program Development*, the discipline remains intensely focused on the task of marketing and selling aerospace products. For purposes of clarity in this volume, we will retain the classical terminology of *Marketing*.

Sometimes modern aerospace firms separate the sales function into an organization called *Business Acquisition*, separate from Marketing. This is a valid and useful organizational structure, because the expertise and qualifications required for technical contracting comprise a separate specialty. However, the process of aerospace marketing is a continuum that has no distinct transition between the marketing phase and the sales phase. Therefore, as we pursue our study of marketing in the industry, we will regularly and unapologetically venture into subjects relating to details of the sales process.

Change is an essential characteristic of the aerospace industry. In an industry culture driven by continuous fast-paced metamorphosis of technology and perpetually evolving political realities, aerospace managers have learned that they must adapt to survive. Business management of the industry, including marketing, has changed in many ways from generation to generation. However, industry practices are a combination of historical context and contemporary circumstances, and it is often valuable to understand historical factors in order to better understand the present. Certainly some of the timeless business principles of the industry are as applicable today as they were in the 1940s. In our examination of marketing methods, we will give appropriate recognition to ideas that were developed in earlier times, but which remain relevant today.

The book is organized into four sections:

Part 1 presents an overview of the marketplace and explores two basic elements of the marketing mix, product and price. It explores market segmentation and stratification by individual product sectors, and evaluates the relative size and structure of the segments. Next is a study of the critical role of the product in the marketing mix, followed by an overview of aerospace pricing strategies and practices.

The aerospace marketer needs to have a basic familiarity with the multi-dimensional marketplace within which he operates. Chapter 1 provides a brief overview of the structure of the international aerospace market, the relative size of national markets, the principal market segments, the dichotomy between civil aerospace and defense aerospace, and the relative size of national aerospace industries. This background information provides a context for the chapters that follow.

In theory, aircraft design is driven by customer requirements. Chapter 2 describes the process by which customer needs are understood by the manufacturer's designers, and are eventually reflected in the final design of the aircraft.

Pricing is one of the four fundamental elements of the marketing mix. Chapter 3 discusses the microeconomic basis of costs and pricing, identifies common pricing strategies, and surveys various factors influencing pricing decisions and practices.

Part 2 identifies, describes, and analyzes tools and resources available to the marketer in the aerospace industry. We survey the use of sales agents, financing techniques, industrial offsets, political lobbying, brand management and advertising, air shows, operations analysis, strategic alliances, and techniques for dealing directly with the customer.

The international aerospace industry has a unique relationship with its foreign sales agents, who are often critical intermediaries with senior government officials and senior executives of airlines. These agents, generally selected because of their political connections, occasionally become involved in financial scandals or other kinds of notorious behavior. Chapter 4 provides guidance concerning the functions of foreign sales agents, and the process of selecting, managing, and contracting with them.

Financing arrangements are often an important discriminator in aerospace sales competitions. The aerospace industry has its own unique financial practices, and the marketer must have a solid general knowledge of these practices in order to compete effectively in the market. These issues are covered in Chapter 5.

A special peculiarity of the international aerospace industry is the practice of industrial offsets, the subject of Chapter 6, which are commonly required by international customers in major contracts. The customer views offset as a means to obtain technology transfer and employment for national industries. From the point of view of the marketer, offsets are an important competitive tool.

As a result of the size, prestige, and technological content of the international aerospace industry, national governments are often intricately involved in the affairs of the industry. Government policy influences subsidies, taxes, export promotion, import protection, defense buying policies, aircraft operating regulations, and many other aspects vital to the well-being of the industry. Chapter 7 describes how the American aerospace industry uses financial contributions to influence its government, and provides an overview of the many government agencies that promulgate policy of interest to the industry.

In common with other industries, aerospace companies carefully manage their brand identities and use advertising to reach their customers. Chapter 8 discusses concepts of brand management, and surveys the risks and benefits of advertising, the various target markets, the aerospace and aviation media, and the content of advertising.

Aerospace is but one of many industries that have trade shows. However, the drama and scale of air shows make them a unique phenomenon. They are a central aspect of the business culture of the industry. Chapter 9 describes the types of shows, how they function, and how marketers use them for the purpose of selling.

In its simplest terms, selling is the process of understanding what the customer needs, and convincing him that those needs are best met by one's own product. In the aerospace industry, operations analysis is the science of dissecting operational and financial requirements and developing solutions to them. Ops Analysis, if artfully done, will help customers better understand their own needs and open dialogues in which the marketer can propose solutions to the customers' needs. This is the subject of Chapter 10.

Moving in parallel with other major capital-intensive industries, aerospace is following a trend towards consolidation and international alliances. Chapter 11 traces the history of aerospace alliances, studies the motivation behind them, and provides a taxonomy of types. The value of alliances to the marketer is discussed.

Ultimately, the crux of the marketing process becomes the challenge of convincing the customer to buy one's product. Chapter 12 provides guidance on how to assess and respond to the peculiar requirements of aerospace customers. Step by step, the chapter describes progressive development of a relationship with a customer, beginning with information gathering, progressing through the collaborative definition of technical requirements, and culminating with protection of relationships after the sale.

In recognizing that aerospace executives must have a means of effectively utilizing and controlling resources in pursuit of objectives, *Part 3* focuses on practices and techniques for the management of marketing in aerospace, including the commercial contracting process.

Like other functions of the enterprise, the marketing discipline must be managed. Chapter 13 provides a nuts-and-bolts summary of management tools and processes widely utilized for marketing in the aerospace industry. Appropriate application of these tools enables marketing managers to add structure to decentralized activities that can quickly become chaotic if they are not monitored and controlled.

No sale is safe until the product is delivered and the money is in the bank. The initial competitive selection by the customer will come under immediate attack by competitors, and is always at risk in the interplay of financial, contractual, technical, and political factors following initial selection. Chapter 14 identifies risk factors that commonly cause sales to unravel and suggests strategies to protect the program.

The aerospace industry uses several standardized methodologies for soliciting offers, making aircraft selections, negotiating, and contracting. Knowledge of these processes is essential for the marketer. Chapter 15 describes the process applying to major direct commercial sales.

Venturing into the administrative framework that relates to aerospace marketing, *Part 4* examines national government practices and institutions pertaining to airworthiness standards and controls over exports of sensitive aerospace material and data. A distinctive aspect of the aerospace industry is the degree of government oversight. Government interest in the industry is attributable to various factors such as public safety of the product, national security implications of some aerospace technology, the economic importance of the industry, and the magnitude of government expenditures on aerospace products. Chapter 16 provides a brief overview of diverse ways in which governments become involved in oversight and control of the industry.

During the first century of its existence, the aerospace market has evolved at the speed of the technology upon which it is based. The second century will be characterized by the same rapid rate of change. Aerospace firms will adapt to the new market characteristics in order to survive. Chapter 17 takes the risk of attempting to project the future of the aerospace business in general, and the marketing discipline in particular.

PART 1
The Aerospace Market and its Basic Elements

Chapter 1

The Aerospace Market:
Supply, Demand, and Segmentation

The market for aerospace goods and services consists of buyers and sellers who create the basic market forces of supply and demand. Marketing, a function of the supply side of the market, is a discipline that attempts to influence buying decisions by the demand side.

In any industry, an effective marketing professional must have a comprehensive understanding of the market in which he or she is working. The purpose of this initial chapter is to provide a brief overview of the aerospace marketplace, by identifying the principal categories of products and customers in the industry, and by identifying some of the major players on the supply side.

Principal Product Segments and Customer Categories

As is the case in any marketplace, the aerospace industry and marketplace are diverse, multi-dimensional spaces. They are by no means compartmentalized, and do not readily lend themselves to classification in well-defined segments.

Part of the problem with defining segments is that the market can be stratified or defined in so many ways. We can identify segments based upon the size of the aircraft, such as airliners, commuter transports, business jets, and general aviation airplanes. Alternatively, we can divide the market into two broad categories of civil products and military products, or by the technological nature of the products, such as avionics, propulsion systems, structural components, hydraulic systems, and flying vehicles. We can divide the market into products intended for outer space and products that operate within the earth's atmosphere. The choices are endless.

One of the issues with any arbitrary system of classification is that most delineations between the categories tend to be ambiguous, and that many products fit into several categories. Obvious examples are that much equipment is used on both military and civil aircraft, and that some equipment is used for space applications as well as conventional aerospace.

Regardless of these limitations, it is evident that the aerospace industry and marketplace is divided into natural major segments. The firms in these segments share common affinities, and governments and economic observers use the segments as practical means of classifying firms and measuring market activity.

The US Department of Commerce (US DoC) uses Standard Industrial Classification (SIC) codes to categorize the industrial activity of all firms in the United States. In this system, the SIC codes are four-digit classifications that are sub-categories of three-digit industry groups of a broader nature. The DoC considers most aerospace activity to fall with industry groups 372, *Aircraft and Parts*, and 376, *Guided Missiles and Space Vehicles and Parts*. The specific SIC codes are shown below. Also shown are corresponding North American Industrial Classification System (NAICS) codes that have recently come into use by the US Office of Management and Budget.

Table 1.1 Aerospace classification codes

SIC	Industry Segment	NAICS
3721	Aircraft	336411
3724	Aircraft Engines	336412
3728	Aircraft Parts	336413
3761	Guided Missiles and Space Vehicles	226414
3764	Space Vehicle Propulsion Units	336415
3769	Guided Missile and Space Vehicle Parts	336419

These broad categories are further refined in other systems of classification, notably by the industry itself. The following breakdown by major product categories and subcategories is typical.

Table 1.2 Aerospace product categories

Category	Products
Military Fixed-Wing Aircraft	Attack
	Bombers
	Cargo/Transport/Refueling
	Early Warning
	Electronic Warfare
	Fighters
	Observation
	Patrol/ASW
	Reconnaissance
	Research/Test Bed
	Training
	Utility
Commercial Fixed-Wing Aircraft	Narrowbody Turbofans
	Widebody Turbofans
	Turboprops

Rotary-Wing Aircraft	Naval
	Scout/Attack
	Tiltrotor
	Training
	Transport
	Utility
Business & General Aviation Aircraft	Turbofan
	Turboprop
	Reciprocating Engine Powered
Gas-Turbine Engines	
Unmanned Aerial Vehicles & Drones	
Space/Launch Vehicles	Manned Systems
	Unmanned Systems
Missiles	Air-to-Air
	Air-to-Surface
	Anti-Armor
	Anti-Ballistic
	Anti-Ship
	Anti-Submarine
	Surface-to-Air
	Surface-to-Surface

Note that this particular classification includes engines, but does not include aerospace electronics, commonly called avionics, or other items of aerospace equipment such as landing gear, hydraulics, control systems, electrical systems, environmental control systems, and aircraft interiors. The value of these product lines is a significant part of the overall aerospace market, and although the firms sometimes classify themselves as members of other industries, such as the electronics industry, they also have a strong identity as part of the aerospace market. The classification also omits aircraft maintenance, repair, and overhaul activities, which are an important segment of the market in terms of transaction value and number of people employed.

Another means of describing market segments involves stratifying the market into tiers. With this approach, the prime contractor, who contracts to deliver the completed aerospace product to the final customer, is at the top of the hierarchy. Below him are subordinate tiers of suppliers that feed intermediate products into the manufacturing process. Buying and selling activities occur at each transition from one tier to the next. This tiered structure is a widely recognized characteristic of the aerospace market, but is imprecise and of limited usefulness in terms of establishing meaningful identification of market segments.

Table 1.3 Contract tiers

Contractual Tier	Characteristics
Prime Contractors	Design, develop, and assemble complete systems
Major Subcontractors	Perform assembly or manufacture of major components of systems
Second Tier Subcontractors	Manufacture subassemblies
Third Tier Subcontractors	Manufacture components
Fourth Tier Subcontractors	Manufacture parts or perform specialized processes

How do the various market segments compare in terms of size and economic importance?

In the European aerospace market, we find that in recent years approximately 45 per cent of value consisted of sales of complete aircraft, and of these complete aircraft, approximately three-quarters of the value was attributable to civil aircraft. The other segments, in declining order of importance, were maintenance, engines, equipment, space, aerostructures, and missiles.

The corresponding data for the American aerospace industry, broken down on a somewhat different basis, shows that sales of complete aircraft comprise approximately 50 per cent of the total market, and that the distribution between civil and military aircraft is roughly even over the long term, although short-term market conditions greatly affect the relative balance. Following the end of the Cold War, in the 1990s demand for military aircraft dropped precipitously, particularly in Europe and Russia. However, American purchases of defense equipment began to rise again following 2001 as American military engagements in Afghanistan and Iraq placed new emphasis on national defense. Demand for civil aircraft is notoriously cyclical, following broader movements of international economic cycles. Airline demand and profits have been affected by widely felt exogenous factors such as petroleum price shocks and terrorist activities, and declines in airline demand are quickly manifested as declines in orders for civil transports.

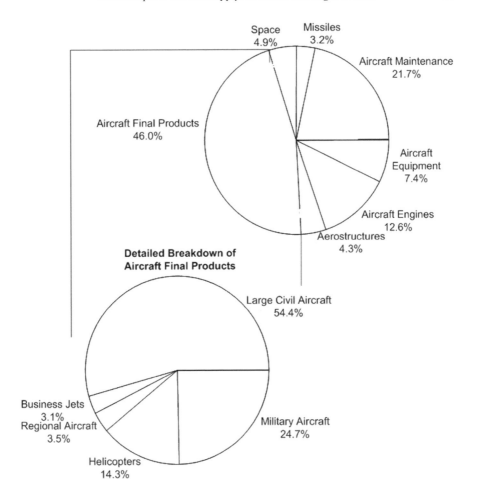

Figure 1.1 Breakdown of relative values of European aerospace industry segments

Source: The AeroSpace and Defence Industries Association of Europe, ASD.

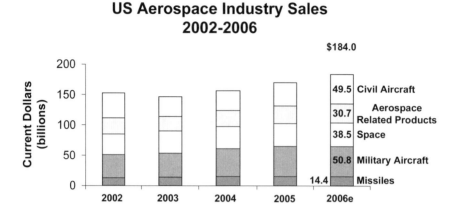

Figure 1.2 Comparative values of American aerospace industry segments
Source: Aerospace Industries Association.

Probably the most visible aerospace segment is the civil passenger airliner category. As the data shows, this segment is relatively more important in Europe, where decline in military spending in the post-Cold War era has been pronounced. In the United States, where high levels of defense spending have persisted, and where exports of military aircraft are promoted aggressively, the value of production for military aircraft continues to exceed production of civil aircraft.

Demand for civil transport aircraft, which is derived from economic wealth and geographical factors, continues to grow. The largest market remains North America, where expansive territory combines with a large, relatively rich population to create strong demand for air travel. The second largest market is Europe, where large populations of rich consumers favor development of airlines. The third largest market, significantly smaller than the two leaders, but growing rapidly, is Asia, where air travel has historically been restricted by the relatively low disposable income of populations outside Japan. Air travel has grown in cadence with the rapid economic development of the region. Airbus and Boeing anticipate that growing Asian wealth, combined with the vast populations and great geographical expanses of Asia, will create a strong future market for commercial aircraft sales.

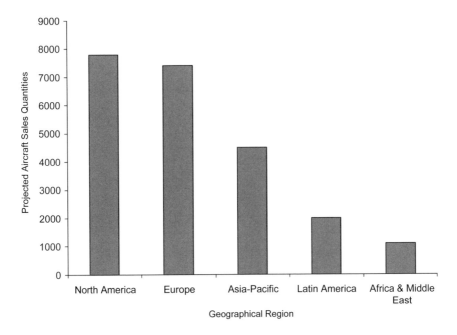

Figure 1.3 Passenger aircraft deliveries by region
Note: North America has long been the biggest market for commercial aircraft, followed by Europe. However, the Asian market is growing quickly.
Source: Airbus.

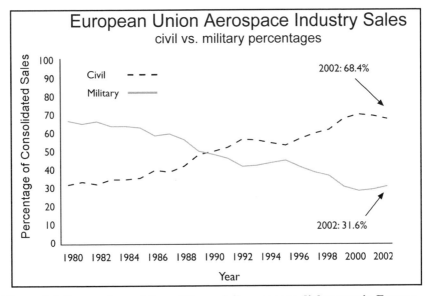

Figure 1.4 Comparison of the military-civil aerospace dichotomy in Europe
Source: The AeroSpace and Defense Industries Association of Europe, ASD.

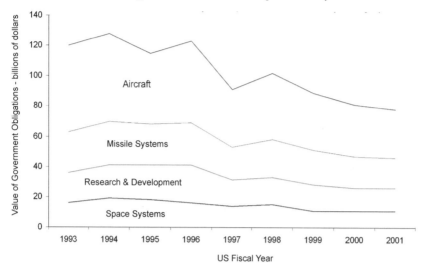

**Figure 1.5 Breakdown of the US military aerospace industry into major
components**
Source: US Department of Defense.

The military aircraft segment of the aerospace market has several striking
characteristics. First, in terms of value it is highly concentrated among a few
countries, principally the United States, Europe, Russia, Japan, and China. Secondly,
it is highly diverse, encompassing a vast array of specialized systems.

The general category of military aircraft is very broad and somewhat imprecise.
Some military types, particularly transports and utility helicopters, have been
certified by civil airworthiness authorities and have been sold in commercial markets
in slightly modified configuration.

The mix of military aircraft types operated by national armed forces varies
dramatically from country to country. At one extreme are the small number of
countries with strategic military roles, notably the United States, the United
Kingdom, Russia, and China, who possess heavy bombers, intercontinental ballistic
missiles, aerial refueling tankers, airborne early warning radars, and other strategic
aeronautic systems. Typical more-or-less industrialized nations generally operate a
more limited variety of aircraft, principally limited to fighters, medium transports,
trainers, and helicopters. The poorest nations likewise attempt to maintain small
inventories of fighters, transports, trainers, and helicopters, but they are often out of
date and of limited quantity.

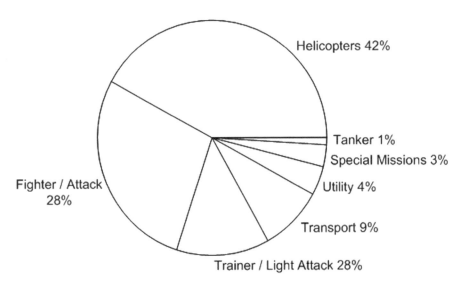

2004 Active Western Military Aircraft Fleet
Total 39,087

Helicopters 42%

Tanker 1%

Special Missions 3%

Fighter / Attack 28%

Utility 4%

Transport 9%

Trainer / Light Attack 28%

Figure 1.6 Breakdown of the military aircraft market by aircraft types
Note: This breakdown is by quantities of aircraft rather than by value. In terms of value, the share of fighters, for example, is much greater.
Source: AeroStrategy.

The Supply Side: Characteristics of Major Aerospace Firms

The engine behind the development of worldwide aerospace industrial capability has been, of course, demand for aerospace products. Consistent year-to-year increases in the planet's economic wealth, combined with advancing capabilities of aircraft of every sort, have produced a relentless growth in demand. Virtually every nation has an operating aviation infrastructure and is a consumer of air transportation. Most nations are also consumers of military aircraft and space technologies, and many nations at even modest levels of economic development have established nascent aerospace manufacturing capability as an industrial strategy for acquiring familiarity with advanced manufacturing technologies.

The global aerospace industry only recently celebrated the anniversary of the first century of existence. In spite of this relatively brief lifetime, the industry has a fascinating history that has progressed from initial flights in rudimentary wooden biplanes to manned exploration of outer space. As technology has advanced, the business structures of the firms themselves have evolved from artisans' workshops to enormous multinational corporations. The history of the aerospace industry is a fascinating subject, but is beyond the immediate scope of this chapter, which will limit itself to a brief survey of the firms in their modern form.

If we compare aerospace industrial activity based upon national identities of the participants, we immediately note that American aerospace sales are vastly greater than other national competitors. In recent years, aerospace sales from the United States were roughly twice the total of the European Economic Community. The three largest individual producers in the EEC were the UK, France, and Germany. In fifth place internationally was Canada, followed closely by Japan.

Several notable countries are not included in the top group, but are important nonetheless. Russia is a major designer and manufacturer of world-class military aircraft, and has historically been an important producer of civil transport aircraft. The Russian aerospace industry is undergoing a period of economic transition to a capitalist economy, and will certainly eventually claim a position as a major business presence in the international industry. China's aerospace industry is the focus of much political and financial support by its national government, and is beginning to design and produce credible aircraft and space systems that eventually will rise to the level of the international competition. Brazil has taken a leading position in the commuter airliner segment of the industry. India has developed an extensive domestic aerospace industry that aspires to compete internationally.

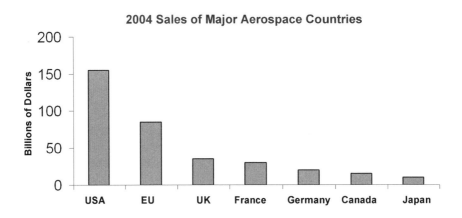

Figure 1.7 The largest national aerospace industries
Source: Society of Japanese Aerospace Companies.

If we examine the individual firms that constitute the industry, we are not surprised to find that they are very large corporations, with sales of many billions of dollars. Reflecting American dominance of the industry, most of the biggest companies are from the United States, but European firms EADS, BAE Systems, Finmeccanica, and Rolls-Royce are also among the top ten. The following ranking is drawn from the 2006 edition of The Forbes 2000, a comprehensive list of the world's biggest and most powerful companies, as measured by a composite ranking for sales, profits, assets, and market value.

Table 1.4 The largest international aerospace companies

Rank	Name	Country	Industry	Sales ($bil)	Profits ($bil)	Assets ($bil)	Market value ($bil)
93	Boeing	United States	Aerospace & defense	54.85	2.56	60.06	59.58
152	EADS	Netherlands	Aerospace & defense	43.09	1.40	76.77	29.14
182	Lockheed Martin	United States	Aerospace & defense	37.21	1.83	27.74	31.78
210	Northrop Grumman	United States	Aerospace & defense	30.72	1.40	34.21	22.27
259	BAE Systems	United Kingdom	Aerospace & defense	18.93	0.95	32.48	23.67
267	General Dynamics	United States	Aerospace & defense	21.24	1.46	18.75	24.81
306	Raytheon	United States	Aerospace & defense	21.89	0.87	24.38	19.34
446	Finmeccanica	Italy	Aerospace & defense	12.18	0.71	28.00	9.24
492	Rolls-Royce	United Kingdom	Aerospace & defense	11.35	0.60	15.26	13.72
641	L-3 Communications	United States	Aerospace & defense	9.44	0.51	11.59	9.93
716	Thales	France	Aerospace & defense	13.96	0.27	14.46	7.84
913	Dassault Aviation	France	Aerospace & defense	4.69	0.42	8.69	7.78
942	Bombardier	Canada	Aerospace & defense	16.41	-0.09	19.45	4.48
1067	Embraer	Brazil	Aerospace & defense	3.85	0.47	5.23	7.26
1129	Goodrich	United States	Aerospace & defense	5.40	0.26	6.45	5.15
1157	Rockwell Collins	United States	Aerospace & defense	3.56	0.41	3.11	9.16
1307	Precision Castparts	United States	Aerospace & defense	3.40	0.32	3.58	7.11
1751	Singapore Technologies	Singapore	Aerospace & defense	2.01	0.24	2.69	5.49

Source: Forbes.com, The Forbes 2000, March 2006.

Virtually all of the largest aerospace firms are the product of industry consolidations that have swept the industry in all countries in recent decades.

Following the end of the Cold War, the US aerospace industry underwent a period of accelerated mergers and consolidations as new technology and market conditions demanded investments and resources beyond the capacity of many of the relatively small historic companies. Firms merged to consolidate their resources, and by the end of the twentieth century, the American aerospace industry was dominated by two enormous firms, Boeing and Lockheed Martin. The second echelon of the US market is occupied by Northrop Grumman, Raytheon, and General Dynamics, firms whose considerable size would make them market leaders in any national market except the United States.

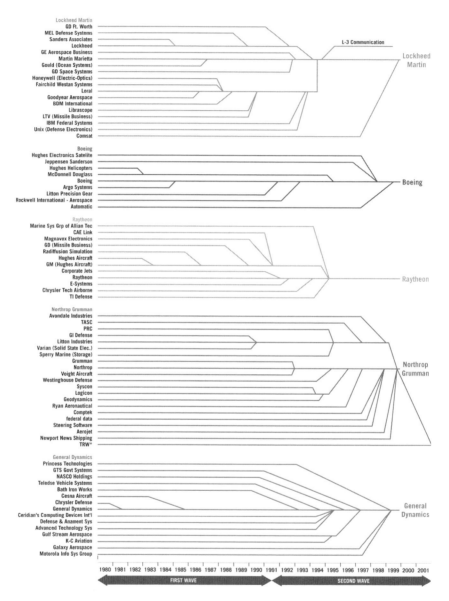

Figure 1.8 Historical trends of consolidation in the American aerospace industry
Note: Consolidation in the American aerospace industry accelerated in the 1990s.
Source: US Government, 'Final Report of the Commission on the Future of the United States Aerospace Industry'.

In Europe, the trend towards consolidation has also been exceptionally aggressive, as the multitude of small national companies have combined into small numbers of national champions, who have in turn merged across international frontiers to create a new phenomenon, the pan-national aerospace firm with a distinct European identity.

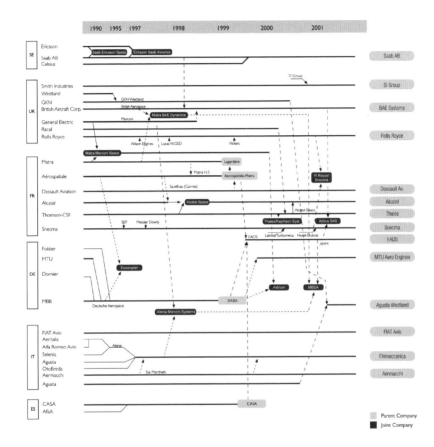

Figure 1.9 Consolidation of the European aerospace industry
Note: The European aerospace industry, like its American counterpart, underwent a period of massive consolidation in the 1990s.
Source: The AeroSpace and Defence Industries Association of Europe, ASD.

Other countries that have a major presence in the international aerospace market are Canada, Japan, Brazil, and Russia.

Canada has a diversified aerospace industry with notable involvement in commuter aircraft, business aircraft, helicopters, flight simulators and advanced gas turbine engines. Led by Bombardier's sales of regional jets, airframes accounted for almost half of Canadian industry revenue in 2003, propulsion 22 per cent, and the balance shared between defense electronics (10 per cent), avionics (7 per cent), space (3 per cent) and others.

Approximately 60 per cent of the companies active in the aerospace industry in Canada are predominantly foreign-owned. Prominent examples are Pratt & Whitney Canada and Bell Helicopter Canada.

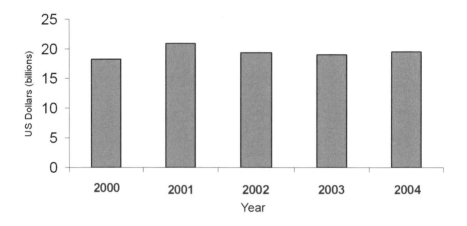

Figure 1.10 Canadian aerospace industry sales
Note: Sales growth, driven primarily by Bombardier, has been dramatic in recent years.
Source: AIAC.

The Japanese aerospace industry is dominated by Mitsubishi, Kawasaki, Fuji, and Ishikawajima-Harima, which together generate approximately two-thirds of overall industry sales. A unique feature of the Japanese industry is that it has significant sales to the well-funded Japan Defense Agency, but exports no defense equipment because of self-imposed restrictions of Japanese law. Most Japanese aerospace exports are generated by Japanese industrial participation as risk-sharing partners in international civil programs. Industrial links between Japan and the United States are particularly strong in the aerospace industry.

Brazil's aerospace industry is overwhelmingly dominated by Empresa Brasileira de Aeronautica, or Embraer, which competes directly with Canada's Bombardier for control of the regional jet market segment. In recent years Embraer has attempted to diversify into defense aerospace, which now represents approximately 20 per cent of annual sales.

Russia has a long an illustrious aerospace history that rivals its Western competitors in Europe or the United States. During the post-World War II era and the ensuing Cold War the Russian aerospace industry supplied enormous quantities of military and civil aircraft to customers within the Soviet Bloc and within the Soviet sphere of influence overseas. Russian civil aerospace has not been successful in international competition since the end of the Cold War, but exports of military aircraft and equipment have continued at respectable levels. There is no doubt that Russia possesses vast resources of aerospace technology, and the country is expected to re-establish itself as a major international competitor after the painful process of reconversion to the competitive international market system is complete.

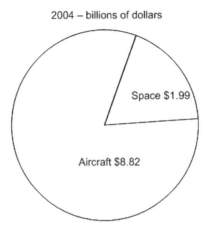

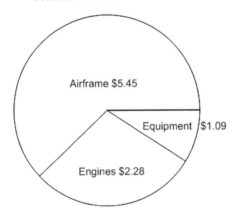

Figure 1.11 Japanese aerospace industry sales
Note: The Japan Defense Agency is by far the biggest customer for the domestic aerospace industry.
Source: Society of Japanese Aerospace Companies.

Since the time of the break-up of the Soviet Union in the 1990s, the aerospace industry of Ukraine has existed independently while continuing historical cooperation with Russian industry. Ukraine's three major aerospace firms are the Antonov aircraft design bureau in Kiev; the Ivchenko Progress aircraft engine design bureau, with its companion manufacturing partner Motor-Sich, both located in Zaporozhye; and the Yuzhnoye rocket design bureau and its companion Yuzhmash Production Association, both located in Dnepropetrovsk.

Table 1.5 Revenues of major Russian aerospace companies in 2005 (million \$)

Company	Revenues
Aircraft Industry	
Sukhoi Company (JSC)	561.91
Irkut Corporation*	711.69
MiG Russian Aircraft Corporation	245.68
Sokol aircraft building plant (Nizhny Novgorod)	356.92
Total	**1876.20**
Helicopter Industry	
Kazan Helicopter Plant	211.55
Ulan-Ude Aviation Plant	199.66
Rostvertol Public Limited Company	166.14
Mil Helicopter Plant (Moscow)	46.56
Total	**623.91**
Engines	
MMPP Salut	402.61
Ufa MPO	369.42
NPO Saturn	306.27
Perm Engine Company	232.20
Total	**1310.50**

* Irkut Corporation data (2004-2005) according to IFRS

Source: Centre for Analysis of Strategies and Technologies (CAST) Moscow, Russia 119334 Leninsky prospect 45, office 480, phone/fax: (+7-495) 775-0418. www.mdb.cast.ru.

Chapter 2

The Product

In the classical study of marketing, the design of the product itself is recognized as one of the four critical elements of the marketing mix: product, price, placement, and promotion. In the aerospace industry, this importance attached to the product certainly is appropriate.

As is typically the case with products of all types, including consumer goods, aircraft and aerospace products tend to follow a life cycle that can be divided into more or less identifiable phases. Because of the exceptional technological content of aerospace products, the product lifetime is greatly influenced by the progression of technology and the product obsolescence that results. This obsolescence is most often felt by customers as new products in the marketplace offer better economic returns or superior performance.

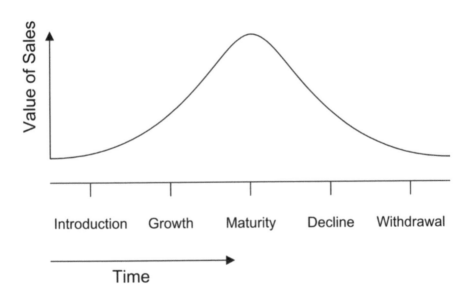

Figure 2.1 The generic concept of the product life cycle

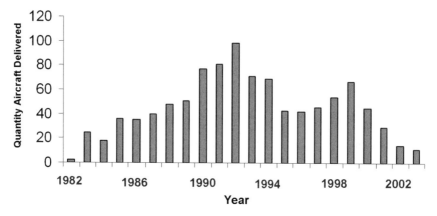

Figure 2.2 Boeing 757 product life cycle
Note: Empirical data pertaining to civil aircraft sales appears to validate the product life cycle concept.
Source: Boeing.

The conventional phases of the product life cycle applied to the context of the aerospace market are described below.

1. *Introduction* is the phase of identifying a market requirement, acquiring insight into the requirement, developing a product to correspond to the requirement, and introducing the product into the market. In the aerospace industry, the steps that precede physical introduction of a new product have exceptional importance, and the implications of these steps are described in detail later in this chapter. The investment necessary to develop and introduce a new aircraft often exceeds the total net worth of the prime contractor, and the period required to amortize the investment can easily be ten years or more. Bad management judgment in product introduction can literally end the existence of the company.

2. In the *Growth* phase, risk-adverse customers have the opportunity to observe the product in service, and familiarity leads to increased sales if the product is good. In the case of aerospace products, the distribution of physical infrastructure and availability of trained pilots makes sales easier. Interoperability is a positive factor for both military and civil products. In this phase, the product technology is still new enough to be a positive selling point, and the initial in-service experience of the initial operators has demonstrated that the product works.

3. As the aircraft reaches *Maturity*, it continues to sell well, but it no longer includes the initial wave of buyers who had a special requirement for the aircraft's capabilities, or who wanted to gain the distinction of being early adopters of the new product. In this phase, the manufacturers often attempt to gain additional sales and prolong the product's lifetime by offering major modifications, mid-life updates, and derivative designs. By this time,

competitors have had an opportunity to introduce similar competing designs, so price competition becomes a significant factor. For a successful product, initial investment in R&D and production start-up will have been amortized by this time.

4. The *Decline* phase occurs as the aircraft's fundamental design technology gradually becomes dated and as a new generation of aircraft is introduced to replace it. Some sales continue to occur to existing customers who want to maintain commonality with their existing fleets or who want commonality with other operators. Often the market requirements for which the aircraft or weapons systems were developed have fundamentally changed. Low production rates tend to cause higher manufacturing costs, sometimes resulting in higher prices that in turn hasten the product's demise.

5. *Withdrawal* eventually results as the production line is shut down and the company focuses on newer aircraft. However, for many manufacturers, especially engine manufacturers, the revenue stream for replacement parts and service extends many years into the future, and sometimes generates cash flow that exceeds the initial sales value of the equipment.

According to academic studies of new product development in the general economy, including work by Philip Kotler at Northwestern University, there are eight major steps in the classic new product development process: *idea generation*; *screening*; *concept development and testing*; *marketing strategy*; *business analysis*; *product development*; *test marketing*; and *commercialization*. The importance of each of these steps has been thoroughly evaluated and is commonly understood by both academics and practitioners of conventional marketing. The concept of the eight steps is generally applicable to the aerospace industry, but requires some adaptation. Aerospace companies don't generally have the luxury, for example, of investing hundreds of millions of dollars to develop a product to support a test marketing stage. By the time the first certified unit is delivered, virtually all of the development costs have been committed.

Certainly one of the distinctive features of aerospace products is their technological content, resulting from exceptional levels of research and development. Sustained R&D by government and industry in the aerospace industry is unparalleled.

In aerospace, as in most other industries, the development of a new product is typically undertaken using a sequential 'stage gate approach', in which the proposed product could be dropped at any stage if marketability or overall profitability become doubtful. At each stage, management has the option of accomplishing some of the stages in parallel rather than in sequence, in a strategy known as parallel development, in order to accelerate the process to ensure an early entry into the market. Parallel development often entails much technological and financial risk, but has historically been common in military aerospace programs in which government customers are willing to bear the risk in order to expedite the fielding of new operational capabilities.

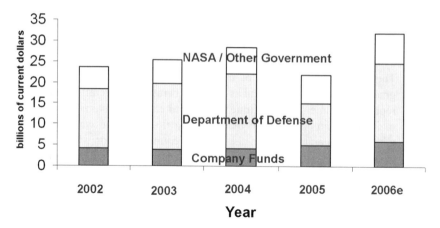

Figure 2.3 Sources of US aerospace R&D funding
Note: A distinctive feature of the aerospace industry is the R&D investment required to bring the product to market. Governments of virtually all aerospace-producing countries share this investment with industry.
Source: Aerospace Industries Association.

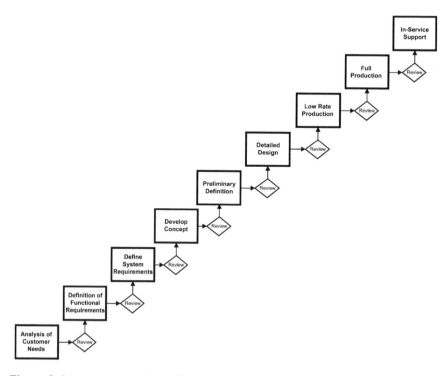

Figure 2.4 Aerospace product life cycle phases and reviews
Note: Development of new aircraft is an iterative process interspersed with reviews intended to protect against misguided strategies and bad investments.

Parallel development and higher levels of risk are generally earmarks of programs that incorporate substantial new technology. Bringing new technology to the market early can generate great financial rewards, as was the case with Boeing's initial 707 jet airliner. On the other hand, because parallel development entails higher-stakes gambling on successful outcome of development work, the financial downside is greater. In the case of military aircraft, where technological superiority often results in advantages in combat, governments are often willing to accept the risks and cost penalties of parallel development. The current US jargon for parallel development is 'spiral development', which implies that the aircraft delivered at the initial phases of the program will lack some capabilities that are expected to be added to subsequent aircraft as advanced technologies become sufficiently mature.

Table 2.1 Spiral development of F-22

Year of Technology Insertion

2004	2005	2006	2007	2008	2009	2010	2014
Initial Operational Capability. F-22 enters service with 50 planes delivered				New Avionics Microprocessor boosts processing power to support new capabilities			
Baseline Spiral 1	Spiral 2		Spiral 3A		Spiral 3B		Spiral 4/Spiral 5
Key Capabilities	Key Improvements		Key Improvements		Key Improvements		Key Improvement Candidates
• Six AIM-120C air-to-air missiles	• Fourth-generation electronically scanned array		• Air-to-ground synthetic aperture radar		• Link 16 tactical data link		• Advanced electronic attack
• Two AIM-9 infrared guided missiles	• Launch JDAMs at supersonic speeds		• Geolocation transmitters		• Small Diameter Bomb integration		• Upgraded air-to-ground radar, including ground moving target indicator
• 20mm M-6 cannon			• Advanced target recognition		• Global air traffic management and anti-spoofing technology		
• Two 1,000-pound Joint Direct Attack Munitions (JDAM)							• Low observable external fuel tanks

Note: In September 2002 the US Air Force decided to add air-to-ground capability to the F-22 Raptor, and to re-designate the aircraft F/A-22. Incorporation of planned improved capability to the aircraft was projected to continue through 2014.
Source: US Air Force.

The case of the Beech Starship illustrates the downside business risk of failed new product development. In 1983, at the National Business Aircraft Association show, Beech presented an 85 per cent scale flying prototype of a revolutionary new business aircraft. The new aircraft, which was a Beech response to chronic criticism of the conservative and utilitarian nature of its prior successful designs, featured an all-composite airframe, variable sweep wing, canard, and twin pusher turboprops. It had striking visual appeal and promised exceptional speed, internal dimensions, and payload. Deliveries to customers were projected to begin in 1985. Orders poured in. Ultimately, when deliveries finally began in 1989, the aircraft was significantly heavier and slower than promised, passenger load had been reduced from ten to eight, and the price had risen more than 30 per cent.

In this ambitious undertaking, Beech had faced the pitfalls of parallel product development. Simultaneously, management was confronted with issues of marketing commitments, design and performance challenges, new production technology, problematic FAA certification, and cost overruns. However promising the aircraft had been in its concept phase, it was a financial failure by the time it entered the market. Weakened by major losses from the program, Beech was acquired by Raytheon Aircraft thereafter.

A manufacturer developing a new product for the marketplace needs to have an accurate understanding of his customers' needs and how those needs can be converted into demand for the product. In technology-driven industries such as aerospace, there is a tendency to assume that the product is the hardware. This emphatically is not always the case. The customer is buying a package of tangibles and intangibles, for reasons that are logical and sometimes illogical.

Every marketer is familiar with the quote attributed to Charles Revson, founder of the Revlon brand: 'In the factory we make cosmetics; in the drugstore we sell hope.' Depending upon the needs and wants of the customer, the nature of the product he is seeking can vary dramatically. He needs hardware, to be sure, but he may also be preoccupied with an industrial offset program; or with post-delivery support in the form of spare parts and technical services; or with the prestige of a brand name; or with strengthening international relationships with governments of certain countries.

All markets are complex, but aerospace has peculiar intricacies involving the interplay among the aircraft manufacturers, aircraft owners, aircraft users, regulatory authorities, airport operators, municipalities, conservationists, and other vested interests and stakeholders. Whenever an aircraft design departs from the contemporary norm, it is subject to unleash reactions, positive or negative, from all of these stakeholders. An excellent recent example is the Airbus A380.

Although design of the A380 was conventional in most respects, the exceptionally large size of the aircraft raised multiple new issues with people and organizations involved, directly or indirectly, with its introduction. Compared to the largest operational airliner of the time, the A380 weighed 30 per cent more, had a wingspan 16 meters wider, was six meters higher, and carried at least 150 more passengers. The positive appeal of the aircraft was, of course, that it could carry larger quantities of passengers on high-density routes, at costs that were projected to be lower than those for smaller contemporary aircraft. However, at the time the A380 launch was announced, virtually no airport in the world could adequately accommodate the aircraft. Runways were too narrow, or were too close together; space between passenger gates was inadequate; hangars were too small; passenger jetways could not reach doors on the upper deck; and customs and baggage-handling facilities were inadequate to handle the surge of passengers. In addition, international airworthiness authorities feared that lingering turbulence created by the enormous aircraft would create flying conditions unsafe for smaller aircraft, so exceptional mandatory runway shutdowns were imposed for several minutes after each A380 takeoff and landing. By 2005, 14 international airports worldwide had committed to make infrastructure investments, estimated at $100 million per airport, to accommodate the new aircraft.

In addition to new operational challenges introduced by the A380, the Airbus manufacturing facilities dispersed throughout Europe were faced with issues involving international transportation of oversize airframe structures among factories. Solutions to these industrial problems involved purchasing specially designed cargo ships, enlarging and deepening shipping channels in Wales, lengthening a runway in Germany, and widening access roads through the French countryside to Toulouse. Airbus successfully developed solutions for all of the new manufacturing issues posed by the new product.

Ancillary product considerations, which in the case of some customers can overshadow the importance of the hardware itself, are discussed in detail elsewhere in this book. Suffice it to say at this point that a winning offer of an aerospace product invariably involves a bundle of elements in addition to the deliverable hardware.

A peculiarity of the aerospace industry is that the interval between introduction of major new designs is exceptionally long. As the cost of developing large civil airliner models has approached $10 billion, the number of new airliner types introduced, never large, has dropped to two or three per decade. Introduction of new military fighter aircraft, which typically have higher development cost than civil aircraft, are similarly infrequent. Major items of aerospace equipment are also expensive to develop, and remain on the market for many years while their investment costs are being amortized.

The small number of new product launches, combined with the exorbitant investment associated with the launches, have combined to create the well-known aerospace industry phenomenon known as 'betting the company'. If company management makes a bad decision when launching a new aircraft, the billions of dollars invested in development will not be recovered. Even if the company survives the financial disaster, it will not have the opportunity to launch another aircraft for many years. The dynamics of the industry are not tolerant of products with poor demand. This reality, described by John Newhouse in 1985, remains equally applicable today.

> The turbulent do-or-die, all-or-nothing environment in which airliners are made and sold is reminiscent of the nineteenth century and some of the entrepreneurial spirits of that era. In deciding to build a new airliner, a manufacturer is literally betting the company, because the size of the investment may exceed the company's entire net worth.[1]

---

1   John Newhouse (1985), *The Sporty Game*, Alfred A. Knopf, New York, p. 4.

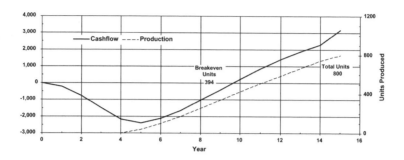

Figure 2.5 Bet-the-company curve
Note: This is a historical version of a bet-the-company curve, at a time when investments were only a few billion dollars. However, the fundamental reality has not changed: hundreds of aircraft must be sold over many years before the investment is recovered.

A consequence of the infrequent birth of new aircraft types is that the aerospace marketer, in contrast to his counterparts in consumer industries, has little short-term flexibility to adjust the fundamental product element of the marketing mix. Boeing, unlike Procter & Gamble, does not introduce dozens of new brands every year.

On the other hand, the aerospace marketer has some product flexibility that sellers of consumer packaged goods do not have. Because of the relatively low production rates of aircraft, it is feasible to incorporate customized features into individual lots of aircraft delivered to specific customers. These features can range from the straightforward plug-in substitutions normal in the automobile industry, such as upgraded radios, to major changes such as relocation of galleys or reconfiguration of fuel systems. Because missions of military aircraft tend to be more specialized than operations of airlines, military customers often demand aircraft that are highly adapted to specific requirements.

Like marketers of consumer goods, marketers of civil aircraft strive to acquire a detailed understanding of their customers so that they can respond to customer requirements. Manufacturers are continuously soliciting customer comments concerning a menu of potential product improvements, derivative designs, upgrades, and new products. Major manufacturers often host joint users' groups conferences to discuss shared interests in product design. Boeing, for example, invites owners of its aircraft to attend meetings which it calls Fleet Team Conferences, where the agenda includes subjects such as maintenance issues, operational practices, and potential design improvements. Meetings of this sort are excellent opportunities for marketers and design engineers to gain invaluable insight into the wants and needs of their customers. In a sense, they are analogous to Procter & Gamble's focus groups of consumer housewives.

Based on information they gather from current operators and potential future customers, combined with proprietary projections of economic trends, lifestyle changes, and so on, the aircraft manufacturers develop detailed projections of market demand in each segment of the market. If future demand in a specific segment is sufficiently large, and if the manufacturer does not have an existing aircraft capable of serving the market, the business analysts, engineers, and production experts will begin work on a business case to justify launch of a new aircraft.

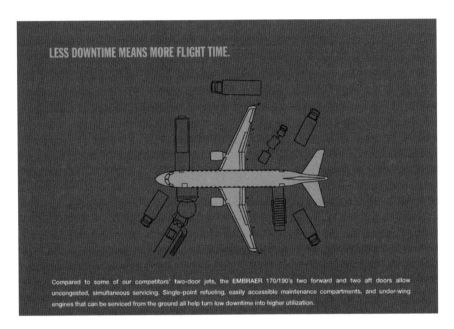

Figure 2.6 Embraer 170 loading doors

Note: For civil aircraft, the product is designed to respond to customer requirements on the ground and in the air.

Source: Embraer.

Table 2.2 Potential market demand for civil tiltrotors, by mission application

Number of Seats	Corporate/ Executive	Public Service	Low Density	Resource Develop- ment	Cargo	High Density	Total Potential Units
6 to 15	475	75	20	0	0	0	570
16 to 25	175	75	50	0	325	0	625
26 to 35	0	35	85	110	80	0	310
36 to 45	0	0	65	85	80	1200	1430
46 to 55	0	0	50	0	120	700	870
56 to 100	0	0	0	0	0	400	400

Note: Size categories are mutually exclusive and cannot be added. This summary data was part of a market survey chartered by the Federal Aviation Administration to assess market acceptance of civil tiltrotor transports.

Source: FAA.

According to aerospace industry folklore, the original Airbus design, the A300B, was conceived partly as a result of design discussions between airlines and aircraft manufacturers in the 1960s. In 1966, Frank Kolk, chief engineer at American Airlines, approached Boeing, Douglas, and Lockheed with a concept for a twin-engined wide-body aircraft that would carry 250 passengers on medium-length domestic routes. For various reasons, none of the US manufacturers was interested in developing such an aircraft. Eventually Kolk spoke to Roger Beteille at Airbus Industrie, which at the time was only an exploratory venture with no aircraft in production. Beteille used the Kolk requirement as support to obtain European government funding for launch of the A300B, which corresponded almost exactly to Kolk's concept, and which eventually was an uncontested commercial success that led the way to development of the Airbus family of aircraft.

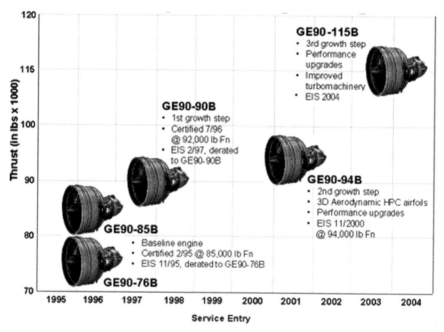

Figure 2.7 Evolution of the GE90 engine family

Note: Over the years, General Electric has built upon the excellent fundamental design of the GE90 to introduce a series of related engines that expand the range of thrust of the original engine and incorporate new technologies and operating efficiencies.

Source: General Electric.

As a way of responding to market opportunities without incurring the full cost of developing new aircraft, manufacturers have long resorted to the expedient of offering derivative designs. Derivatives are aircraft that are based on earlier designs, but are modified to correspond to specific market requirements. In the case of civil airliners, derivatives most commonly have lengthened or shortened fuselages to accommodate more or fewer passengers. Changes in fuselage length often entail corresponding changes to wing area and empennage. Airliner derivatives have traditionally been designated by Boeing with dash numbers (such as the 747-400), and by Airbus by incrementing or decrementing the model number by one digit (such as the A318, 319, 320). In the case of military aircraft, derivatives commonly involve the development of capabilities for new missions, such as adapting an air-to-air fighter so that it is optimized for air-to-ground roles.

Introduction of aircraft based upon derivative designs has strong appeal to the manufacturer:

- Derivative designs require less investment because much of the investment for the initial design, such as design work and factory facilitization, can be re-used for the derivative.
- Derivatives can generally be brought to market faster than entirely new designs. Lead times are shorter because much of the work done for the initial design can be transferred quickly to the derivative. Getting the aircraft to market faster is often a major marketing advantage.
- Recovery of costs may be faster because unit recurring costs of the aircraft can theoretically be lower than for an initial new design. This is because of positive learning-curve effects that are transferred throughout the manufacturing process from the initially produced aircraft. Suppliers who have manufactured hundreds of specially designed equipment items can continue to produce the same items on efficient production lines, and the derivative aircraft assembly line can utilize the same trained and experienced workers who have built many units of the similar original design.

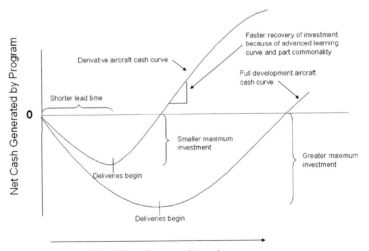

Figure 2.8 Investment costs for derivative aircraft

Note: The aerospace industry uses derivative designs as a means of introducing new features to a product without incurring the full cost of investment in an entirely new product.

Figure 2.9 The Airbus A320 family
Note: The Airbus A320 is the basis for an entire family of derivative aircraft.
Source: Airbus.

To gauge market reaction, manufacturers sometimes circulate new product concepts to their customers. Because development costs for new civil aircraft are customarily funded by the manufacturers themselves, the normal practice is to withhold introduction of new aircraft or major upgrades until a threshold quantity of launch customers is committed. Invariably the launch threshold is insufficient to entirely amortize development costs, but is sufficient to demonstrate the existence of solid demand for the product.

Often, new product concepts are circulated as part of competitive strategies, particularly as a means of distracting customer interest from new products being introduced by competitors. At the time of the Airbus launch of the Airbus A380, for example, Boeing widely promoted a technologically dramatic concept called the Sonic Cruiser, a medium-sized transport that would cruise just below the speed of sound, thus enabling premium passengers to cut several hours from trans-Pacific trips. The concept received much international attention, possibly to the detriment of the A380, but was suspended when the airline financial crisis following September 2001 created an atmosphere in which premium service and large investments became less attractive to the airlines and the aerospace industry.

The process of incorporating engineering design into the product is somewhat different when military aircraft are involved. As an almost invariable rule, manufacturers do not launch major new military aircraft programs unless the military establishment in their home country has given them a commitment to buy.

Military aircraft programs are very rarely launched as speculative investments using company money, and the rare examples of such speculative investments have frequently been failures. A significant example was the Northrop F-20 Tigershark of the late 1970s and early 1980s. The company produced two prototypes that were widely promoted as inexpensive export fighters for international allies of the United States. The program was eventually cancelled when no sales materialized. An example of an apparently successful company-funded military aircraft program was the C-130J, a major redesign of the Hercules transport undertaken by Lockheed after the US Air Force declined to fund the development program. The program survived major unplanned costs caused by problems involving avionics, stall characteristics, and integration of new engines and propellers. Sales to export customers have been good, and the US Air Force eventually bought large quantities of the aircraft.

Table 2.3 Significant Boeing new product studies

Aircraft Designation	Timing	Description	Outcome
7J7	Late 1980s	Small, ultra-fuel-efficient design based on new unducted fan engine technology	Concept shelved when fuel prices dropped
777	Early 1990s	Large, efficient, long-range twin-engine wide-body	Successfully launched
737 NG	Mid 1990s	Major redesign, including new wings, of classic single-aisle 737	Successfully launched as 737-600, -700, -800, -900
747X	Late 1990s	Major growth derivative of 747 intended to counter Airbus A380	Concept shelved after firm launch of A380. Boeing later launched the more modest growth derivative 747-800
Sonic Cruiser	Early 2000s	High speed subsonic transport with unconventional layout, introduced at time of A380 launch	Concept shelved after airline crisis following September 2001
7E7	Early 2000s	Medium-sized wide-body with improved operating efficiencies from new engines, new materials, design enhancements	Successfully launched in 2003 as the 787

Note: Of the numerous design concepts that aerospace manufacturers explore with their customers, few reach the production phase.

The advantages of having a military customer at the outset of the program are many. In most countries the government pays the contractor to design the aircraft and to prepare for manufacturing, so up-front investment risk to the contractor is minimized. If the program enters the production phase, the contractor can usually expect years of assured manufacturing work.

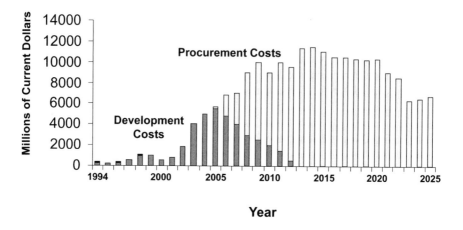

Figure 2.10 Payment of non-recurring costs on US Government contracts
Note: Standard government practice on military contracts is to pay defense contractors for development costs as they are incurred as depicted by this data for the JSF program. (Contrast this with the 'Bet Your Company' risks involved in launching new civil aircraft.)
Source: US Government Accountability Office.

To outside observers, technical concepts for design of military aircraft appear to originate from within the government defense establishments, who issue the technical requirements for the aircraft. In fact, these requirements are the result of lengthy iterative processes involving communication among operators, contractors, and technical agencies that form an idea of what is technically feasible.

When military customers are ready to engage contractors in acquisition activity, the customer issues a request for proposal that generally specifies required parameters of performance, size, weight, and some technical characteristics. Competing contractors then propose either existing aircraft, modified versions of existing aircraft, or new designs. If new design work is required, engineers, marketers, business managers, and the program manager work together to formulate the optimal technical offer to the customer, based on trade-offs between capability, cost, reliability, supportability, and so on. This process involves reconciliation of contrasting perspectives. The engineers instinctively promote the most elegant technical solution, which frequently is the most expensive alternative. The business managers characteristically prefer the lowest-risk alternative, which often is a low-technology alternative, with prices padded with reserves to protect against unknown eventualities. The marketer can be expected to promote the idea of offering an elegant engineering offer at an unrealistically low price. Ultimately the final content of the offer is decided by the program manager and by senior management of the business unit. This decision process is described in Chapter 13 of this book, devoted to the subject of marketing management.

Table 2.4 Product development funding

	Major New Design	Major Block Upgrade	Standard Options	Custom Options
Civil Transport Aircraft	• Investment risk by manufacturer and industrial partners. Investment recouped over production deliveries.	• Investment risk by manufacturer and industrial partners. Investment recouped over production deliveries.	• Sometimes investment made by manufacturer. • Sometimes investment paid by former buyer of custom option.	• Development costs generally paid by specific customer for the option.
Military Aircraft	• In Europe and USA, development costs are funded by government customer. • In Japan, industry funds development costs after receiving assurances that production program will ensue. • Rarely, development is funded at risk by manufacturer.	• In Europe and USA, development costs are funded by government customer. • In Japan, industry funds development costs after receiving assurances that production program will ensue. • Rarely, development is funded at risk by manufacturer.	• Usually investment paid by former buyer of custom option. • Sometimes investment made by manufacturer.	• Development costs generally paid by specific customer for the option. • Original customer may insist on recoupment if same option is sold to subsequent customers.

Note: Funding for product development is handled differently in different segments of the market.

In the design phase of an aircraft, often it is possible to provide for future marketing eventualities at negligible extra cost. In the basic design of a military transport aircraft, for example, it is not costly to incorporate many of the features required by civil airworthiness authorities for commercial transports. In the event that a civil derivative of the military aircraft is brought to market in the future, as was the case, for example, with the Lockheed C-130, the costs of additional development can be greatly reduced. Likewise, if coproduction of the aircraft is envisioned, the aircraft can be designed so that it can be manufactured in modular units that can be easily transported between factories. In the very early days of the F-16 program, the CEO of General Dynamics at the time, David Lewis, personally directed that the final aircraft design incorporate a modular concept in order to facilitate an anticipated large-scale coproduction program with European industry.

The importance of getting the product concept right is matched by the importance of building and delivering the product on time. Aircraft operations are complex undertakings that require customers to commit to plans years in advance. In accordance with contractual delivery dates of aircraft, airlines invest heavily to establish route structures, build infrastructure, train aircrews, develop branding, and make commitments to dispose of older aircraft. Customers whose businesses are seriously impacted by late delivery of aircraft are not happy.

An example of the serious negative marketing consequences that result from late product deliveries was illustrated by the Airbus A380 program. Well after launch customers had obtained contractual commitments for the aircraft, Airbus announced that deliveries would be delayed approximately six months due to technical problems encountered in the development phase of the program. Because of the unique nature of the aircraft, A380 customers had invested heavily in preparation for deliveries, but were forced to modify their own operating plans to accommodate the late deliveries. Several important customers made public statements about their unhappiness, and demanded (and received) financial compensation from Airbus to cover cost impact of the delays. Perhaps coincidentally, Airbus experienced a lull in A380 orders from new customers.

As with all complex technological undertakings, development and manufacturing of aerospace products requires fastidious planning and detailed internal schedules governing every aspect of the task. Typical aerospace programs have multiple layers of schedules, in which schedules for the smallest tasks are subordinate to larger tasks, which in turn are subordinate to even larger tasks, until schedules for major components feed into the master schedule that governs completion and delivery of the aircraft or end-item itself.

Internal master schedules are often used by aerospace companies to communicate program information to their customers and other stakeholders. Particularly in the launch and developmental phase of programs, simplified master schedules are used to show status and to build program credibility.

As the A380 experience illustrates, complex aerospace programs involve large numbers of intricate events, many of which are difficult to predict with accuracy. Because there are marketing advantages to being early to market with a new product, there is an understandable tendency to formulate optimistic delivery schedules, and to offer products to customers accordingly. This is risky practice. Missed schedules have a serious downside for the seller in terms of soured customer relations and financial penalties. Schedules should be aggressive, but they should always be realistic, and should not be based upon overly optimistic forecasts or expectations.

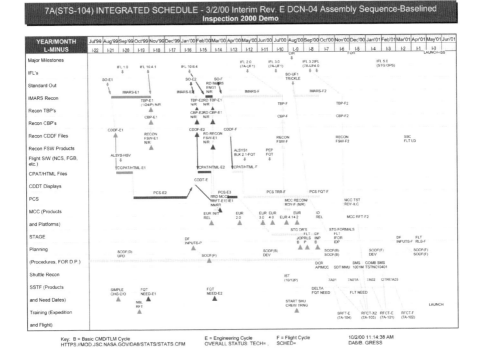

Figure 2.11 Program master schedule

Note: A schedule such as this for a deliverable assembly would feed into a higher-level master schedule, and would in turn be supported by subordinate schedules for smaller tasks. KIDASA Software's Milestones Professional project planning and presentation software is widely used in the aerospace industry.

Source: KIDASA www.kidasa.com.

Figure 2.12 Simplified 7E7 program schedule
Note: This simplified program schedule, derived from a more detailed internal master schedule, is used to communicate fundamental information to customers and other stakeholders.
Source: Boeing.

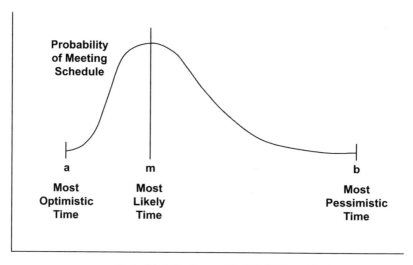

Beta Distribution with PERT Time Estimates

Figure 2.13 Probability of schedule being met
Note: It is very unlikely that delivery schedules will be met if they are based upon highly optimistic projections. They should be aggressive but realistic.
Source: US DoD.

The product is of primary importance in any business, and aerospace is no exception. The development of aerospace products is an iterative process of understanding customer requirements, formulating design concepts, communicating the concepts to the customer, refining the concepts, establishing cost and price targets, expanding a business case, obtaining program approval from top management, marketing and selling to customers, manufacturing, and supporting delivered products. As we have seen, it is a complex, time-consuming process with major financial consequences, positive or negative.

Chapter 3

Pricing in the Aerospace Industry

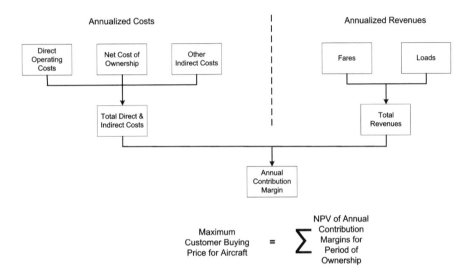

Figure 3.1 Aircraft buyer price assessment
Note: The rational commercial operator will only buy if the price is low enough to enable a profit. If competing aircraft are available, the customer will buy the one that yields the largest projected profit.

To the eternal regret of most salesmen, they do not have the privilege of determining prices for the products they are selling. Price and technical configuration are generally the two primary factors that determine the outcome of competitions in the aerospace industry. Technical configuration is complicated and time-consuming to change, but pricing can be adjusted with the stroke of a pen. Nothing can have greater immediate impact upon a sales campaign than a big price change.

The theoretical objective of aerospace firms in the private sector is to maximize long-term profitability. Pricing strategy is one of many elements that management uses to achieve that objective. However, the concept of pricing for long-term profitability is not as straightforward as it seems. The concept of 'long-term' is sometimes murky and controversial; individual product lines have strategic implications that affect their pricing; future uncertainties introduce a substantial element of subjective judgment in pricing strategies; competitors' actions cause changes to market demand; and so on.

Furthermore, the aerospace industry is characterized by traditional pricing practices that are diverse and particularly complex. Individual segments of the market have pricing methods that often are entirely different from other segments. For example, the market for commodity aerospace hardware is much like commodity markets in other industries, with intense price competition and increasing use of on-line auctions. In contrast, commercial airliners are generally sold on the basis of formal list prices that are heavily discounted, depending upon circumstances of the sale. Military aircraft are often priced on the basis of audited manufacturing costs plus fixed profit percentages.

The circumstances of every sale are unique, and the pricing strategies of the sellers reflect these circumstances. Buyers, of course, also have vital interest in the sales price, and invariably attempt to use their market power to negotiate prices downward. Particularly in the case of commercial air transporters, the question surrounding purchase price is very simple: Can he make a profit if he buys the aircraft at the sales price?

Pricing strategies can generally be effectively divided into two main categories: *market-based strategies*, and *cost-based strategies*.

Whatever pricing strategy a firm employs, sooner or later management of the company must come to grips with the fundamental concept of *breakeven analysis*. In its simplest form, this concept observes that costs consist of upfront initial investments (*non-recurring costs*) and variable costs (*recurring costs*) incurred as each unit is manufactured. Revenues, on the other hand, are received gradually as each unit is sold or as progress payments are received. Eventually the total of revenues must exceed the total of costs, or the program will be unprofitable and will be shut down. Over the long run, it is not helpful to increase sales by lowering prices to a point below recurring cost. Under these circumstances, the firm will never reach its *breakeven point*.

As an example of the consequences of a pricing strategy that positions prices at a level too low to allow the revenue line to cross over the cost line, consider Fokker Aircraft's history with the F-100 program. Because of various factors, including adverse trends in the dollar-guilder exchange rate, Fokker was compelled to sell its aircraft at prices roughly equivalent to its recurring costs. Year after year, the company missed planned breakeven points, and program profitability became more and more remote. Eventually the program and the company were shut down by German parent Daimler-Benz.

In commercial sales of aircraft and major equipment items, sales prices often result from a confluence of both market-based and cost-based strategies.

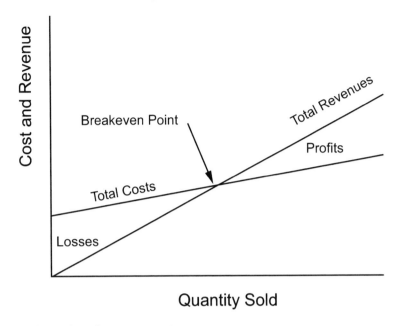

Figure 3.2 The breakeven concept
Note: Reaching the breakeven point in the aerospace industry is exceptionally risky and difficult because of the enormous initial investment required to bring new aircraft to market.

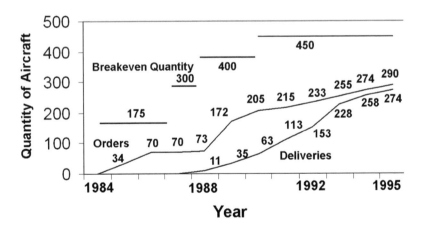

Figure 3.3 Fokker 100 planned breakeven point
Note: As Fokker was forced to offer uneconomical prices in order to sell, its breakeven point continued to recede into the future as revenues did not sufficiently recover costs.
Source: Netherlands Ministry of Economic Affairs.

Boeing and Airbus both publish annual list prices for airliners in their product lines. The Airbus listing for 2001-2005 is shown in the table below. These list prices, which take the form of maximum and minimum prices for each model type, are based upon manufacturing costs. The differences between maximum and minimum prices reflect cost variations attributable to differences in technical configuration and optional installed equipment.

Nominal prices may venture outside the list price range if the buyer specifies exceptional options involving installation of additional equipment or amenities. Specialized avionics systems, customized galleys and toilets, luxury passenger fittings, crew rest compartments, and high-end entertainment systems are common cost additives that can easily add $2-3 million to the cost of a narrowbody or $5 million to a widebody.

List prices change from year to year as costs escalate. To add transparency to price changes, the manufacturers sometimes raise prices based upon annual changes in published economic indices related to aerospace manufacturing costs. Sometimes, as exceptional external factors affect manufacturing costs, the increases depart from standard escalation formulas. In addition to inflation, costs rise (and sometimes decline) because of design changes to the aircraft.

Although formal list prices for aircraft are generally cost-based, the manufacturers almost always negotiate discounts to the list price. The amount of the discounts depends on demand factors.

In 2003, in the midst of the weakest demand in years, industry observers estimated that Airbus Industrie granted an average discount of 30-40 per cent to buyers. Easyjet, for example, was reported to have paid a unit price of well below $30 million for a quantity of A319s listed at a minimum price of $40.7 million.

In 1999, prior to the temporary collapse of demand for passenger aircraft, typical Airbus discounts were estimated to be approximately 25 per cent from list. When demand is strong and manufacturers have several years of backlog, they have less incentive to discount, although fear of loss of market share to competitors provides a perennial incentive to maintain low prices. The invisible hand of competition is at work.

Market-based Pricing Strategies

Simply put, market-based strategies ignore cost factors, and strive to sell product for the highest price that market circumstances will permit. In the aerospace industry, this type of pricing is sometimes referred to as *commercial pricing*. Aerospace sales to domestic governments, in contrast, are often required by law to be cost-based, in order to protect governments from cost gouging that sometimes results from market-based pricing strategies.

Many observers of the aerospace industry believe that pricing of commercial aircraft follows an evolution that is in concert with the life cycle of the product itself. In the initial *launch* phase of a new aircraft, the manufacturer tends to offer an aggressively low price in order to garner sufficient orders to reach critical mass to launch the program. In the face of enormous start-up investments, the builder also wants to maximize early orders to get positive cash flow. The second phase, *demand growth*, allows the seller to raise prices as the marketplace accepts the new aircraft and demand strengthens as airlines vie to acquire the new model. The third phase, *consolidation*, allows sellers to maintain firm pricing as the aircraft becomes commonly established among operational fleets. In the final phase, *oldie-but-goodie*, the aircraft remains capable of rendering credible service, but is eclipsed by newer models. Price reductions are its primary means of competing against younger challengers.

Table 3.1 Nominal catalog prices for Airbus aircraft

Model	US$ mil 2001	US$ mil 2002	US$ mil 2003	US$ mil 2004	US$ mil 2005
A300B4-600	106.9	109.3	111.8	114.4	117.0
A310-300	84.4	86.3	88.3	90.3	92.3
A318	40.9	41.8	42.8	43.8	44.8
A319	47.0	48.1	49.2	50.3	51.5
A319CJ	38.9	39.8	40.7	41.6	42.5
A320	52.2	53.4	54.6	55.8	57.1
A321	57.8	59.1	60.5	61.8	63.2
A330	131.9	134.9	138.0	141.2	144.4
A330-200	121.7	124.5	127.3	130.2	133.2
A330-300	131.9	134.9	138.0	141.2	144.4
A340	126.3	129.2	132.1	135.2	138.2
A340-200	123.8	126.6	129.5	132.4	135.4
A340-300	126.3	129.2	132.1	135.2	138.2
A340-500	161.1	164.8	168.5	172.4	176.3
A340-600	161.1	164.8	168.5	172.4	176.3
A380	257.7	263.6	269.6	275.8	282.1

All aircraft prices are in US$. They are averaged figures based on the high and low list prices published by the manufacturer. The prices vary in function of the configuration, engines, avionics, special features, options included in the final airplane and the quantity ordered.

Note: Airbus Industrie list prices from 2001 to 2005 showed a continuous upward trend in prices. In fact, major discounts were routinely offered during the period, and actual sales prices were declining dramatically.
Source: AirGuide.

Within the broad category of market-based pricing, a number of distinct sub-categories of pricing strategies are frequently applied. Although these strategies are dissimilar, it is important to recognize that they share a common characteristic: they are primarily oriented to the *demand side* of the market, and they consider factors such as activities of competitors, expected behavior of customers, market share, and so on.

Market Penetration

Market share is a very important consideration in the aerospace industry. The industry is characterized by exceptionally high capital investment requirements, perhaps greater than any other industry. In order to amortize this capital investment, long production runs at reasonably high rates are required. The small number of oligopolists fight mercilessly for market share in order to generate production volume necessary to enable capital amortization and low production costs.

In addition, manufacturers are faced with enormous fixed costs of supporting their aircraft and equipment after delivery. By their very nature, aircraft are expected to be geographically dispersed, and manufacturers are obligated to sustain facilities worldwide to provide immediate support in terms of technical services and spare parts. The cost of these facilities varies somewhat according to the number of aircraft to be supported, but the basic infrastructure, and its associated cost, has to be maintained whether the worldwide fleet of aircraft is small or large.

Aircraft operators have compelling reasons to maintain loyalty to a single aircraft manufacturer rather than operate mixed fleets of aircraft from several suppliers. Operational costs are lower for single-source fleets because cockpits and controls are similar, resulting in lower pilot training costs and flexibility in assigning pilots to fly multiple aircraft types. Ground operations are cheaper because much ground support equipment is common. Spare parts inventories are lower because aircraft from the same vendor tend to utilize common parts and systems.

Consequently, aircraft suppliers attempting to penetrate a new market, or sell to a new customer, face formidable barriers to entry. Often their single most powerful tool against these barriers is pricing. At some price point, the customer's economics will favor purchasing dissimilar aircraft from a new supplier, regardless of all negative considerations involving support and operating costs.

This is the logic of pricing for market penetration. The seller prices his aircraft or equipment at a level, often below short-term cost, that enables him to sell in a market that would otherwise be closed to him. The objective is to eventually raise production rates and deployment efficiencies to the point where the seller can compete on equal terms with existing suppliers.

Airbus Industrie is a textbook example of effective application of pricing for market penetration. Entering a 1970s airliner market dominated by Boeing and McDonnell Douglas, Airbus had no choice but to compete on the basis of pricing. Supported heavily by financial assistance from European national governments, the supplier gradually clawed its way toward a significant market share, and after more than 20 years achieved market parity with Boeing. Airbus did not report consolidated profit and loss statements during the early decades of its existence, so no definitive public information about profitability is available. However, most knowledgeable observers believe that Airbus' financial losses in the 1970s, 1980s, and 1990s were large. Regardless, the Airbus strategy to gain market share was ultimately successful.

The future challenge for Airbus is to convert its hard-won market share into eventual long-term profitability.

Skimming

This practice is relatively rare in the aerospace industry. In theory, a firm introducing a new and exceptional product can temporarily sell at a high price to capture the business of customers who have a particular interest in acquiring the new product. Later, after the early-adapters have paid the high price, the supplier lowers his price to capture the broader market.

This practice is observed to exist in consumer marketing, but its occurrence in aerospace is not common. Occasionally a product will have such novelty (in-flight entertainment systems) or performance advantages (zero-zero ejection seats) that initial customers will be willing to pay price premiums. But, for the most part, civil aerospace customers take a conservative outlook on new technology, and prefer to wait until a technology is proven in use before adopting it. The military is more aggressive about incorporating new technology into combat capability, but the traditional cost-based pricing methodology imposed upon government contractors discourages the use of skimming unless the technology was developed at private expense.

Monopoly Pricing

This type of pricing, also relatively rare in the aerospace industry, involves companies that are the sole suppliers of a specialized type of equipment, and who take advantage of the lack of effective competition to price their products so that they earn exceptional profits. For years, customers and competitors were heard to complain that Boeing's pricing on the B-747 was monopolistic because of the lack of any effective competition for very large civil transports. Generally, the rare perceptions of monopolistic pricing occur in smaller, more specialized segments of the industry, where the volume of business is inadequate to support multiple suppliers. Sometimes, suppliers of specialized RF antennas are accused of monopoly pricing, for example.

According to economists, true monopolistic power does not exist unless barriers to entry effectively prevent other competitors from entering the market. In fact, the perception of monopolistic profits often is an incentive to other firms to compete. Airbus' introduction of the A-380 super widebody is a perfect example of a strategy to counter monopoly pricing by a competitor.

Matching Competitor Pricing

Economists describe markets characterized by a small number of large sellers as oligopolistic markets. A common practice in oligopolistic markets is price matching. The few firms involved want to avoid aggressive price competition that will reduce profits for all, and they tend to offer list prices that are in the same range for similar products.

However, when one or more of the oligopolistic firms becomes dissatisfied with his market share and chooses a strategy to increase market share, or when the size of the overall market is in decline, price competition becomes more severe. Although price competition among oligopolists is good for the customer, it does not necessarily yield the desired outcome to the original price-cutting supplier. Typically, the other oligopolists, remaining true to the traditions of their industry, match the price cuts of the original firm, eliminating any competitive advantage, and reducing profits for all sellers.

Responding to Customer Affordability

At the outset of a planned competitive procurement, customers sometimes announce the quantity of aircraft they intend to buy and the budget that has been approved for the procurement. Often this procedure is a calculated bluff by commercial operators who are seeking a bargain, but sometimes, particularly when government procurements are involved, the budgetary limit is real and non-negotiable.

When the customer has directly or indirectly communicated the maximum price he is willing to pay, the supplier has several possible courses of action. One choice is that he can meet the customer's price, regardless of whether the price enables a normal profit. A second choice is to withdraw from the competition if he concludes that a sale at the customer's price would be a money-losing proposition with no compelling strategic value. Or, third, he can remain in the competition at a price higher than stipulated by the customer, with the hope that the customer will eventually find a way to increase his available budget to cover the higher price offered by the supplier.

Buying-in

For reasons discussed above, it is often problematic for aerospace customers to abandon initial suppliers, even if later developments make other competitors more attractive. Because suppliers recognize this, they often offer extremely aggressive pricing to win initial competitions in programs that are expected to have subsequent follow-on buys. The concept is that profits foregone or losses incurred on the initial program can be recaptured by means of higher prices on subsequent rounds of procurement. Intentional use of this pricing strategy is illegal under some circumstances, such as when selling to the US Government. Other customers understandably will be unhappy if they know their supplier has an explicit plan to raise prices after an initial commitment is obtained.

Pricing to Maximize Spares and Maintenance Revenue

This strategy, sometimes known as the 'give-away-the-razor-but-sell-the-blades' strategy, considers product pricing in the context of the long-term revenue stream that will result from selling spare parts and post-delivery support for in-service aircraft and installed equipment.

The volume of business resulting from post-delivery support is substantial. The US Department of Defense, in studies involving life cycle costing, estimates that the cost of operating and maintaining military aircraft will be from three to seven times the initial purchase price of the aircraft. Much of this cost results from spare parts and technical services provided by the original manufacturer.

The relationship between initial sales price and future spares and maintenance revenue varies greatly between types of equipment. Jet engines, which last many years and require many spare parts and maintenance actions, offer prime examples of how the pricing strategy can work effectively, and jet engine manufacturers are known for heavily discounting their products in order to assure future lucrative sources of support business. The same is true of manufacturers of helicopter dynamic components such as transmissions, rotor hubs, and swashplates, which require relatively frequent overhauls. On the other hand, major civil aircraft prime contractors are less likely to be heavily involved in post-delivery support. Airframe structure can last indefinitely without replacement, and often aftermarket maintenance, repair, and overhaul specialist companies (MROs) capture much of the maintenance business. The equipment items that require replacement or overhaul are generally provided by subcontractors who compete for the repair and replacement business themselves. Consequently, the expectation of future support business is not a major consideration in the pricing strategy of many aircraft prime contractors.

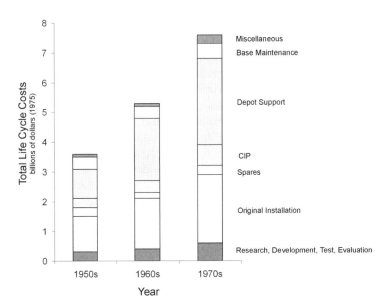

Figure 3.4 Life cycle costs for jet engines

Note: For many equipment items such as jet engines, the cost of spare parts and maintenance over a lifetime will exceed the initial purchase price. This reality is an incentive for sellers to price their product low in order to profit from support business.

Source: Institute for Defense Analyses.

Cost-based Pricing Strategies

In a competitive marketplace, price is determined by the interplay of supply and demand. Cost has a bearing on the supply side of the market. In the long run, the price at which suppliers are willing to offer their products will depend upon their investments and cost of manufacturing.

The ability of the seller to reduce prices by reducing costs is in large part dependent upon the time horizon. When an imminent sale of an existing product is at hand, costs are generally known and are difficult to reduce in the short term. The seller might chose to reduce prices, but realistically he is not going to be able to implement immediate cost reductions of any significance. In contrast, at the beginning of a new program, in which all design and manufacturing decisions remain to be made, the manufacturer has a great deal of freedom to select design characteristics and manufacturing plans that will have enormous impact on cost.

However, as we saw in the example of Airbus list pricing at the beginning of this chapter, supply-side factors rarely determine the final selling price. If demand is weak, the manufacturer may be faced with a choice of temporarily lowering his price below his breakeven point, or not making a sale.

A predictable characteristic of aerospace costs is that manufacturing hours per unit tend to decrease over time as the cumulative quantity of aircraft manufactured increases. This phenomenon, which has been widely studied, is the *learning curve* effect. A theoretical corollary of this effect is that, to the extent that pricing is based upon costs, early buyers will pay more than later buyers. When this is true, the outside observer might believe that the supplier is engaged in the demand-based pricing strategy of skimming, described above. In fact, any relationship between learning curves and skimming pricing is generally remote. The reality is that, because declining cost tendencies related to learning curves are often offset by inflation over the same period, aerospace prices historically have risen over time.

One important segment of the aerospace market in which cost-based pricing is regularly used is defense contracting in NATO countries. In most major defense contracts, the government customer makes separate incremental payments for non-recurring costs such as engineering research and development and manufacturing tooling. Because of technological uncertainties, costs for R&D are notoriously difficult to accurately predict, and thus are customarily paid for by the customer on a cost-reimbursement basis rather than as a fixed price. Later, as aircraft or systems enter full-scale production, the government customer is entitled to believe that, because he owns much of the technology and production equipment, he has a right to limit the manufacturer's profits to a reasonable level.

Defense contractors in NATO countries are normally required to maintain meticulous cost records that are periodically audited by government officials. These records form the basis for cost-based pricing.

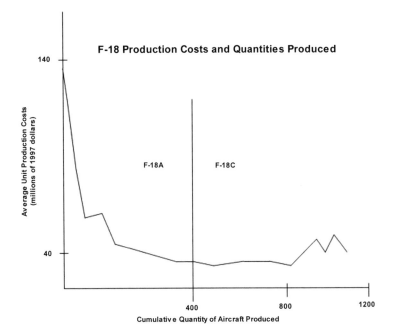

Figure 3.5 F-18 learning curve effect
Note: Because of the learning curve effect, cost per unit tends to decline as the cumulative number of aircraft produced increases. Note that prices for this curve are in constant dollars. If inflation had been considered, costs would have tended to rise over much of the time period.
Source: US Department of Defense.

Penalties for 'Overpricing' to the US Government

On August 27, 2003, the US Justice Department announced that it had reached a $37.9 million settlement for alleged overcharging by Lockheed Martin on sales to the US Government of airborne targeting pods that were destined to be resold to an international customer through Foreign Military Sales (FMS) channels to Saudi Arabia and Greece.

The mischarging came to light as a result of a whistleblower lawsuit filed in Federal court by a former Lockheed employee. According to the lawsuit, Lockheed was trying to offset cost overruns on an unrelated US Air Force contract by falsely charging costs to the FMS contract.

Lockheed Martin denied any wrongdoing and said it settled the dispute to avoid the costs and distraction of further litigation. Under the settlement, the whistleblower was awarded $8.75 million.

An exception to cost-based pricing in the defense industry is when the product and its underlying technology have been developed by the supplier at his own risk and expense. In this case, the government customer has no rights of access to cost data, and the supplier is permitted to quote demand-based prices.

Return-on-sales Targets

In defense aerospace, the most common pricing method involves simply adding a standard profit percentage onto projected costs. The government customer allows a profit percentage, generally around 12 per cent, that is somewhat negotiable depending upon anticipated risks and program difficulties. This concept of *ROS*, primitive though it might be, is a widely used benchmark to measure the financial health of aerospace businesses.

Return-on-investment Targets

In an effort to more accurately relate profit to financial resources required to deliver a product, modern aerospace managers customarily calculate profit as a function of investment. The most traditional of these methods, return on investment, or *ROI*, compares discounted anticipated cash flow from sales against time-phased investment. By assuming a target ROI such as 20 per cent, financial analysts can specify the sales price that must be maintained in order to meet the target.

Cost Plus Fixed Profit, Cost Plus Incentive Fee, and so on

These variations on the theme of cost-plus contracting have justifiably become controversial because their weak incentives for contractors to control costs have resulted in out-of-control spending on numerous programs that have become part of the folklore of the aerospace industry. The basic methodology is that the contractor is reimbursed for his costs and receives additional profits. The profits can be a specific amount, a percentage of cost, or a sliding fee inversely proportional to the level of costs.

Other Factors Affecting Pricing

Traditionally, civil airliners have been priced in US dollars, regardless of the country of origin of the manufacturer. Recently, as a gesture of European nationalism, Airbus has begun to offer its aircraft priced in euros as an alternative, but the overwhelming majority of international sales remain denominated in dollars.

For manufacturers and customers located outside the United States, financial effects of currency exchange rates can sometimes have significant unexpected impact for the better or worse. Companies whose costs are in non-dollar currencies but who sell in dollars are at risk of wide swings in revenue and earnings fluctuations as dollars are converted to their home currency at varying exchange rates. Although risks of short-term currency swings can be minimized by classical hedging techniques, longer-range currency movements can have devastating effects.

Management of the legendary Dutch aircraft manufacturer Fokker attributed much of the blame for the company's bankruptcy in 1996 to unfavorable trends in the dollar-guilder exchange rate throughout the 1990s, during a period when the company was heavily leveraged financially as it introduced its new F-50 and F-100 transports. As the chart below shows, the dollar declined from a high of 2.2 guilders to a level below 1.6, during the period, resulting in a negative impact to Fokker guilder-denominated revenues of more than 20 per cent.

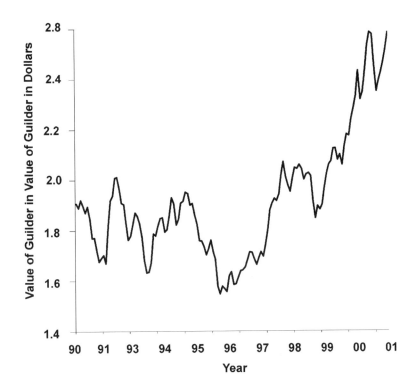

Figure 3.6 US dollar vs Dutch guilder exchange rate
Note: At Dutch bankruptcy hearings to investigate the causes of the collapse of Fokker, this chart was presented as evidence of the negative financial impact of dollar-guilder exchange rate changes.
Source: Netherlands Ministry of Economic Affairs.

More recently, Embraer of Brazil, another major aerospace manufacturer whose national currently fluctuates in relation to the dollar, reported similar negative impact to its earnings as the dollar-real exchange rate moved in an unfavorable direction.

Ultimately, companies such as Fokker and Embraer are compelled by economic circumstances to deal with the consequences of exchange rate changes as best they can. One common strategy is *hedging*, a financial technique in which companies commit to contracts to sell dollars at fixed dates in the future at the exchange rate prevailing when the contract was signed.

Dealing with Unavoidable Price Increases

Price increases are painful but are sometime unavoidable. As is often the case when bad news is involved, negative consequences and hard feelings can be minimized if the increases are handled in a thoughtful and businesslike way, with the supplier paying particular attention to the needs and perspective of the customer.

Guidelines for raising prices:

1. *Maintain a sense of fairness.* The aerospace business is based on long-term relationships. If cost factors cause a supplier to raise prices, the customer will expect the increase to be imposed in a way that shares the pain between the supplier and the customer. Particularly in instances where the customer is committed to the supplier because of technical factors or reasons of fleet compatibility, the customer will react very badly if he believes that the supplier is abusing his power in the relationship by passing all of the cost increase on to the customer. This principle of fairness may temporarily result in reduction of historical profit rates as the supplier absorbs cost growth rather than raising prices the full amount of the growth. Financial managers will protest temporary reductions in profit, but the long-term profitability of the supplier's company will not be well served by alienating a customer by giving him reasons to feel that he has been treated unfairly.

2. *Give customers adequate advance warning.* If price increases are unavoidable, give the customer as much advance warning as possible so that he has time to manage his business to minimize the impact of the increase. Executives and financial managers are under pressure to meet financial projections. Given sufficient advance warning, they can adjust their business plans and financial projections to partially offset the impact of a pricing increase that might have devastating effects if it takes them by surprise.

3. *Explain the circumstances behind sharp price increases.* Transparency is important. As part of your long-term relationship with your customer, you owe him an explanation for exceptional price increases. Even if he does not like the increase, he can empathize with unavoidable business circumstances that cause prices to rise. He will be less sympathetic, incidentally, of cost increases caused by self-inflicted actions such as reorganizations, mergers, or general mismanagement.

4. *Before increasing list prices, cut other customary price concessions.* As we have seen, in some segments of the aerospace industry, list prices have a tenuous relationship with actual sales price. This disconnect between the two can serve to blur the extent of a price increase. By reducing non-listed factors such as discounts, free services, or below-market financing, the effective price can be raised without changing the list price. But do not fool yourself – the

customer will know that he is paying more.

5. *Use escalation clauses if possible.* Because major cost factors in the aerospace industry are well known and are tracked by published economic indices or other objective measurements, it is sometimes possible to reach advance agreement with customers that prices will increase in accordance with specific escalation formulas. This approach has many advantages. It generally appeals to the sense of fairness of both parties, it offers pricing transparency, and it provides adequate advance notification that prices will rise, even if the exact amount of the increase will not be known until the periodic indices are published.

Year	Aerospace Deflators (1987 = 100)					
	Composite	SIC 3721	SIC 3724	SIC 3728	SIC 3761	SIC 3764,9
1972	33.7	39.9	30.1	36.6	39.7	34.4
1973	37.7	41.2	30.9	38.1	39.4	35.6
1974	41.5	44.8	34.9	44.0	41.6	40.5
1975	46.6	48.3	42.3	51.6	45.2	49.2
1976	51.0	52.8	45.9	56.5	50.4	53.8
1977	54.6	56.2	49.1	58.7	55.6	58.2
1978	57.5	59.3	54.6	55.2	60.7	63.6
1979	63.5	65.3	60.9	58.9	69.7	70.0
1980	70.6	72.9	66.3	65.3	78.9	78.5
1981	79.5	80.8	77.0	74.9	87.1	89.5
1982	87.9	89.8	85.2	84.3	93.4	97.2
1983	92.2	94.4	89.5	87.9	98.6	101.5
1984	99.8	105.9	98.1	93.6	100.7	102.9
1985 [a]	98.7	100.7	99.2	94.4	102.4	103.2
1986	99.8	100.6	99.3	97.9	103.5	102.4
1987	100.0	100.0	100.0	100.0	100.0	100.0
1988	101.5	102.2	103.0	103.5	98.6	98.4
1989	105.5	111.0	105.8	106.8	97.1	97.7
1990	108.6	116.8	111.7	109.8	93.4	98.2
1991	111.4	121.3	117.0	113.6	90.5	101.9
1992 [b]	116.9	125.2	122.7	118.0	88.4	104.8
1993	120.2	129.5	124.7	120.9	90.9	109.6
1994	122.7	133.9	128.0	123.5	88.0	107.1
1995	124.5	138.3	129.9	124.4	84.3	104.2
1996	126.7	141.5	132.4	128.8	81.8	103.6
1997	127.8	143.4	133.7	131.4	77.8	103.5
1998	128.5	143.8	134.7	133.0	78.3	102.4
1999	129.4	145.1	135.7	134.3	76.8 [r]	103.1 [r]
2000 [r]	133.3	151.6	138.6	135.4	78.1	102.8
2001	136.7	156.9	142.8	138.5	76.4	102.5

Source: Aerospace Industries Association, based on data from: Bureau of Labor Statistics, Producer Price Indices; Bureau of Economic Analysis, Chain-Type Price Indexes and Implicit Price Deflators; and International Trade Administration.

a The International Trade Administration has discontinued its reporting of the Aerospace Deflators with 1986. Subsequent composite deflators computed by AIA and deflators for 1985 and 1986 revised for consistency.

b The Bureau of Economic Analysis discontinued its reporting in 1995 of the National Defense Purchases Deflators (used in AIA's Composite calculations). 1992-1994 revised using 1992 fixed weights and BEA's Chain-Type Price Indexes for National Defense Investment and Consumption Expenditures.

Key: SIC = Standard Industrial Classification; SIC 3721 = Aircraft; SIC 3724 = Aircraft Engines and Engine Parts; SIC 3728 = Aircraft Parts; SIC 3761 = Missiles and Space Vehicles; SIC 3764 = Space Propulsion; SIC 3769 = Space Equipment not elsewhere classified.

Figure 3.7 Price deflators for the aerospace industry

Note: Aircraft prices are sometimes subject to annual escalation for inflation, particularly in the case of military contracts that use cost-based pricing methodology. The specific amount of escalation is generally based upon published indices.

Every industry has its war stories, and aerospace certainly has its share. The following story depicts a sales battle between Boeing and Airbus for an airliner sale to Spanish national carrier Iberia. The story, drawn primarily from *Wall Street Journal* reports at the time, illustrates the importance of price to the customer, and shows how the customer benefits when two companies hungry for sales engage in ruthless competition.

Price Competition for a Strategic Sale – A Brief Case Study

In 2002 and 2003, Boeing and Airbus competed head-to-head for a major aircraft order from Iberia, the Spanish national carrier. This period was a cyclical low in the airline business, as the industry was reeling from negative consequences of the 2001 terrorist attacks in New York, but Iberia was one of the few major international carriers that had remained consistently profitable. Iberia had completed a thorough restructuring before being privatized in early 2001. It fortuitously escaped many of the negative consequences of the 2001 attacks because it flew few routes to North America, where air travel experienced a particularly severe downturn, and by dominating the large Latin American market, which was largely unaffected. Iberia was the world's 18th largest airline in passenger traffic, with a fleet of 145 planes.

Because of the prevailing dearth of aircraft orders, the Iberia order was a particularly attractive prospect for both aircraft manufacturers.

Enrique Dupuy de Lome, Iberia's chief financial officer, who led the selection process for the new aircraft, structured a rigorously competitive framework to ensure that Iberia could squeeze the most attractive possible offers from the two suppliers.

In several important ways, Airbus began the competition from a stronger position. The company had sold Iberia more than 100 airplanes since 1997, including an order in June 2002 for three Airbus A340s. Aircraft commonality is important to airlines for many economic reasons, so Boeing was at a disadvantage in trying to displace Airbus as Iberia's preferred aircraft supplier. In addition, the Spanish aerospace industry was a part of EADS, European Aeronautics Defense & Space Co., which owned 80 per cent of Airbus. Although Iberia and EADS theoretically were entirely independent of each other, the Spanish Government was a shareholder of both.

The Iberia requirement was to replace six Boeing 747-200s more than 20 years old. It planned to buy as many as 12 new planes to complete a ten-year modernization program for Iberia's long-haul fleet. Based on list prices, the 12-plane order was valued at more than $2 billion.

Because Airbus was so thoroughly entrenched at Iberia, which had last bought a Boeing aircraft in 1995, Boeing considered skipping the competition altogether. However, Dupuy de Lome met with Toby Bright, Boeing's marketing vice president for commercial aircraft, at dinner in London, and convinced Boeing that Iberia would seriously consider buying Boeing aircraft.

In November 2002, the two competitors submitted their initial offers for the Spanish requirement. Airbus offered the A340-600, against Boeing's 777-300ER. The A340 had slightly greater range, but the 777 offered more seats and lower fuel consumption. The catalogue price of the 777, at $215 million, was approximately $25 million more than the A340.

As the competition began, Dupuy de Lome notified both manufacturers that he expected to obtain discounts of at least 40 per cent from list prices.

Toby Bright, the Boeing sales lead, promoted the 777 as a superior profit-maker. Because it contained more seats and consumed less fuel, Boeing calculated that their airplane could generate $8,000 more earnings per flight than the A340. The Airbus executive responsible for marketing, John Leahy, advocated the A340 on the basis that it was less expensive and would enable Iberia to have a standardized Airbus fleet, which would enable the airline to save money on spare parts, maintenance, and crew training.

Leahy, whose Toulouse headquarters was a one-hour flight from Madrid, made a series of visits to build relationships and pass information to his customer. He particularly attacked Boeing's contention that the 777 could accommodate 400 seats rather than the 350 planned for the A340. This issue of revenue-earning seat capacity was central to the competition between the two companies. Airbus, offering the less expensive aircraft, preferred to compete on price. Boeing, at a higher sales price, argued that the price difference would be eclipsed by the 777's much greater earning potential over its lifetime. Boeing also contended that its wider fuselage was more comfortable for passengers.

Dupuy de Lome applied price pressure on Leahy with another factor. When Airbus had sold 18 smaller A340 models to Iberia in 1995, Leahy had agreed to a contract in which Airbus guaranteed a minimum resale price if Iberia resold the aircraft in the future. As negotiations for the new sale advanced, Dupuy de Lome threatened Leahy with the prospect of an expanded buy of 777s to replace Iberia's existing fleet of A340s. In such an eventuality, Airbus would not only lose its position as Iberia's sole supplier, but would also have to pay the differential between the sale price and guaranteed price for the 18 second-hand A340s.

In early December 2002, while Leahy and an Airbus team were in Madrid presenting detailed information about operating costs, Dupuy de Lome informed them that a team from Iberia was traveling to evaluate a group of late-model 747-400s that had recently been taken out of service by Singapore Airlines and was available for lease. The Singaporean aircraft supposedly was another competitive contender for the Iberian contract.

At the same time, Iberia had concluded a technical evaluation of the two competitors. The Boeing aircraft was projected to have an 8 per cent lower operating cost, which would represent a saving of millions of dollars over the period of ownership. The Iberian engineers concluded that the 777 could fit 24 more seats than the A340, which would generate significantly greater earnings. However, the A340, with four engines, was expected to operate better at some high altitude airports that Iberia served in South America. Cost factors in Airbus' favor were the A340's lower price and operational benefits to Iberia of having an all-Airbus fleet.

In the second week in December, a Boeing sales team presented a comprehensive technical offer with pricing to Iberia. Dupuy de Lome responded that the price was too high. On 18 December, Bright made a personal visit to Dupuy de Lome, who dictated the price he wanted. Bright declined, and the two broke off discussions.

Although the Iberia board of directors had been pressing for a selection decision before the end of the year, Dupuy de Lome contended that both prices were still too high, and obtained permission to pursue further the possibility of the second-hand Singaporean 747s.

On 4 January 2003, Dupuy de Lome drove to France for further price negotiations with Leahy. During their four hours of talks, Dupuy de Lome asked for concessions to match the 50 per cent price concessions that the press was reporting Airbus had given British carrier EasyJet for a major sale. Leahy denied the accuracy of the press reports and declined to reduce his prices significantly.

Separately, Dupuy de Lome contacted Bright with the suggestion that the two meet at Boeing in Seattle to continue negotiations. Bright responded that Dupuy de Lome would be welcome, but that Boeing would make no further price concessions. On 14 January Dupuy de Lome and a small team arrived and had dinner with Bright and Boeing's chief executive for commercial aircraft, Alan Mulally. During the dinner, Mulally urged Bright to work to find a way to meet Iberia's requirements.

The next day, Boeing presented an improved offer that included a somewhat reduced sales price, improved financing terms, and more attractive arrangements for spare parts, maintenance, and training. Both sides agreed that they were getting closer to an acceptable deal.

On 17 January, Dupuy de Lome met with Leahy and Airbus President Noel Forgeard in the office of Iberia Chairman Xabier de Irala. Forgeard agreed to reduce the Airbus price somewhat, and said that he believed a deal was possible.

Iberia scheduled a board meeting for 30 January to make the selection decision. In the days leading up to the decision, Boeing maintained constant contact with Dupuy de Lome, and cut its price a further 10 per cent after wringing concessions from leasing firms and the engine manufacturer, General Electric. At the same time, Dupuy de Lome remained in constant contact with Leahy, making sure that Airbus was aware that Boeing continued to make price reductions.

On the day of the board meeting, Bright contacted Dupuy de Lome with an offer to make a final price reduction if Iberia would agree to an immediate handshake deal. Dupuy de Lome declined to deal until he had seen the final Airbus offer. Bright extended the price reduction anyway.

Later in the day, Airbus President Forgeard telephoned Iberia Chairman Irala, who said he was still waiting for Airbus to meet two Iberia demands involving financial terms and economics. As a final concession, Forgeard agreed to meet Iberia's conditions for asset guarantees and limits on Iberia's cost of maintenance of the aircraft. In response, Irala told Forgeard that he would recommend to his board that the Airbus offer be accepted.

That evening, after the Iberia board meeting, Boeing was notified by Iberia that the Spanish company had agreed to buy nine Airbus A340-600s, with options for an additional three.

PART 2
Marketing Tools, Techniques, and Resources

Chapter 4

Overseas Agents and Sales Consultants

Knowledge of the local market is valuable for marketers in any industry. In the aerospace market in particular, the characteristic complexity of the decision-making process makes detailed local knowledge indispensable.

In addition to local knowledge, the marketer also needs a network of effective business contacts with access to the customer and other important decision-makers.

In international competitions, most marketers do not personally possess the intimate knowledge of the customer and high-value business contacts required to operate effectively independently. To gain the benefits of specialized knowledge and contacts, aerospace marketers commonly enlist local supporters to assist in the marketing effort. The nature of services provided by these local allies ranges from simple advice-giving, to active intervention in the marketing process, and can include direct involvement in the sales process as a distributor or re-seller. Methods of compensation and payment to these local allies are as varied as the nature of their responsibilities.

Foreign marketing representatives are often utilized even by aerospace firms that have their own in-country offices staffed by expatriates or locally hired employees. The marketing representative, as a well-connected insider without many of the corporate constraints of his client, generally operates in a different orbit than the staff of the local corporate office. Nevertheless, some degree of rivalry between the representative and the local office can emerge if the two groups do not work together in a cooperative spirit.

When dealing with foreign representatives, it is good practice to bear in mind that a disgruntled former representative can often do serious harm to future marketing efforts. Firing a representative is likely to be contractually messy and to cause hard feelings, and a vindictive former agent can cause serious harm to ongoing marketing campaigns. As in marriage, it is a good idea to avoid a commitment until one is reasonably sure that a sound basis for a fruitful long-term relationship exists.

International marketing assistance provide by independent specialists can be categorized into three general roles. These roles exclude purveyors of general services, who are involved in furnishing routine administrative services such as translations, transportation, arranging exhibits, printing, and so on.

1. *Consultants and advisors* are often highly knowledgeable insiders who provide invaluable guidance and recommendations to marketers, and who intervene behind the scenes, utilizing their personal network of contacts to influence the sales process. Consultants and advisors are theoretically excluded from

direct action to influence the customer on behalf of the companies that employ them.

2. *Agents and representatives*, also knowledgeable insiders, have a more direct role in the marketing process. They are contractually delegated to act on behalf of their employers, and are expected to interact directly with the customer.

3. *Distributors and re-sellers* are direct parties to the sale. They generally purchase product directly from the aerospace manufacturer for resale to the final customer. Under this arrangement, the manufacturer essentially becomes the wholesaler, and the distributor becomes the retailer.

These three roles have important distinctions for the company attempting to sell. Because these local allies are generally independent companies, the aerospace firm is faced with an important choice concerning how much legal authority and autonomy to transfer to the ally. Agents and representatives are legally authorized to act on behalf of the aerospace firm, and consequently can put the firm in legal and financial jeopardy if they act improvidently or abuse their position of trust. Distributors and re-sellers typically do not legally act on behalf of the original equipment supplier, but they have direct control over how the manufacturer's products are managed and marketed in the local market, and thus can potentially have a major impact on success or failure in the market. Because they are often independent licensees, they often have a great deal of autonomy from the manufacturer, and can be problematic if they act in a manner that is not compatible with the wishes of the manufacturer. Consultants and advisors are generally specifically proscribed from acting on behalf of the seller, and are not allowed to represent or commit the seller. These restrictions on consultants are appealing to many aerospace companies who wish to minimize risk.

In spite of the legal and contractual distinctions between the three roles, in fact their activities often tend to blur and overlap. Consultants and advisors, for example, who nominally are limited to furnishing guidance to marketers, frequently are used as direct interlocutors with the customer, acting in a capacity very similar to that of agents and representatives. Sometimes marketers erroneously believe that they can repudiate any eventual harmful or inappropriate actions of rogue consultants and advisors, because they are not contractually authorized to act on behalf of the seller. In fact, most legal rulings in court have held that the seller is fully liable for most actions of paid advisors and consultants, particularly if the seller could reasonably be expected to be aware of those actions.

It is important to recognize this reality: in most countries, the seller has some degree of civil and criminal liability for the acts of his paid supporters, even if they are contractually acting as only advisors or consultants. Also, international anti-corruption legislation such as the US Foreign Corrupt Practices Act (FCPA) holds employers responsible for corrupt action by consultants and advisors under many circumstances. For this reason, it is indispensable that any party who is paid to act in a supporting role in the marketing process be carefully investigated and evaluated in the context of business ethics as well as marketing effectiveness.

India Press Information Bureau; issued Feb. 19, 2003 – New Delhi

Transparency In Defence Deals

In order to bring greater transparency to the whole procurement process and realising that the presence of an Authorised Representative/Agent would improve the delivery of services and follow up post contractual obligations, the Ministry of Defence have, on November 02, 2001, issued Supplementary Instructions on the appointment of Indian Authorised Representatives/Agents of foreign suppliers.

The Authorised Representatives would make available information of latest technologies, assist during trials and help in post contractual servicing

The salient features of these instructions are:

--All foreign suppliers who wish to appoint Indian Authorised Representatives/ Agents would register them with the Ministry of Defence.

--The Authorised Representative/Agent could be an individual, a partnership, an association of persons, a limited company Private or Public.

--The agent must be an income tax payee.

--The foreign supplier appointing an agent must furnish copies detailing Agreement/terms of appointment.

--The obligations of an Authorised Representative/Agent will flow from the contract entered with the Ministry of Defence.

--The foreign supplier will have to declare the payments made to the Authorised Representative/Agent.
 Particulars relating to agency commission would be reported to the Enforcement Directorate of Central Board of Direct Taxes.

--The Agent will be appointed with the approval of the Secretary of the Department.

--These instructions will be applicable for future contracts only.

--The new policy has been successful and the Ministry of Defence has been receiving requests from various firms for the guidelines issued by the Government in this regard.

--This policy is applicable to all the defence deals.

This information was given by the Defence Minister Shri George Fernandes in a written reply to Shri PK Maheswari in Rajya Sabha today. (ends)

Figure 4.1 Indian Government directive on the use of sales agents
Note: The Government of India, after suffering through a series of corruption scandals involving defense aerospace in the 1990s, briefly outlawed the use of sales agents, but later authorized their use under controlled conditions.

Under the US Foreign Corrupt Practices Act, firms can be prosecuted not only for direct corrupt payments but also for indirect corrupt payments made by third parties if there is actual knowledge of the intended results or if there is a conscious disregard or deliberate ignorance of known circumstances that should reasonably alert the offender to the high probability of violation of the Act.

In the early 1980s, a New Jersey firm known as W.S. Kirkpatrick & Co. was engaged in efforts to sell ejection seat trainers, disorientation simulators, and general aero medical equipment to the Nigerian Government. The equipment was to be installed at the Aero Medical Center at Kaduna Air Force Base in Nigeria. The total value of the sales contract was $10.8 million.

Kirkpatrick hired a local sales agent, who paid bribes of $1.7 million to several Nigerian officials, including the defense minister, senior air force officers, politicians in the National Party, and officials of the Medical Center. The agent arranged to pass the payments through two Panamanian corporations that he controlled.

The US Government obtained information about the payments and in 1985 charged Kirkpatrick with violation of the Foreign Corrupt Practices Act, contending that Kirkpatrick officials had knowledge of the bribes. The company pled guilty and was fined $75,000, to be paid over a five-year period. The former chief executive officer of Kirkpatrick pled guilty to a single count of bribery of a foreign official. He received a suspended sentence, was placed on probation for three years, was fined $10,000, and was required to do community service work.

To simplify discussion in this chapter, we use the terminology representative to broadly include the complete spectrum of consultants, advisors, agents, representatives, distributors, and re-sellers. In cases in which there are important distinctions between the individual classifications of this broad group, they will be mentioned.

In the aerospace industry, representatives are generally utilized as a routine part of international marketing. The role of representatives, who have become institutionalized in most international aerospace marketplaces, tends to vary from country to country, depending upon business cultures and historical factors. Often representatives are small sole proprietorships consisting of one or two influential principals supported by a few administrative support staff. In contrast, some representatives are large corporations with large numbers of technical professionals.

In Japan, for example, major aerospace companies are traditionally represented by large Japanese trading companies that often have annual revenues that exceed the revenues of the aerospace companies themselves. The role of the trading companies is institutionalized to the extent that the Japan Defense Agency is legally required to utilize trading companies when procuring foreign military equipment, unless the equipment is procured directly from a foreign government.

Payment and compensation to in-country representatives can take numerous forms. Some of the most common compensation arrangements are described below. These arrangements are not mutually exclusive, and manufacturers' contractual agreements with representatives often contain compensation terms that are a combination of several of these individual arrangements:

- Retainers involve a fixed monthly payment for services rendered.
- Hourly charges involve billing by the representative on the basis of time spent in support of the client.
- Commissions involve payment to the representative of a specified percentage of the sales value.
- Bonuses are lump-sum payments paid to representatives that meet specific targets defined in advance.
- Mark-ups, used particularly in cases in which the representative is acting as a distributor, involve resale by the distributor at a price above the manufacturer's price.
- Reimbursements for expenses, as the language implies, are theoretically not revenue-generating compensation, but are intended to repay the consultant for costs of conducting business. In fact, representatives in some countries incur significant recurring expenses for entertainment and social events, and generous reimbursements of general expenses can often relieve the representative from important financial overhead costs.
- Payment for linked services is often used as an expedient method of channeling money to a representative if government regulations or other constraints limit the amount that the representative can be paid in commissions. Sometimes this practice is illegal, and plans to pay representatives for performance of linked services should certainly be reviewed thoroughly before they are implemented. Examples of linked services might be an arrangement in which the representative provides ancillary technical services after the sale, or provides arrangements for temporary housing and transportation for in-country contractor teams. Standards of legality for such arrangements vary from country to country, but generally such arrangements are expected to be justifiable as legitimate services rendered rather than as pure subterfuges for unearned payments.

In-country representatives are often small business operators, and they may request that their clients make payment to them in ways that have beneficial effects for financial management of their individual business entities. Sometimes special payment arrangements are perfectly legitimate and legal, but sometimes they may be subterfuges intended to evade taxes or obscure visibility by government officials. For this reason, client companies should be particularly wary of representatives' requests for unorthodox payment arrangements. Examples of such special arrangements are: payments into offshore bank accounts; payments divided into several smaller amounts that are paid to companies with different names; and commissions earned in a single year but paid on a deferred basis over several years.

Table 4.1 Japanese trading companies

Trading Company	Companies Represented	Commercial Aircraft	Companies Represented	Military Aircraft And Helicopters
Nissho Iwai	Boeing	*Airliners*	Boeing	*F-4, F-15 and Apache helicopter*
	Bombardier	*Commuter airliners and biz jets*	Raytheon	*Missiles*
Itochu	Raytheon	*Beechcraft*	Boeing	*767 AWACS, 767 Tanker, Chinook Helicopter, F-18*
	Boeing	*747/767 VIP*		
			Bell-Boeing	*V-22 Tiltrotor*
Mitsubishi	Pratt & Whitney	*Engines*	Raytheon	*T-400*
			Lockheed	*Tactical aircraft, F-22, F-35, C-130*
			Sikorsky	*Helicopters*
			Pratt & Whitney	*Engines*
Mitsui	Airbus	*Airliners*	Boeing	*C-17*
			Airbus	*Transport aircraft*
			Bell	*Helicopters*
			Bell-Boeing	*V-22 Tiltrotor*
Tomen			MD Helicopters	*Helicopters*
Marubeni	Gulfstream	*Biz jets*	EH Industries	*Helicopters*
	Embraer	*Commuter airliners*	Honeywell	*Engines*
			Airbus	*310 Tanker*
			Rolls-Royce	*Engines*
			Gulfstream	*U-4*
Kawasho	Cessna	*Biz jets*	Eurocopter	*Helicopters*
			Turbomeca	*Engines*
Corns	Zeppelin	*Dirigibles*	Thales (UK)	*Avionics*
Kanematsu	Raytheon	*Biz jets*	BAE Systems	*Tactical aircraft*
			Raytheon	*U-125*
Yamada			GE	*Engines*
			Northrop Grumman	*E-2C*

Note: In Japan, where traditional and legal restrictions have discouraged direct sales of aerospace products by foreign manufacturers to customers such as the Japan Defense Agency, international firms are often represented by major Japanese trading companies.

Recruiting a Foreign Sales Representative

The US Department of Justice and the US Securities and Exchange Commission have defined a number of specific circumstances that they believe should arouse suspicion that a foreign sales representative may be, or may intend to be, involved in illicit payments to government officials or decision-makers. Obviously these circumstances should elicit increased scrutiny from a prospective client before he engages in a contract with the representative:

- Requests for payments 'substantially in excess of the going rates' for similar services rendered.
- Payments involving a country with a history of FCPA violations or notorious widespread corruption.
- Activity in industries, such as aerospace, that are notorious for bribery (other notorious industries are construction, petroleum, and defense).
- Requests for financial transfers to third countries, particularly developing countries with weak government controls of financial institutions.
- Situations in which the representative is known to have a close relationship, family or otherwise, with an important government official.
- Requests for payments in cash, or through complex procedures with no obvious legitimate explanation.
- Requests for unusual bonuses for operational managers of the representative.
- The proposed representative is new to the business or lacks facilities and staff that would normally be expected to provide legitimate services.

National laws pertaining to in-country representatives vary dramatically, and it is not uncommon for such representatives to be expressly prohibited altogether. Before a marketer takes any initiative to involve a representative in his marketing efforts, he should obtain a professional legal opinion from a local law firm concerning the conditions under which representatives can be used in the target market.

As a search for a qualified local representative begins, the first step is to identify a list of potential candidates. At this point, it is often useful to arrange a meeting with the economic affairs counselor attached to the local embassy of the marketer's country. Most embassies maintain reference lists of sales representatives in major industries in the local economy. Although the embassies are generally prohibited from giving formal endorsement of individual representatives, they often will know if any of the listed companies have experienced legal problems or have been involved in customer-relations problems that resulted in serious consequences such as black-listing.

Other good sources of information about potential representatives are other aerospace companies with which the marketer has good relations, local expatriate business associations such as the American Chamber of Commerce or other international equivalents, and local law firms.

Sometimes the customer himself will recommend a qualified sales representative, particularly if he is asked. Although the selection of a friend of the customer as sales representative might appear to be a move that would enhance sales prospects, there are significant risks in involving the customer in the search. An obvious risk is the potential for conflict of interest and appearance of corruption if a friend of the customer is chosen for the job. Another problem is that, if the customer's recommended friend is eventually rejected in favor of a better-qualified candidate, hard feelings may result. Furthermore, a representative preferred by a single individual in the customer's organization may not be a popular choice among other influential people in the same organization or in other organizations involved in the selection process.

In the current age of large and diverse aerospace conglomerates, some corporations have attempted to implement policies of eliminating multiple sales representatives in individual countries. As the conglomerates have acquired new product lines through mergers, they have often acquired new groups of international marketing representatives different from the representatives for their heritage product lines. Although there are administrative benefits in working with a smaller number of representatives, it is often the case that specialized product lines are best represented by specialized representatives. It is also true that small marketing representatives, who can effectively represent one or two accounts, can quickly lose their effectiveness if they are overwhelmed by having numerous new accounts thrust upon them as the result of mergers. Generally, the best policy following a merger is to avoid tampering with the historical alignment of local marketing representatives until enough time has passed to fairly evaluate the effectiveness of each. In a deliberate fashion, less effective representatives can be identified and phased out. Thoughtful action is likely to produce better results than an aggressive initiative to pursue a questionable goal of eliminating all but one representative.

After a list of apparently qualified candidates is compiled, a formal process of interviews and evaluation should be conducted. This process should be conducted by a small team from the client company, rather than by a single individual. Payments to foreign representatives often involve large payments, and reasonable business practices dictate that no single individual should have unilateral control over the selection process. The aerospace industry is rife with stories of international salesmen and their foreign representatives who have fashioned schemes of mutual enrichment involving favoritism in the hiring process in return for kickbacks following eventual aircraft sales.

Embassy of the United States of America
Welcome to the Office of Defense Cooperation (ODC) Malaysia
376 Jalan Tun Razak, 50400 Kuala Lumpur. Tel: 603-2168-5000 ext. 4827 Fax:
603-2141-1080
E-mail: odc_my@po.jaring.my

Chief: LTC Benny E. Woodard, U.S. Army
Deputy Chief: Major Carlton Douglas Dawson, U.S. Air Force

The **Office of Defense Cooperation (ODC)** is the Department of Defense point of contact for U.S. Contractors who wish to do business with the Malaysian defense community. The ODC is primarily responsible for managing all Foreign Military Sales (FMS), Defense Cooperation in Armaments (DCA) programs, Title 10 Conferences, and International Military Education and Training (IMET) programs for the Department of Defense with Malaysia. The ODC works primarily in a government-to-government role or directly with U.S. defense companies. Provided below is the assistance U.S. defense contractors can expect to receive from ODC - Malaysia.

Assistance To U.S. Defense Contractors

The purpose of this note is to outline assistance available from the embassy to U.S. companies marketing defense products in Malaysia. The embassy stands ready to provide all appropriate assistance to U.S. companies seeking to fill Malaysia's defense requirements. When two or more U.S. companies seek to meet a single requirement, we are committed to providing even-handed assistance to all.

In general, assistance from the embassy is available from any section. The sections specifically charged with assisting companies marketing defense products are the Office of Defense Cooperation (ODC), the Foreign Commercial Service (FCS), and the Defense Attache's Office (DAO). The ODC can assist by providing insight concerning Ministry of Defense (MINDEF) procurement procedures; the FCS can provide detailed information regarding doing business in Malaysia, assist in Malaysian Government contacts outside MINDEF, and provide information on local agents through their Gold Key Service or by completing an FCS Advocacy Form; and the DAO can provide information on Malaysian defense requirements.

We request that U.S. companies marketing defense products make contact with the embassy through the ODC. The ODC will arrange for appointments with the FCS and DAO if requested.

We recommend that companies which have identified a specific Malaysian requirement, and believe they have a good chance of being selected to fill it, use a local agent. Local agents can greatly facilitate appointments with Malaysian government officials and can provide constant feedback and support.

Figure 4.2 US Embassy in Malaysia recommendation on the use of sales agents
Note: The US Embassy in Malaysia offers typical services to American firms attempting to sell in Malaysia. In this example, the Office of Defense Cooperation recommends the use of sales agents for military sales to the Malaysian Government, and offers to support marketing efforts.

Interviews should preferably take place on the premises of the individual candidates, so that the interviewers have a chance to evaluate physical facilities, workspace, and general working atmosphere. The candidate will be asked in advance to prepare a briefing of his background, qualifications, and assessment of the market. The interviewers will ask him a prepared list of questions that should be fundamentally the same for each candidate. The purpose of the interview is to assess the personality, style, and professionalism of the candidate, but also to obtain the following information:

- An understanding of why the candidate seeks to act as representative for the company and product line.
- An assessment of the candidate's background and skills.
- A preliminary assessment of the candidate's financial resources.
- An understanding of the size and capability of the candidate's organization.
- The identification of any potential conflicts of interest involving competitors or customers.
- The identification of any past legal problems or serious business problems with customers or government entities.
- A list of references.
- The identification of any subcontractors or associates that the candidate would propose to use in support of marketing or lobbying activities.
- An assessment of the candidate's understanding of anti-corruption legislation, such as the FCPA, to which the client is subject.

Sometimes inexperienced marketers proceed under the assumption that the most effective sales representatives are retired senior officials of the customer organization. This is not always true. Although retired executives and senior military officers often retain excellent relationships with their former colleagues, they sometimes leave a legacy of ill-will or professional rivalries within their former organizations. Another consideration is that, particularly in countries where the culture places great emphasis on social rank, former senior officials are often unable to initiate contact with former colleagues who were previously subordinate in rank. In South Korea, for example, it would be extremely awkward for a retired general to directly telephone an active-duty major to solicit information or ask for a favor. In any case, professional relationships are highly perishable, particularly in the military, where reassignments cause wholesale turnover of personnel after a few years. Generally, the most effective long-term marketing representatives are individuals with wide-ranging relationships and broad general knowledge of how local governmental and industrial decisions are made.

Following the initial selection process, the winning candidate undergoes a rigorous due diligence process that involves checking his business and financial references, verifying that he has had no significant legal problems, and generally checking the accuracy of the information considered during the selection process.

If no unexpected problems arise during the due diligence, a formal contract is drafted.

The contract between the selling company and the international representative is a legally enforceable agreement for the latter to provide professional services for the former. Much of the content is straightforward, but the document should specifically prohibit the representative from engaging in actions, such as corrupt behavior, that could cause problems for the seller.

A typical agreement between an aerospace company and a foreign sales consultant would contain sections defining the following conditions governing the relationship:

- The term of the contract.
- The products for which the consultant will provide marketing assistance.
- A general description of the consultant's duties, supplemented by a specific statement of work.
- A definition of specific reports that the consultant must furnish, at defined intervals.
- Specific limitations on the consultant's authority, with particular caveats that he must not obligate the seller in any way, and must not convey the impression that he has the authority to act on the seller's behalf.
- A specific commitment that the consultant will obey all applicable laws in the customer country and in the country of the seller.
- A definition of record-keeping requirements.
- Terms of compensation and payment.
- Terms of reimbursement of expenses, if any.
- The territory covered by the agreement.
- A non-compete clause.
- A non-disclosure clause.
- Terms and conditions of termination of the agreement.
- Government approvals required.
- Exclusivity or non-exclusivity.
- Governing law.
- A specific declaration by the consultant that he is familiar with the Foreign Corrupt Practices Act, and will abide by its conditions.
- A declaration by the consultant that he will not use government employees in his marketing efforts.
- Agreement to provide records and documentation in case the seller's government conducts an inquiry.
- Agreement to provide certificates and registrations as required by the consultant's home country.

Working with Marketing Representatives

A well-prepared contract between the marketing representative and the client company will contain a rigorous, detailed, statement of work. However, it is invariably left to the front-line marketer to define the nature of the day-to-day work that the representative actually performs. This point is worth emphasizing.

The campaign should be managed by the client rather than by the representative. A competent marketer will listen carefully to the comments and advice of his in-country representative, but will not abdicate responsibility to him for developing strategy or planning marketing activities.

Ideally, the relationship between the marketer and his representative will be one of consensus and close cooperation. The two parties share an overwhelming common interest – both have the same objective, which is to close the sale.

Frequent and continuous communication is essential. Real potential for misunderstanding exists because of language barriers and cultural differences, and regular discussion is the best means of exchanging information and coordinating action. A good practice is to agree on a specific time for a recurring phone conversation several times a week. Depending upon international time differences, this standing appointment is likely to be early in the morning or late in the evening.

The client and the representative should regularly exchange routine information by e-mail, fax, or conventional mail. The client should forward to the consultant routine internal company reports of interest, such as program status reports, announcements of major organization changes, sales announcements, relevant statements to the press, and news of major engineering developments. The representative should forward information such as customer organizational changes, released customer financial statements, announcements involving operational matters, and so on.

When a marketing strategy for the campaign is formulated, the representative should be a major source of information about the customer's decision-making process, and should identify key personalities with control over specific decisions.

When the client visits the international customer, the agenda of visits should be fully coordinated between the marketer and the representative, and the representative should be expected to arrange meetings and make many of the logistical arrangements. In the minds of many marketers, the measure of the effectiveness of their representative is his ability to obtain access to important high-level officials. The extent of reimbursement of costs associated with visit agendas will depend on the terms of the contract between the two parties.

In advance of the arranged appointments, the marketer and the representative should agree on the appropriate message to be conveyed to the customer. Normally the marketer will prepare the presentation materials, perhaps with assistance from the representative's office with details such as translations into the local language.

A major part of the representative's job is to obtain insider information, within the limits of the law. As the marketer wends his passage through the customer's arcane planning and purchasing process, he relies on the representative to keep him informed of what is actually going on within a system that may be opaque to outsiders.

An effective and smoothly functioning relationship between an international marketer and an in-country representative is often a decisive factor in international marketing campaigns. A good working relationship, based on mutual trust between two competent professionals who communicate well and empathize with each other's circumstances, is a substantial asset.

Chapter 5

Financing and Leasing

Financing is a discriminator in the sales process. Aerospace is a competitive industry, and aircraft operators generally can choose among several aircraft that will adequately meet their operational needs. As a result, aircraft buyers, driven by financial considerations, often make their aircraft selections based upon ancillary considerations such as financing arrangements and after sales support. The marketer whose company works most aggressively with the customer to understand his financing needs, and who uses industry knowledge to structure the most attractive financial offer, significantly increases his chances of success. At a minimum, anyone involved in the process of marketing and selling aircraft will be expected to have a basic understanding of aircraft financing mechanisms and financial terminology.

Virtually all large civil aircraft sales are financed. Generally the financing arrangements are handled by third-party lenders or leasing companies, although major manufacturers such as Boeing and Airbus have their own in-house finance companies that are essentially stand-alone specialty banks.

Because aircraft acquisitions have enormous financial implications for the operator, the financial structure of the ownership arrangement is a primary consideration of all parties involved. The enormous aggregate value of the worldwide inventory of commercial aircraft has given rise to a specialized financial services industry focused on aircraft leasing and financing.

With the possible exception of ocean-going ships, no major assets are more international in nature than large transport aircraft. As aircraft flying on international routes enter the airspace and territory of different countries during the course of a single day, they fall under different legal jurisdictions with different concepts of property, ownership, and debt. This physical transition among legal regimes presents problems for the lenders and lessors who have ownership rights to the aircraft. Particularly when aircraft fly to nations outside the well-understood legal domains of Europe, North America, Australia, and Japan, aircraft owners have experienced chronic problems of aircraft seizure by creditors of airlines, regardless of whether the airline itself is the owner of the property. The problem was illustrated by incidents in 2003 and 2004, when a small company registered in Cyprus, which had pressed legal claims against the Ukrainian Government, arranged to have Ukrainian civil transport airplanes seized in Canada and Belgium as the aircraft were in transit.

Table 5.1 The ten largest aircraft leasing firms in 2001

Rank	Lessor	Fleet Value ($billion)	Total Fleet	Twin-aisle Jets	Single-aisle Jets	Turbo-props
1	GECAS, Stamford, USA	22.1	1,040	136	866	38
2	ILFC, Los Angeles, USA	19.8	498	161	335	2
3	Flightlease, Zurich, Switzerland	4.4	95	41	54	0
4	debis Air Finance, Amsterdam, NL	4.2	198	20	144	34
5	Babcock & Brown, San Francisco, USA	3.0	110	15	95	0
6	Ansett Worldwide, Sydney, Australia	2.6	107	21	86	0
7	GATX Capital, San Francisco, USA	2.4	94	12	82	0
8	CIT Aerospace, New York, USA	2.3	124	20	76	28
9	Pegasus Capital, San Francisco, USA	2.3	197	29	167	1
10	BAE Systems, Woodford, UK	1.7	390	0	103	287

Note: The world's ten largest leasing companies owned aircraft valued at $64.8 billion in early 2001.

Source: Frost & Sullivan.

Creative Financing Influences Czech Aircraft Selection

In December 2001, the Czech Government announced that the Saab Aerospace/BAE Systems consortium called Gripen International had won the country's international competition to provide 24 fighter aircraft to the Czech air force. The program was valued at about 50 billion Czech crowns, or $1.37 billion at prevailing exchange rates. The selection decision was to be followed by detailed contract negotiations.

According to news reports at the time, a major discriminating factor that prompted the Czech Government to select the JAS-39 Gripen fighter was an impressive financing and offset program put together by Saab Aerospace and BAE Systems. During the competition, Gripen had faced the Lockheed F-16, the Boeing F/A-18, the EADS Eurofighter, and the Dassault Mirage 2000.

BAE Systems and Saab offered the Czech Government a 15-year payment schedule for the aircraft, and provided the Czechs with a five-year grace period before payment of the first installment.

A loan from an international banking consortium headed by Germany's Commerzbank was offered to cover 85 per cent of the total cost of the aircraft procurement, not including weapon systems and upgrades. Other banks in the consortium included HSBC, KBC and Bayerische Landesbank. The UK and Swedish governments agreed to fully guarantee the loan.

The remaining 15 per cent of the financing was to be provided by a loan from a consortium of Czech banks headed by CSOB, and including Ceska Sporitelna and Interbanka. All financing arrangements were subject to final Czech parliamentary approvals and guarantees.

BAE Systems offered export financing conditions under which the Czech Government would not be required to make any substantial payments for the Gripen until 2006, after it had completed paying for an earlier procurement of 72 Aero Vodochody L-159 light combat and training aircraft. The consortium proposal allowed the Czech Government to select the currency in which it would pay.

BAE Systems committed to provide a 100 per cent guarantee for currency fluctuation, in recognition of the expectation that the Czech Government would choose to pay for the aircraft in Czech crowns rather than US dollars or British pounds. BAE Systems and Saab Aerospace crafted the proposal to satisfy conditions insisted on by the chairman of the Parliamentary Defense and Security Committee, who insisted that no military procurement program should draw more than Kcs4 billion annually from the state budget.

Under the terms of the grace period offered by the seller, the Czech Government would not have to pay more than 4 per cent of the cost of the aircraft four years after execution of the final negotiated contract. The Kcs50 billion procurement cost was to include the aircraft, training of pilots and ground crew, and spare parts for three years.

This chaotic international legal situation increased uncertainty in the financial markets, and the corollary of uncertainty is always higher prices. In the case of the airline industry, lenders and lessors were compelled to raise their financing rates in order to insure their assets or otherwise cover their risk of seizure. The ultimate effect was that airlines worldwide were being prevented from conducting their business in an orderly fashion.

In attempts to resolve this issue, the national governments worked through the forum of the International Civil Aviation Organization, or ICAO, to establish an international agreement to standardize rights and procedures for aircraft owners, lenders, and lessors worldwide. The result was the Protocol to the Convention on International Interests in Mobile Equipment on Matters Specific to Aircraft Equipment, better known as the Cape Town Agreement, signed and approved by the parties in 2005. Under the Cape Town Agreement, aircraft owners for the first time can expect standard legal terms to apply to financial issues in all international locations where the aircraft operate.

Debt

Many large commercial aircraft are acquired by operators through leasing structures, rather than by debt, because of tax advantages and accounting factors that often favor leasing. However, access to capital through debt remains an effective and time-honored means for airlines to acquire aircraft. Government-guaranteed loans through *export credit agencies*, or *ECAs* (see below) are a mainstay of the aircraft financing industry. Because leasing structures are often convoluted and require commensurate administrative costs, bank loans can be a low cost option for an operator, if capital is available at less than a percentage point above *LIBOR*, the London InterBank Offering Rate. Banks are also sometimes involved in transactions that involve debt in the form of *commercial paper* that is handled jointly with third-party conduits.

Leasing

Simply stated, a lease is an agreement whereby one party (the lessor) gives exclusive rights to use and possess a piece of equipment to a second party (the lessee) for a fixed period of time in exchange for a regular payment – typically a monthly fee.

As government deregulation has made airlines more free to respond to market forces, the airlines experience relatively short-notice requirements for aircraft and crews to serve new markets. Outright ownership of aircraft, which entails major capital commitments over long periods of time, is not always suitable for the increasingly dynamic nature of the industry.

An industry of specialized aircraft leasing companies has arisen to respond to the financial needs of commercial aircraft owners. The leasing companies offer airlines the option of obtaining operational aircraft, sometimes on short notice, for a monthly fee. Obviously the amount of the monthly fee varies depending on the circumstances of the lease, but for large passenger aircraft a rough rule of thumb is that the monthly payment for a basic aircraft will be approximately 1 per cent of the value of the aircraft. Actual charges increase or decrease depending on factors such as prevailing interest rates, credit worthiness of the lessee, services provided by the lessor, guarantees provided by the lessee, term of the lease, termination conditions, and so on. An additional significant determinant of the lease fee is the projected residual value of the aircraft at completion of the lease.

For the lessor and the lessee, the attractiveness of alternative leasing arrangements is generally determined by arbitrary rules and standards established by government agencies and quasi-official organizations. These organizations define how financial transactions must be officially reported, and how taxes will be imposed. Of particular importance are:

- *Financial Accounting Standards Board (FASB)*, the committee established by the American accounting profession to define accounting standards. It gives lessors and lessees detailed guidance for presenting lease transactions in financial statements. Each industrialized country has its own equivalent to the FASB, and national accounting guidelines vary accordingly, but there is an international trend towards convergence of national accounting standards.
- *Internal Revenue Service (IRS)*, the American tax-collection agency, and its international counterparts. Following national legislation, these tax-collecting agencies define their own rules for tax treatment of leasing arrangements. Often the national tax agencies issue regulations that differ from recommended accounting practice promulgated by the FASB and its international counterparts. Because national tax laws vary significantly, there are often important tax advantages to arranging leases or aircraft ownership in specific countries.
- *State, provincial, and local governments* are concerned with collecting personal property and sales taxes on leased equipment. Their definition of legal ownership may differ from those of the FASB and the IRS. Obviously localities with oppressive tax regimes should be avoided by aircraft owners and financiers.

Convoluted leasing arrangements tend to blur ownership of aircraft. Consequently, the FAA and its international airworthiness counterparts have established guidelines for determining aircraft ownership so that accountability can be clearly established for purposes of enforcement of airworthiness regulations. The FAA generally determines the lessee to be the registered owner if the lease meets any of the following three conditions:

- The purchase option is 10 per cent or less of the value of the aircraft.
- The lessee is obligated to pay a residual value or termination sum equal to or exceeding the purchase option price.
- The option price is less than the lessee's reasonably predictable cost of performing under the lease agreement if the option is not exercised.

The FAA also insists that, in order for lessees to be registered as aircraft owners, the lessee must be obligated to ensure aircraft maintenance, insurance, taxes, operations, and the risk of loss, and the conditions of the lease must not permit the lessee the unilateral right to terminate the lease without economic penalty.

Wet Leases and Dry Leases

Depending on the needs of their customers, the leasing companies offer packages ranging from bare aircraft to aircraft with complete crews and planning support. Prices vary accordingly. In the parlance of the industry, a *dry lease* involves the aircraft only. A *wet lease* includes the aircraft and a complete crew. A further hybrid, the *damp lease*, generally includes the aircraft and cockpit crew, excluding the cabin crew. The most comprehensive lease, in which the lessor provides aircraft, crews, maintenance, and insurance, is called *ACMI*.

Financing Leases and Operating Leases

The terms of leases are structured according to the needs and resources of the customer. The *financing lease* is, in reality, secured financing of an aircraft purchase by an airline. The leasing company buys the aircraft and delivers it to the airline. Thereafter, the aircraft is considered to be an asset of the airline, and is reported as such on the airline's financial statements. Lease payments due are also included as short-term liabilities and long-term liabilities on the financial statements. At the completion of the lease, the residual value of the aircraft remains as an asset on the airline's balance sheet. The aircraft will normally be registered with the FAA or international airworthiness authority in the name of the lessee under a financing lease.

Under an *operating lease*, ownership of the aircraft remains with the lessor, and the aircraft often carries an international registration number of the lessor's home country rather than the airline's country. Operating leases are appropriate for shorter term airline requirements that are likely to result in transfer of aircraft to other operators before the useful life of the aircraft is exhausted. Thus, this type of leasing structure is appropriate for airlines that expect to respond to changing market conditions by frequently adding or removing aircraft from their networks as cyclical conditions warrant.

Another very significant attribute of operating leases is that the leased aircraft generally remain as assets on the lessor's balance sheet rather than the lessee's. Because the leases typically are short term, the lessee does not incur large long-term liabilities on his financial statements. Consequently, the leasing airline benefits from a favorable indicated ROI (return on investment), because its assets are understated, and a favorable debt-to-equity ratio, because its liabilities are understated. These two key indicators of financial health are closely watched by investors and creditors. Operating leases are also attractive to airlines that, for whatever reason, are unable to take advantage of the considerable tax advantages offered by depreciation of owned aircraft. For example, unprofitable airlines will often not be able to fully deduct depreciation from taxable revenue. By means of leasing arrangements, the tax deduction can effectively be transferred from the airline to the leasing company, with suitable financial accommodation for the airline.

A variant of the financing lease is the *synthetic lease*, in which the lessor is obligated to take possession of the aircraft at the completion of the lease, unless the airline exercises an option to purchase the aircraft at a pre-determined price. The purpose of the synthetic lease is to qualify as an operating lease for accounting purposes, but qualify as a loan for tax purposes. The lessee is able to reduce his tax liability because the lease payments are classified entirely as expenses. At the same time, the aircraft are excluded from the airline's balance sheet. The aircraft is registered in the name of the lessee under a lease with a purchase option. In cross-border leases, where the lessor is located in a different country than the lessee, the transaction may be structured so that each party is able to claim tax benefits in its own country. Obviously national tax laws must be thoroughly considered before cross-border leases are executed.

When dealing with cash-strapped airlines with weak financial positions, lessors generally consider the operating lease a more attractive alternative because it does not require them to acquire long-term commitments from borrowers with questionable credit ratings. Additional risks associated with operating leases to weak lessees are reflected in appropriate risk premiums attached to leasing fees.

A common leasing phenomenon used by airlines in precarious financial situations is the *sale and lease-back*, in which an airline simultaneously sells its aircraft to a leasing company, but retains physical possession of the aircraft by becoming a lessee. This maneuver allows the airline to convert the asset value of the aircraft to cash, without losing the revenue-generating potential of the aircraft.

Leveraged leases are complex financial arrangements in which a third party lends money to the lessor, who puts in some equity to buy the aircraft. The lender bases his credit decision on the creditworthiness of the lessee and makes the loan to the lessor on a non-recourse basis. The lessor keeps all the tax benefits and uses the leverage to create a high return on investment.

In *lease-in/lease-out* arrangements, the airline leases out its aircraft to an investor, then leases them back in a structure maturing between 50-60 per cent of the assets' useful life. Though US tax rules require a straight-line amortization, the investor realizes income statement benefits, while the airline enjoys a net present benefit from the transaction.

An historically important form of the leveraged lease has been the *Japanese Leveraged Lease* or *JLL*, which during the 1980s and 1990s was a very stable and popular cross-border leasing product. However, low yen interest rates in Japan, competition from other markets, and tax changes have combined to reduce the JLL's share of the global leveraged lease market. Because the JLL's attractiveness to investors has primarily derived through Japanese tax benefits, October 1998 tax reforms in that country negatively impacted the JLL by reducing the corporate tax rate (thus making tax deductions less attractive) and imposing less advantageous straight line depreciation.

Like most leasing arrangements, the *Japanese Operating Lease*, or *JOL*, is structured to maximize tax advantages for its investors. Because of the ambiguous nature of some aspects of Japanese tax regulations, JOL arrangements are diverse, but have a similar fundamental structure. The company that owns the aircraft leases it to the operator. The owner's purchase is financed through a combination of equity investment and a loan, which is limited in recourse to rentals payable under the lease. The loan is generally secured by a mortgage on the aircraft and an assignment of lease payments. As with the JLL, the lessor avoids the Japanese withholding tax on interest payments by routing the debt through a French *groupement d'interet économique*, or *GIE*, which is a type of partnership. The GIE sells the aircraft to the Japanese lessor under an installment sale agreement. Thus non-Japanese banks that do not have Japanese branches are able to participate as lenders into JOL transactions. Sometimes, the lenders will have the benefit of a residual value guarantee.

Changes in German tax regulations have led to the gradual disappearance of the *German Leveraged Lease*, or *GLL*, a once-popular structure that enabled airlines to convert owned aircraft to leases, and often enabled lessors to claim tax advantages in two countries. The *German Operating Lease*, or *GOL*, which is a relatively straightforward operating lease structure, has now largely replaced the GLL.

Using Debt and Lease-back to Improve an Airline Balance Sheet

Malaysia Airlines (MAS) was one of the many Asian carriers that suffered financially from the 1997 Asian economic crisis and the resulting depreciation in Asian currencies. The airline operated at a loss for five consecutive years following the crisis, and by January 2002 was carrying total debt of 10 billion ringgit ($2.7 billion).

To address the mounting debt problem, airline management announced an aggressive plan to convert assets to cash to be used to pay down liabilities.

Part of the strategy to shed assets consisted of sales of real estate, including the airline's 35-story office building in the heart of Kuala Lumpur's financial district, an office complex at Subang Airport and various other properties, including a computer center, training school and the carrier's administration complex at the new Kuala Lumpur international airport.

The second major thrust of the debt-reduction plan involved a plan to raise 5.6 billion ringgit ($1.5 billion) from the sale of six 747-400s and two 777-200ERs in a lease-back agreement. Of the eight aircraft to be sold, three of the 747s and both 777s had been ordered by the airline but not yet delivered. The sale was to Aseanbankers Malaysia Holdings; and the accompanying leaseback was for 12 years. The aircraft sale was expected to raise 4.1 billion ringgit.

The airline announced its intention to apply the revenues to pay off various Japanese loan instruments totaling 50 billion yen ($384.6 million) that were due in May 2002. The remainder of the funds were earmarked to be used as working capital until the airline returned to profitability and began to generate positive cash flow.

To restore operating profitability, the airline had developed a plan to cut international routes that were generating losses. However, the Malaysian Government had asked MAS to rethink its plans to cut some international services to Cairo, Istanbul, Beirut, Auckland, Zurich and Manchester, which the Government considered important to the country for reasons of economic development and international prestige.

By comparison with the JLL or GLL, the total number of cross-border *French Leveraged Leases*, or *FLL*s, of aircraft is relatively small. One reason for this is that, under French law, so-called *credit-bail* transactions (the leasing of an asset for professional use with a purchase option in favor of the lessee) are legally available only to banks or financial institutions registered as banks. This restriction limits the total pool of equity investors who are able to participate in credit-bail transactions. However, because aircraft leased under the FLL often provide lessors with the infamous *double-dip* (tax advantages in two countries, as long as the countries do not have mutual tax treaties), the FLL is often attractive to airlines and lessors.

Securitization

In the aircraft leasing industry, *securitization* is the process of creating marketable securities that are backed by the value of leases in one form or another. Securitization enables financial firms to raise additional capital to expand the scope of their operations. Securitization reduces the risk of financing or leasing aircraft, if the aircraft offered as collateral have predictable value in the resale market. To assure this predictable value, finance companies prefer common aircraft with well-established second-hand values. Ideally, they prefer to spread their risk over a number of aircraft types considered to be solid values. The simplest form of securitization is the issuance of corporate bonds secured via the aircraft. Secured bonds are a straightforward example of *asset-backed securities*. As with other types of asset-based financing, lenders generally will provide financing for only part of the asset value, with the expectation that the borrower or lessee will obtain the balance of the investment through internal funds or from a secondary lender. Generally asset-based financing of aircraft is limited to 75 per cent of aircraft value.

Other forms of securitization are more complex. *Equipment trust certificates*, or *ETC*s, are promises to pay, secured by lease receivables and the leased aircraft. A newer financial structure, the *enhanced equipment trust certificate*, or *EETC*, is considered a safer security from the point of view of the lender. EETCs have three characteristics. First, the borrower is rated highly by the credit agencies, and is effectively insulated from an eventual bankruptcy of the aircraft lessee. Second, the loan is rated according to the collateral provided by the projected residual value of the aircraft. And third, a liquidity facility is provided to ensure the continued payment of interest on the EETCs during the remarketing period following an eventual default by the lessee. An essential element of EETCs is that they are structured to ensure that the lessor has legal rights to repossess the aircraft under the US Commercial Code, thus ensuring the availability of the collateral. Because of the added credit protection afforded by EETCs, they tend to have credit ratings significantly higher than the corporate credit rating of the lessee. EETCs have become a dominant form of leasing structure in the United States, where Section 1110 of the US Bankruptcy Code allows creditors to proceed with fast repossession. In Europe, where national bankruptcy laws vary, and where repossession is less common, EETCs are less popular.

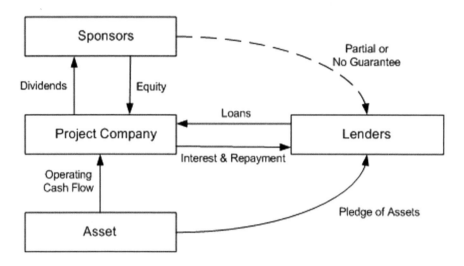

Figure 5.1 Asset-based Finance
Note: Asset-Backed credit reduces risk to lenders.

In contrast to the EETC structure, a *portfolio securitization* relies on a diversified portfolio of aircraft on operating leases to a number of airlines, both in the US and in other countries. Rather than enhancing a single corporate credit, the ratings of the debt securities issued in a portfolio securitization are based on the existence of a worldwide aircraft leasing market and the projected residual values of the aircraft in the portfolio. The actual levels of the ratings depend on a number of factors, including the age, initial value and diversity of the aircraft in the portfolio, the diversity (both individually and geographically) of the lessees of the aircraft and (to a lesser extent) their credit quality, the initial level of lease rents, assumptions as to the timing and costs of defaults and remarketing and other relevant factors. Credit support in a portfolio securitization is tailored to the particular needs of the aircraft and lessees involved, such as coverage for potential Eurocontrol liens, major maintenance costs, compliance with noise regulations and similar factors.

An important element in portfolio securitization is the quality of the servicer of the portfolio, in monitoring the performance of the lessees and in re-leasing and selling the aircraft both at the normal expiry of leases and in the case of lease defaults. The rating agencies also may require that a back-up servicer be identified and committed to act in appropriate circumstances.

Enhanced Equipment Trust Certificates Appear on the Aircraft Financing Scene

In September 1997, Continental Airlines announced that it had arranged financing at attractive rates for a major purchase of Boeing aircraft. The news was noteworthy because Continental had a long-standing record of poor profitability and consistently received poor scores from New York credit rating agencies.

The explanation for Continental's favorable borrowing terms was an innovative arrangement known as an enhanced equipment trust certificate, or EETC. The financing technique, which was not widely used at the time, was expected to become widely used because of its capability to effect a dramatic reduction in borrowing costs.

Observers correctly anticipated that the prospect of obtaining low interest rates on large portions of new debt would be alluring to many airline executives. The preferential interest rates resulting from the top-tier credit ratings could be secured by airlines that could obtain a guarantee from an institution with a high credit rating. The institution providing the guarantee had to agree to pay up to 18 months of interest on the debt if the carrier could not do so. For example, ABN AMRO Bank N.V. and Westdeutsche Landesbank Girozentrale guaranteed 18 months of interest payments for the $752 million in debt securities issued in 1997 by Continental. In turn, AMRO and Westdeutsche Landesbank Girozentrale would be the first creditors paid if an aircraft needed to be sold to pay off Continental debts.

The guarantees by the two banks to cover 18 months of interest payments qualified Continental for a higher credit rating than it otherwise could have obtained. Continental used the financing method to receive attractive interest rates between 6.8-6.9 per cent on three tranches – or segments – of pass-through certificates used to finance the new Boeing aircraft. Tranche A certificates received a high AA+ credit rating from Standard & Poor's and an A1 from Moody's Investors Service. The less senior tranche B certificates gained ratings of A+ from Standard & Poor's and A3 from Moody's, while weaker tranche C certificates earned ratings of BBB+ from Standard & Poor's and A3 from Moody's.

The financial markets believed that splitting the debt into different tranches with varying credit ratings avoided the problem of offering huge amounts of debt at a single rating and saturating the market.

However, markets identified risks of EETCs. Airlines that incurred millions of dollars of new debt through EETCs would obviously lose some degree of financial flexibility. Risk associated with the loss of flexibility could hurt an airline's credit rating for unsecured debt. Market-makers also expressed concern that access to EETC financing could also lead some airline executives to put less emphasis on improving credit ratings for senior, unsecured debt.

Aircraft Lease Portfolio Securitization History

Standard practices in the financial services industry often become implanted as a result of innovative experiments that are tested and proven to be successful. This was the case with aircraft lease portfolio securitization, which first appeared on the scene in the form of Aircraft Lease Portfolio Securitisation Limited 92-1, known as ALPS 92-1, sponsored by GPA Group plc. Prior to ALPS 92-1, which closed in June 1992, lease securitizations had involved large portfolios of small ticket items and were more similar to mortgage and credit card receivables securitizations. ALPS 92-1 was the first securitization of extremely high-value items of leased personal property, specifically aircraft, with values from $15 million to $80 million.

ALPS 92-1 involved a portfolio of 14 aircraft on lease to 14 lessees in 12 countries outside the USA, having an aggregate appraised value of $521 million. The aircraft were sold to ALPS 92-1, which issued $417 million of senior and mezzanine debt. There was substantial credit support in the form of a 'supermezzanine loan', available to fund shortfalls of principal and interest, with repayment of such loan subordinated to the senior debt.

Standard & Poor's carried out particularly intense due diligence in ALPS 92-1. Each country in which a lessee was located was completely vetted from a legal standpoint, and each lease was carefully reviewed to ensure that it met exacting legal standards. A similarly high legal standard was applied in the actual aircraft deliveries.

Except for the one relatively small class of amortizing bonds, the ALPS 92-1 debt was to be paid from aircraft sales in the 18 months before the maturity date, during which period ALPS 92-1 was in effect required to create a sinking fund by selling aircraft. If ALPS 92-1 were to fail to meet specified sales goals, it effectively would be put into a voluntary workout, with the senior debt holders having the ability to sell aircraft at levels sufficient to pay only the senior debt.

This financial structure forced aircraft sales within a limited period and required that sales proceeds be held in low-risk investments. The requirement for sale within a specified fixed period imposed an undesirable risk: the possibility that the fixed remarketing period could occur during a significant recession or even a period when very few aircraft sales were being closed, as had happened following the Gulf War in 1991. However, ALPS 92-1 in fact refinanced its debt without adverse circumstances at the beginning of the remarketing period in 1996, through Aircraft Lease Portfolio Securitization 96-1 Limited.

Essential Elements of Lease Agreements

Leases are rigorous legal documents replete with terms and conditions, but at a minimum they specify the term of the lease, penalties and conditions for early termination, fees, and subleasing conditions.

The practice of aircraft leasing has advantages and disadvantages that affect the parties in different ways. From the point of view of the airline, it is advantageous in many ways to avoid the financial risks and burdens of aircraft ownership, leaving airline management free to focus on the operation of the airline. Values of aircraft fluctuate dramatically as markets experience cyclical phases, and airline managers sometimes prefer to pass this risk to third parties. As leasing companies have grown in recent years, they have become volume purchasers of new aircraft, with commensurate negotiating weight vis-à-vis the aircraft manufacturers. In theory, because of this negotiating power, the leasing companies pay lower-than-market prices for their aircraft, and some of this price advantage is passed to lessees.

Export Credit Agencies

National governments attach inordinate importance to the success of their domestic aerospace industries, and commonly government policy includes official measures to support the industry. Prominent among government policy in support of aerospace is the use of *export credit agencies*, or *ECA*s, which are government agencies or government-protected agencies that ensure subsidized export financing for aerospace sales. Every year, a very significant volume of commercial aircraft financing passes through the ECAs.

Because ECA activity is a form of national subsidy of export industries, the ECAs potentially can cause distortion to international trade. Recognizing this threat, the major aircraft exporting countries (principally the United States, the United Kingdom, France, and Germany) have reached a formal agreement to limit the extent of ECA subsidies. This agreement, formulated within the framework of the Organization of Economic Cooperation and Development, or OECD, is known as the *Large Aircraft Sector Understanding*, or *LASU*.

LASU establishes the terms, conditions, and special guidelines of export credit support that OECD governments can extend to buyers of large aircraft. It sets the minimum cash payment at 15 per cent, a market-based interest rate for loans extended by an export credit agency, and a maximum 12-year repayment term.

ECA / Country	Normal maximum percentage of cover		Unconditional cover	Fixed rate at CIRR available	Foreign currency financing possible	Bond Insurance: Insurance against unfair calling	Bond Support: Support for the issuance of bonds	Lines of Credit	
	Political risk	Commercial risk						General purpose	Project
CESCE Spain	99	94	N	Y	Y	Y	Y	N	N
COFACE France	95	95	N	Y	Y	Y	N	N	Y
ECGD UK	100	100	Y	CBC	Y	Y	N	Y	Y
EDC Canada*	100 for direct loans up to 75 for guarantees	100 for direct loans up to 75 for guarantees	Y	Y – but no interest make-up on guarantees	Y	Y	Y	Y	Y
EKN Sweden	100	90	N	Y	Y	Y	Y**	Y	Y
EXIM BANK USA	100	100	Y	Y – Direct Loans N – Guarantees	N – Direct Loans Y - Guarantees	N***	N***	Y	Y
ATRADIUS Netherlands	98 (95 in 2002)	95	N	N	Y	Y	Y	Y	Y
EULER HERMES (KfW*) Germany	95	95	N	Y (CBC in 2002)	Y	Y	N	Y (N in 2002)	Y
NEXI Japan	97.5	95 (90 in 2002)	N	Y	Y	Y	?	N	Y
SACE Italy	95	95	N	Y	Y	Y	N	Y (N in 2002)	Y

FINANCING PRODUCTS

* Direct lenders
** EKN - In the form of counter guarantees for contract guarantees (bonds).
*** Exim's Working Capital Guarantee Program has permitted that its "revolving line of credit guarantee" be utilized as a counter guarantee against a commercial bank's stand-by letter of credit on a case-by-case basis.

Figure 5.2 Products of export credit agencies

Note: Although the ECAs of industrialized nations are similar in many ways, the financial products they offer have significant differences.

Source: ECGD.

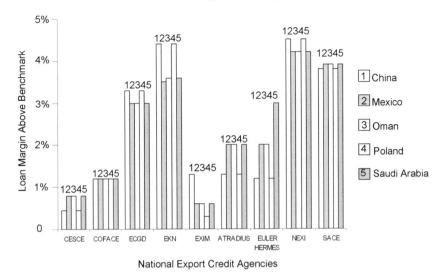

Figure 5.3 ECA risks and prices
Note: Part of the function of ECAs is to provide coverage for risks that deter commercial lenders, but ECA pricing reflects the perceived risk in the borrowing market.
Source: ECGD.

After the advent of LASU, aerospace industries and their national agencies continued to search for ways to compete on the basis of aircraft financing, by means of financing agencies that did not fit the definition of ECAs, but which were nonetheless able to offer some advantages of government support. These agencies are known as *market windows* because they supposedly are fully exposed to market forces, as contrasted to the ECAs themselves, known as *official windows*. The two most active market windows are the German Kreditanstalt fur Wiederaufbau (KfW) and the Canadian Export Development Corporation (EDC). In the example of KfW, which operates as the market window alter-ego to the German official window ECA Hermes Kreditversicherungs-Ag, KfW does in fact have significant government-provided advantages over the private sector banks against which it supposedly competes. These advantages include:

- KfW capital is provided by the German Government.
- KfW borrows with the full faith and credit of the German Government, thus greatly reducing the cost of its access to funds.
- KfW does not pay dividends to shareholders.
- KfW pays no taxes on its profits.

The largest of the national ECAs is the Export-Import Bank of the United States, known as Ex-Im Bank, although it is not strictly speaking a bank. European ECAs are the UK's Export Credits Guarantee Department (ECGD), France's Compagnie Francaise D'Assurance pour le Commerce Exterieur (COFACE), and Germany's combination of Hermes Kreditversicherungs-Ag (Hermes) and Kreditanstalt fur

Wiederaufbau (KfW). Typically the three European ECAs work together to assure export financing for Airbus. In one of the ironies typical of the tortured political relationships in the international aerospace industry, the three European agencies also provide support for US manufactured engines in Airbus airframes, and the amount of that support is split among the three agencies. In cases in which the aircraft are powered by Rolls-Royce engines, however, the proportion of the support provided by ECGD is higher.

Although all of the ECAs are involved in a broad range of export activities and international project finance, aerospace exports are a major part of their portfolios. In the year 2000, for example, the agencies participated in large aircraft loans with a total value of $9.5 billion.

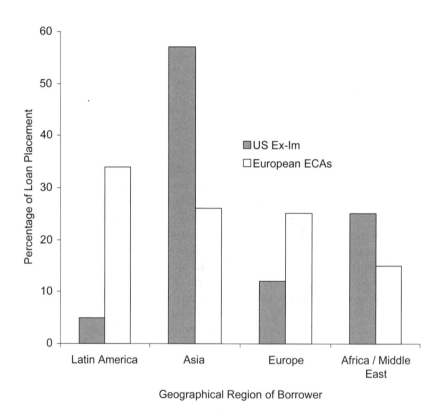

Figure 5.4 ECA loans by geographical area
Note: International loan arrangements reflect aircraft sales, with Ex-Im supporting American aerospace manufacturers and the Euopean ECAs supporting their domestic producers. The total value of ECA loan guarantees in specific regions varies drastically from year to year.
Source: US Ex-Im Bank.

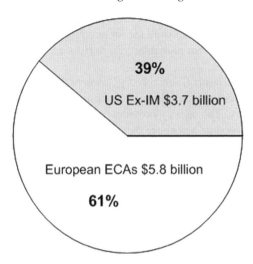

Figure 5.5 Relative volume of financing by Ex-Im and European ECAs
Note: In the year 2000, total large aircraft financing by European and American ECAs was roughly $10 billion, more than half of which was from Ex-Im. As Airbus' relative share of the market has increased, European ECA participation has increased proportionately.
Source: US Ex-Im Bank.

Ex-Im Bank offers financial support for the export of new and used US-manufactured commercial and general aviation aircraft, including helicopters, under its direct loan, guarantee, and insurance programs. It typically guarantees loans that have been extended by a financial institution to either the borrower directly or to facilitate a finance lease. The credit decision rests on the creditworthiness of the airline/lessee and/or the guarantor, plus the additional security provided by the financed aircraft. As stipulated by the OECD, Ex-Im offers up to a maximum of 12-year repayment terms. Repayment may be structured as either a level principal or mortgage-style amortization. In all cases, Ex-Im reserves the right to make the final determination on the profile of the debt repayment schedule. The maximum financed amount equals 85 per cent of the US contract price net of all manufacturer credit memoranda. However, the financed amount may be reduced in cases where the risks are considered significant.

Ex-Im may allow the inclusion of spare parts, related ground equipment, training costs, and transaction expenses in sovereign guaranteed large aircraft transactions. Generally, these items are not included in asset-based transactions, but they may be considered on a case-by-case basis when a substantial asset value to loan margin exists and the airline is a suitable credit risk.

By law, Ex-Im is prohibited from supporting the sale of military aircraft or civilian aircraft that will be used for military applications. In order to qualify for support, Ex-Im must be satisfied that all aircraft sales to military or quasi-military buyers are intended to be used for primarily civilian or humanitarian purposes.

The exposure fee charged on a particular transaction reflects Ex-Im's assessment of the creditworthiness of the borrower and/or guarantor and the risks presented by the transaction. The exposure fee may be included in the financed amount supported by Ex-Im. Ex-Im's minimum exposure fee for new large aircraft transactions is 3 per cent. Transactions that present particularly high risks are assessed an exposure fee greater than the minimum.

ECGD, the Export Credits Guarantee Department, Britain's official export credit agency, is a separate government department responsible to the Secretary of State for Trade and Industry. The agency provides loan guarantees and export financing insurance for British-source aerospace exports, as well as extensive non-aerospace related financial support of British exports.

ECGD provides credit guarantees for aircraft importers in the form of buyer credits that can extend to 100 per cent of the total credit amount, which can be 85 per cent of the aircraft value. The bank of a qualifying British exporter receives an ECGD guarantee that all sums lent to the overseas buyer will be repaid in full. Further, the ECGD will pay the difference between the fixed rate and the future commercial floating rate if the latter is higher. ECGD guarantees can also extend to contractual termination settlement and arbitration expenses and awards.

ECGD export insurance can cover up to 95 per cent of the value of any loss suffered due to non-payment in connection with individual aircraft exports, including political and commercial risks.

The *Compagnie Française d'Assurance pour le Commerce Extérieur (COFACE)*, the official export credit agency of the French Government, insures French exporters on commercial terms against short-term non-payment risks, and also supports French exporters in markets that conventional insurance companies are not willing to cover due to perceived risks. These involve large projects, such as aircraft financing, as well as high-risk markets. In these cases, COFACE acts on behalf of and with the backing of the French Government. This category includes market survey insurance, medium-term credit insurance on large-scale projects and capital goods, investment risks in foreign countries, and exchange rate guarantees on major contracts or large amounts. Under these agreements, COFACE acts as the manager for the French Government.

Acting as a private insurer or on behalf of the French Government, COFACE insures French companies against the risk of non-repayment of customer debt attributable to customer insolvency or default on the part of the buyer due to other causes, including broadly defined political risks. It also provides cover against fluctuations in exchange rates.

German Government-sponsored financial guarantees for the promotion of exports by German industry are administered by a consortium consisting of *Hermes Kreditversicherungs-AG* and *C&L Deutsche Revision Aktiengesellschaft Wirtschaftsprüfungsgesellschaft*. Hermes is the senior member of the consortium.

Press release by ECGD, Export Credits Guarantee Department, Britain's official export credit agency, an agency of the UK government

25 February 1999

TRADE MINISTER WELCOMES ECGD BACKING FOR LARGEST EVER
AIRCRAFT FINANCING DEAL

Brian Wilson, Minister for Trade, today announced that ECGD had agreed to provide backing for the UK portion of the largest aircraft financing deal in history. A US$4.327 billion umbrella facility, arranged and lead managed by Halifax plc, Group Treasury, is to support the delivery of 75 Airbus aircraft over the next three years.

Mr Wilson said:

'This is superb news for British Aerospace. The orders to be financed under the ECGD-backed loan facility will provide the company with valuable work for some time to come and should secure jobs in Bristol and Chester and for BAe's many sub-contractors up and down the country. I am absolutely delighted that this co-operation between Government and industry has produced such an excellent result for Britain.'

As part of the overall facility ECGD has agreed to support up to US$1.123 billion of export credits to help Airbus Industrie provide a subsidiary of US-based operating lessor International Lease Finance Corporation (ILFC) with a range of aircraft for on-lease to a number of airlines around the world.

ECGD has started to issue a series of guarantees for loan repayments in respect of deliveries to individual airlines, e.g. Air Canada, Dragonair, Swissair. A variety of Airbus models will be involved, e.g. A319, A320, A321, A330, A340. The remainder of the financial backing is being supported by Coface of France and Hermes of Germany.

The other Lead Managers for the financing facility are Societe Generale of France (on behalf of Coface) and Commerzbank AG of Germany (on behalf of Hermes).

This facility enables Airbus Industrie to place aircraft with a wide range of airlines worldwide in the knowledge that the lessor (ILFC) has a top quality credit rating.

Airbus aircraft are built by a European consortium comprising British Aerospace (who provide the wings), Daimler Chrysler Aerospace of Germany, Aerospatiale of France and CASA of Spain. On occasion Britain also provides Rolls-Royce engines.

ECGD, the Export Credits Guarantee Department, Britain's official export credit agency, is a separate Government Department responsible to the Secretary of State for Trade and Industry. One of its main functions is to underwrite bank loans to enable overseas buyers to purchase capital and project related goods/services from Britain.

Figure 5.6 ECGD backing for largest ever aircraft financing deal

The Hermes consortium guarantees loans for aircraft and aerospace equipment for direct sales to buyers in the private sector, or buyers in the public sector and government-owned enterprises. The guarantees may cover risk of insolvency by the purchaser, political events, transportation, delays, manufacturing risks, and fees and premiums. Hermes also offers insurance against bad debts and fraud, and provides bond guarantees.

Germany's *Kreditanstalt fur Wiederaufbau (KfW)* is a true bank, in contrast to Hermes. It is publicly owned, but is not an ECA. On behalf of the German Government, it functions as a conventional bank to provide export credit under guarantees written by Hermes. It is also the country's *market window*, as defined above, to enable the Government to assure attractive export loans that are not constrained by the LASU convention. Loans under these conditions do not have Hermes coverage guarantees.

Inevitably, the large sums of money involved in ECA transactions have resulted in instances of corruption by buyers and sellers. To control this problem, OECD ECAs have subscribed to a number of international conventions that expressly prohibit certain corrupt practices.

OECD (Organization for Economic Cooperation & Development) Initiatives to Eliminate Corruption in ECA Transactions

December 2000 - **ACTION STATEMENT ON BRIBERY AND OFFICIALLY SUPPORTED EXPORT CREDITS**

In recognition of the Convention on Combating Bribery of Foreign Public Officials in International Business Transactions and the 1997 Revised Recommendation, the Members of the OECD Working Party on Export Credits and Credit Guarantees (ECG) agree:

1. Combating bribery in international business transactions is a priority issue and the ECG is the appropriate forum to ensure the implementation of the Convention and the 1997 Revised Recommendation in respect of international business transactions benefiting from official export credit support.
2. To continue to exchange information on how the Convention and the Recommendation are being taken into account in national official export credit systems.
3. To continue to collate and map the information exchanged with a view to considering further steps to combat bribery in respect of officially supported export credits.
4. To take appropriate measures to deter bribery in officially supported export credits and, in the case that bribery as defined by the Convention was involved in the award of the export contract, to take appropriate action, including:

- All official export credit and export credit insurance providers shall inform applicants requesting support about the legal consequences of bribery in international business transactions under its national legal system including its national laws prohibiting such bribery.
- The applicant and/or the exporter, in accordance with the practices followed in each ECG Member's export credit system, shall be invited to provide an undertaking/

declaration that neither they, nor anyone acting on their behalf, have been engaged or will engage in bribery in the transaction.

- The applicant and other parties receiving or benefiting from support remain fully responsible for the proper description of the international business transaction and the transparency of all relevant payments.
- The applicant and other parties involved in the transaction remain fully responsible for compliance with all applicable laws and regulations, including national provisions for combating bribery of foreign public officials in international business transactions.
- If there is sufficient evidence that such bribery was involved in the award of the export contract, the official export credit or export credit insurance provider shall refuse to approve credit, cover or other support.
- If, after credit, cover or other support has been approved, an involvement of a beneficiary in such bribery is proved, the official export credit or export credit insurance provider shall take appropriate action, such as denial of payment or indemnification, refund of sums provided and/or referral of evidence of such bribery to the appropriate national authorities.

These actions are not prejudicial to the rights of other parties not responsible for the illegal payments.

5. To continue to exchange views with appropriate stakeholders.
6. To review periodically actions taken pursuant to this Action Statement.

Any of the actions mentioned above have to be realised in accordance with the legal system of each ECG Member country taking into account its specific judicial instruments and institutions to implement its penal laws.

Figure 5.7 OECD initiatives to eliminate corruption in ECA transactions

Financing Military Aerospace Sales

Almost all sales of military aircraft take place through one of two alternative contractual arrangements:

- In direct commercial sales, the manufacturer or an agent sells directly to the military customer
- In government-to-government sales, one national government sells equipment directly to another national government. Under this arrangement, the selling national government may be acting as an intermediary for a manufacturer in his own country, or he may be selling surplus aircraft or equipment from his own inventory.

Commercial sales of military aircraft are most commonly structured as cash sales in which the customer provides progress payments to the manufacturer to cover manufacturing costs during the work-in-process phase prior to aircraft delivery.

However, creative financing arrangements for military aircraft are becoming increasingly common for sales to customers of all types.

Some military equipment sales are financed through arrangements that closely resemble civil aircraft sales, with the notable exception that the customer for military equipment is almost always a sovereign government rather than a private party.

The major European exporting nations handle military aircraft export financing in a manner very similar to export financing of civil aircraft, by utilizing their respective export credit agencies. Britain's ECGD, Germany's Hermes, and France's COFACE all carry major portfolios of guarantees for export military equipment, and in fact in some years ECGD's military-related guarantees exceed the value of guarantees for civil exports.

In the United States, where Ex-Im is legally prohibited from financing arms exports, sales of military equipment and aircraft can be financed through government institutions that exist exclusively for the purpose of accommodating international arms sales. The principal American Government mechanisms for financing arms sales are the Defense Export Loan Guarantee (DELG) program, and the Foreign Military Financing (FMF) program. Operation of DELG is similar in many ways to Ex-IM, and credit support is theoretically available to a wide range of US exporters and their customers. FMF, in contrast, is essentially a tool of American foreign policy, and is normally available only to customers for whom the American Government wants to provide foreign aid for national defense purposes. It is therefore inaccessible to the vast majority of military aircraft customers.

Chapter 6

Industrial Offsets

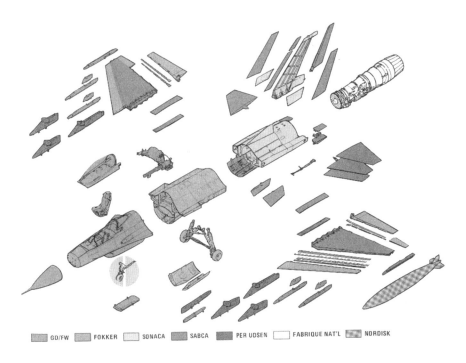

GD/FW   FOKKER   SONACA   SABCA   PER UDSEN   FABRIQUE NAT'L   NORDISK

Figure 6.1 Industrial worksharing under the F-16 offset program in Europe
Source: Lockheed Martin.

In large-scale international aerospace sales, the customer may insist that the aircraft seller provide the buyer's country with certain kinds of industrial benefits as a condition of sale. Commitments to provide these compensatory industrial benefits, known as *offsets*, are often a condition of sale.

The involvement of offset agreements is particularly common in sales of military aircraft, where the buyer is normally a sovereign government that has an interest in promoting the interests of its domestic industry.

The use of offset came into widespread practice in the aerospace industry in Western Europe in the period following World War II, when the shattered European aerospace industry was struggling to rebuild, but was often dependent upon American industry for military aircraft. European governments wanted to acquire work for their domestic aerospace industries, and at the same time wanted to offset the enormous negative balance-of-payments effects of importing foreign aircraft. To compensate for the loss of financial reserves and aerospace jobs that resulted from aircraft imports, European governments began to insist that part of the manufacturing work involved in aircraft manufacture be transferred to Europe. As time passed, the concept of offsets became more complex and spread to other parts of the world. As the modern fully developed European aerospace industry began to export military aircraft to international markets, it also began to include offset commitments in its sales contracts.

In industry parlance, the term *offset* is generally taken to mean the entire range of industrial and commercial benefits provided to foreign governments as an inducement or condition to purchase *military* goods or services, including benefits such as co-production, licensed production, subcontracting, technology transfer, in-country procurement, marketing and financial assistance, and joint ventures. Offsets sometimes become involved in purchases of civil aircraft, particularly when government-owned airlines are the purchaser, but offsets are primarily a characteristic of military sales.

A defining characteristic of both defense and commercial offsets, per the above definition, is that the foreign *government* plays a role (either directly or through state-controlled companies) in obtaining the benefits from the exporter.

Large amounts of money are involved in major international sales of aircraft, and the value of offsets is proportionately high. The US Commerce Department compiles data on offsets, and reports that during the decade of the 1990s, total defense-related offsets, most of which involved the aerospace industry, consistently exceeded $2 billion per year, and sometimes exceeded $3 billion. Comprehensive data applying to offsets offered by the European aerospace industry is less readily available, but it is safe to assume that European-source offsets are proportional to the volume of European exports of military aerospace equipment.

The chart on page 99 shows the value of US defense offset transactions each year over 1993-2004. 'Value', in this context, means the amount of offset credit awarded to US exporters by offset-receiving nations.

Because national governments are almost always the final customer when exports of defense equipment occur, this type of export is frequently subject to government offset demands. However, data compiled by the US Government shows that the defense aerospace industry is particularly prone to becoming involved in transactions that carry offset commitments. In the period 1993-1998, 89 per cent of defense offsets (measured by value) were associated with the export of aerospace goods or services by US firms. During the same period, US defense aerospace exports accounted for approximately 70 per cent of all US defense exports, indicating that aerospace was disproportionately represented in defense offset transactions.

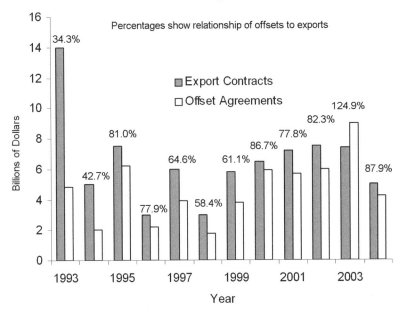

Figure 6.2 Value of industrial offsets, 1993-2004
Note: The value of industrial offsets is enormous, and is expected to grow as offset practices become institutionalized throughout the world.
Source: US Department of Commerce, Bureau of Industry and Security.

Categories of Offsets

Offset arrangements appear in many forms, dictated primarily by the industrial policy needs of the buyer country and the imagination of the parties to each transaction. Although new forms are constantly evolving, they fall into two principal categories, direct and indirect offsets. Direct offsets are arrangements in which the benefit provided to the buyer country is directly related to the aerospace system sold in the underlying transaction. For example, in a sale of military aircraft, the seller might be required to assemble part of the aircraft structure in the buyer country instead of in the prime contractor's facility in the United States. Because this side agreement is directly related to the underlying aircraft sale, it would be considered a direct offset.

Indirect offsets, by contrast, involve activities unrelated to the system sold in the underlying transaction. In the example of an aircraft sale, an indirect offset arrangement might require the vendor to purchase its office furniture from a company within the buyer country. This would be termed an indirect offset because, even though office furniture is in no way related to aircraft, the furniture sale is nonetheless a component of the underlying aircraft sale.

The US Government Accountability Office (GAO), one of several US Government institutions that has studied the impact of aerospace offset practices on the American economy, has identified a number of sub-categories of offset arrangements:

1. *Co-production and subcontracting.* In the co-production arrangements studied by GAO, US vendors contracted with one or more companies in the buyer country to assemble, build, or produce articles related to the underlying sale. In the subcontracting arrangements, US vendors agreed to buy goods or services related to the underlying sale from suppliers in the buyer country. Co-production and subcontracting offsets appeared in 20 per cent of the transactions reviewed by GAO.

An example of a co-production offset program was the 1991 Korean Fighter Program, in which the Government of South Korea and General Dynamics concluded a $5.2 billion transaction involving the purchase of F-16 fighter aircraft. The parties structured the deal so that the Government of South Korea purchased 12 of the aircraft off-the-shelf and bought 36 in the form of aircraft kits to be assembled in Korea. In addition, South Korea obtained the right to manufacture an additional 72 F-16s under license.

An example of an offset program involving subcontracting was the sale of Apache attack helicopters to the United Kingdom in the 1990s. As part of the sales agreement, valued at nearly $4 billion, McDonnell Douglas agreed to purchase from British firms $350 million worth of equipment for the helicopters.

2. *Other procurement.* In this type of indirect offset arrangement, the prime contractor agrees to purchase goods and services unrelated to the aerospace item sold. According to GAO, this form of offset was present in 9 per cent of the transactions reviewed.

An example of procurement involving indirect offset was Lockheed Martin's agreement, as part of its sale of C-130 aircraft to Canada, to purchase assemblies and avionics from Canadian industry for Lockheed's C-5 transport plane.

3. *Technology transfer.* In these cases, US vendors transfer technology, technical assistance, or training to the buyer country. The technology is in some cases unrelated to the underlying aerospace item sold. In GAO's review, this form of offset appeared in 48 per cent of the transactions studied.

An example was Lockheed's agreement, as part of its sale of F-16 fighter aircraft to South Korea, to transfer manufacturing and assembly expertise, enabling South Korea to assemble from kits and manufacture many of the aircraft sold as part of the deal.

4. *Marketing assistance.* In this form of offset, aerospace contractors help foreign companies market their products overseas. The basis of this type of offset arrangement is the assumption that the firm with the offset obligation has greater marketing expertise or market access than the foreign firm that benefits from the agreement. Such offsets were present in 23 per cent of the transactions reviewed by GAO.

An example was McDonnell Douglas' agreement, as part of its $3 billion sale of F/A-18 fighters to Finland, to provide international marketing assistance for the REDIGO training aircraft produced by the Finnish company Valmet Aviation, Inc.

5. *Financial assistance/investment/joint venture.* In this form of offset arrangement, US contractors took equity positions, provided start-up financing, or provided other services to support a new or existing business entity in the buyer country. According to GAO, such offsets appeared in 13 per cent of the transactions reviewed.

An example was McDonnell Douglas Helicopter Company's initiative to enter into several joint ventures in the United Arab Emirates as part of its sale of Apache attack helicopters to that country. The joint ventures, mostly unrelated to aerospace, developed products to clean up oil spills and recycle printer cartridges used in photocopiers and laser printers.

The main types of offset transactions, by value, are: the counter-purchase of goods from the offset-receiving country, which is usually a type of indirect offset; subcontracts provided to companies in the offset-receiving nation for items used in the product being exported, which is direct offset; and direct transfer or licensing of technology, which may be either direct or indirect offset. Many counter-purchases are similar to subcontracts in that the goods or services purchased by the US exporter are then used by the exporter in its own operation, rather than being directly resold to a third party. For example, the US exporter of a military aircraft may fulfill offset obligations by counter-purchasing navigation equipment from a source in the customer country, using the navigation equipment in production of civil aircraft unrelated to the initial sale of military aircraft.

As shown in Figure 6.2, the dollar value of US defense offset agreements as a percentage of the export sales with which they are associated ranged from 34 percent to 124 percent from 1993 to 2003, and, while volatile, shows no obvious upward or downward trend during this time period.

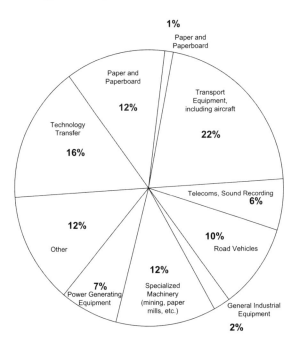

Figure 6.3 The mixture of indirect offset projects executed by McDonnell Douglas associated with its sale of the F-18 fighter to Finland in the 1990s

Source: US Government Accountability Office.

How Important are Offsets to the Marketer?

Beyond any doubt, offsets are a very important ingredient in international marketing of defense equipment. In an era of relative international peace, it is often difficult for national governments to justify the overwhelming investments that defense equipment entails. To obtain government funding for new aircraft programs under these circumstances, it becomes necessary for defense ministers to seek political support from other cabinet members and political interest groups. To enlist support from organized labor, industry, and the technological community in the buyer's country, an appealing offset program is essential. In fact, a common problem among aerospace executives is that they sometimes do not fully understand the nature of the product they are offering to international buyers. They mistakenly believe that their product is narrowly defined military hardware that they are selling to an independent government defense establishment, whereas in reality they are selling a package of benefits that includes military aircraft, but also includes jobs, technology transfer, profits for industry, and so on. The customer for this broadly defined product is the overall constituency of the government. The relative importance of military capability versus industrial benefits varies from country to country. Israel, for example, where national defense is an exceptionally high priority, places great weight on the operational capability of the military aircraft that it buys. Denmark, on the other hand, where the populace does not consider itself to face a military threat, heavily emphasizes industrial benefits when it selects imported military aircraft.

The political importance of offsets in Western Europe was succinctly described by Bernard Udis of the University of Colorado in a study he performed in 1994 on the subject:

> Defense ministry officials in all countries were quick to observe a major political issue – to keep the Parliament contented which, in turn, requires that public opinion be willing to support the expenditure of public funds to buy weapons and equipment from abroad with ostensible benefits to foreign workers and industry. To counter the impression that such foreign gains come at the expense of domestic interests, offsets are presented to show a longer term gain to the national economy, national defense and the Alliance, and to indicate that such gains are spread to the general economy as well as to the domestic defense sector.[1]

In order to successfully sell, the military aircraft marketer must understand how offset is factored into the customer's evaluation process; what is necessary to satisfy the customer's offset requirements; and how he can marshal the resources available to him to offer a winning proposal.

In the year 2000, the US Commerce Department surveyed major American defense firms that had recently made international defense sales, to gauge the importance of offset in international sales of military aircraft. The survey asked the firms to guess the hypothetical outcome that would have befallen them if they had not offered an offset package as part of their sales proposal. Results of the survey were:

---

1   Bernard Udis (1994), *Offsets in Defense Trade: Costs and Benefits*, University of Colorado, Boulder, p. 34.

- In 11 per cent of the responses, the surveyed firms believed that they would have won the competition anyway.
- In 22 per cent of the responses, the firm believed that it would have lost the competition, but that the sale would have been awarded to a rival American firm that had offered an offset package.
- In none of the responses did the firm believe that the international customer would have procured the equipment from an internal domestic source.
- In 59 per cent of the responses, the firm believed that it would have lost the competition, and that the contract would have been awarded to a non-US firm that had offered an offset package.
- In 8 per cent of the responses, the firm believed that the customer would have cancelled the requirement and bought nothing.

This survey appears to reinforce the universal perception of knowledgeable international marketers in the industry: if you do not offer a competitive offset program, you lose.

In international sales of civil aircraft, offsets are less pervasive than in the military aircraft market, and are certainly much less formalized. Perhaps this is because of the increasing body of international agreements that greatly restrict the practice. Another important factor is that the advent of Airbus Industrie has enabled the European civil aerospace industry to reach approximate parity with its American counterpart, thereby eliminating the need for trans-Atlantic civil offsets. A third factor is that, as the trend towards privatization of national airlines has accelerated, government ownership has diminished accordingly, and private ownership of airlines generally is not enthusiastic about interjecting offset requirements into their aircraft purchase contracts.

Three international agreements restrict the use of offsets in commercial trade. The first of these is the General Agreement on Tariffs and Trade's (GATT) 1979 Government Procurement Code, now known as the World Trade Organization's (WTO) Agreement on Government Procurement. Article XVI of the agreement provides that signatories 'shall not, in the qualification and selection of suppliers, products or services, or in the evaluation of tenders and award of contracts, impose, seek or consider offsets'. This prohibition on offsets does not apply to the procurement of defense goods or services which involve essential security interests.

As of the end of 1997, 26 countries had signed this agreement, including the United States, the European Economic Community and its member countries, Japan, and other countries. Developing countries signing the agreement are allowed to negotiate conditions under which they may use offsets, and these signatory countries have in some cases negotiated an exemption for their procurement of telecommunications and transportation products.

The second international agreement limiting offsets is GATT's 1979 Agreement on Trade in Civil Aircraft, signed by the United States, the EC and its member countries, and other countries, for a total of 24 signatories. Article 4.3 of this agreement states that: 'Signatories agree that the purchase of products covered by the Agreement should be made only on a competitive price, quality and delivery basis', which implicitly proscribes purchases requiring offsets. Responsibility for enforcement of the GATT agreement has more recently been transferred to the World Trade Organization.

The third applicable agreement is the bilateral 1992 U.S.-EC Agreement on Trade in Large Civil Aircraft. This agreement interprets Article 4.3 of the GATT Agreement on Trade in Civil Aircraft (discussed in the previous paragraph) as prohibiting offsets by stating that:

> …the signatories agree that Article 4.3 does not permit Government-mandated offsets. Further, they will not require that other factors, such as subcontracting, be made a condition or consideration of sale. Specifically, a signatory may not require that a vendor must provide offset, specific types or volumes of business opportunities, or other types of industrial compensation. Signatories shall not therefore impose conditions requiring subcontractors or suppliers to be of a particular national origin.

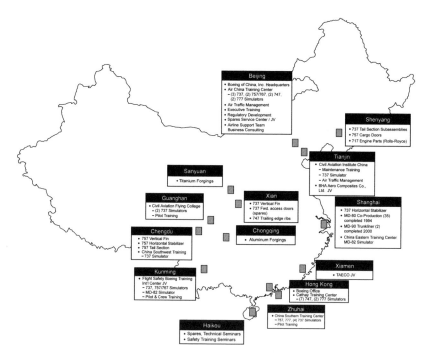

Figure 6.4 Boeing industrial activity and technology transfer in China
Note: Although sales of commercial airliners are not normally tied to formal offset requirements, the aircraft manufacturers often strive to place industrial work in the country of the purchaser, in order to strengthen relationships with the local government. This is especially true in countries such as China, where the national government exercises significant influence over aircraft selection.
Source: Boeing.

Apart from official international agreements that prohibit offsets related to civil aircraft sales, the offsets continue to occur under various guises, although they are rarely referred to as offsets. Aerospace firms recognize the importance of nurturing beneficial long-term relationships with the countries in which they aspire to sell, and they often use industrial cooperation as a way to gain local recognition and governmental support. Boeing Commercial Aircraft, which is a master at developing broad long-term international relationships, has extensive manufacturing subcontracts on the national territory of most of its major international customers, notably Japan and China. Airbus Industrie endeavors to do likewise.

The Controversial Nature of Industrial Offsets

Understandably, the practice of transferring industrial work overseas by means of offset agreements is controversial. Organized labor, in particular, has often expressed the view that offsets are detrimental to the interests of domestic industry because they result in lost jobs in the selling country. Likewise, government critics have registered concern that offsets of technology transfer result in loss of indigenously developed technical advantages of the exporting country. American labor contends that the resulting shift of the nation's jobs overseas constitutes a permanent economic loss that outweighs the business and competitive rewards reaped by individual US aerospace contractors, subcontractors and shareholders from foreign weapons and aircraft contracts. Aerospace industry representatives, on the other hand, have generally held the view that international aerospace exports are net creators of many thousands of jobs in the home country, and that manufacturing tasks transferred overseas are typically a small part of the overall export contract. Industry also maintains that technology transfers overseas generally involve technology that is available through other channels, and rarely involves highly advanced, state-of-the-art technical knowledge.

It is noteworthy that the major industrial nations that place offset work overseas are sometimes themselves beneficiaries of incoming offsets. In the United States, for example, the official position of the Department of Defense is that it does not demand offsets. In practice, foreign companies that want to sell military equipment to the US often have to grant a license to a US prime contractor for the production of their aircraft and weapons. Examples include the British Harrier jet and the Swiss Pilatus trainer aircraft, both of which were purchased by the DoD but manufactured in the USA. To European suppliers, such requirements were considered to be pure offset obligations.

How to Manage Offsets in a Marketing Campaign

Now that we have explored the nature of offsets in the aerospace industry, we can address the subject of offset management. Offsets are frequently a required condition of sale for international exports of military aircraft, and the quality of the offset program is likely to influence the customer's selection of aircraft. Proceeding from this basis, how do we manage offsets to our benefit in the sales process?

It is important to recognize that industrial offsets add cost to most programs. There are identifiable costs involved in administrative management of offsets, as well as industrial costs attributable to actions such as establishing second manufacturing sources overseas. Part of the art of managing offsets involves finding good economic matches between the industrial capabilities of the customer country and the industrial team of the prime contractor. If the economics of the buyer and seller are a good match, production can be carried out efficiently, and add-on costs can be minimized. Normally, for estimating purposes, aerospace companies anticipate that the overall cost of the aircraft program will increase by approximately 5 per cent if offset is required by the customer. To recover this cost, it must be added to the cost build-up that results in the final price proposed to the customer. In a 1999 US Commerce Department survey of American defense contractors, the contractors claimed that their costs of offset ranged from 4 to 10 per cent of total contract value.

Following is a normal progression of steps that the marketer takes as he puts together a competitive offset offer to the customer. Note that many of these steps are closely related to actions described in Chapter 13, relating to overall management of the marketing process.

1. Understand the opportunity

This is the normal first step in any marketing campaign, intended to give reasonable assurance that the customer is credible, has a realistic requirement that can be satisfied by our product line, and has access to funding. We also want to know supporting information such as nominal quantities, delivery schedules, budget targets, and so on. Obviously the amount of detailed information available depends upon the program's position in the customer's planning and programming process. If it is a fully funded program for which a request for proposal has been written, we can expect complete details. If, however, the program is in the phase of requirements definition, we will expect information of a hypothetical nature. Information about the opportunity is available from sources such as the media, the economic counselor in the seller's local embassy, a local agent, a network of contacts in the aerospace industry, or procurement offices of the customer country.

2. Get organized

If the company is engaged in large-scale international aerospace sales, particularly involving military equipment, it should have an organizational unit devoted to offset management. This is a specialized function that should be part of the marketing department. Offset managers should have close working relationships with Production, Subcontract Management, and Procurement. The offset management unit should be organized so that it can accomplish four essential functions:

- Before the sale, effectively gather information about the customer's requirements.
- Before the sale, put together an effective offset program (which involves intense coordination with suppliers, business partners, and internal units of the prime contractor), and sell the offset program to the customer's offset-management agency.

- After the sale, supervise implementation of the offset program to ensure that commitments are met.
- After the sale, work with the customer offset agency to keep score of progress towards accomplishment of the commitment.

3. Contact the customer's offset management authority to learn the formal rules

When marketing planning reaches a point that the marketer needs to acquire specific information about a customer country's offset practices, a meeting with the customer country's official offset authority should be arranged. Contact information about the national offset authority can be obtained through the seller's local embassy or from other aerospace companies that have experience in the country. Most countries that are regular buyers of new military aircraft have formal policies about offset. These policies generally include identification of a government agency, normally in the ministry of finance or the ministry of defense, that has responsibility for administering offset programs. In developed countries, this agency usually publishes guidelines that stipulate parameters such as offset percentages required, required percentages of local content, qualifying types of work, special multipliers for special technologies, penalties for non-performance, and so on. In less developed countries, offset practices tend to be less well-defined and less consistent in application.

The sidebar gives some examples of fundamental guidelines promulgated by government authorities in Canada, Finland, South Korea, Switzerland, and the United Kingdom.

- Canadian offset policy requires offsets of at least 100 per cent of the contract value for all contracts for imports of defense systems over C$ 100 million (US$ 67.5 million).
- Finland's Industrial Participation program requires 100 per cent offsets on any defense procurement over FIM 50 million (US$ 8.8 million).
- For South Korea, any defense procurement contract greater than US$ 10 million must participate in the country's offset program. All contracts above this amount are required to contain some kind of offset proposal, which must be more than 30 per cent of the contract value in order for a bid to be eligible for selection.
- Switzerland's offset policy requires a combination of co-production and indirect offsets totaling 100 per cent of the procurement contract for contracts valued at 50 million Swiss francs (US$31 million) or more.
- Under the United Kingdom's Industrial Participation program, foreign bidders on defense procurement contracts are invited to submit an offsets proposal, and the official stance is that offset is only one of many items considered when assessing bids. (In practice, large non-domestic bids without any type of offset proposal are generally not selected. It is not explicitly spelled out, but 100 per cent offset obligations are required. Although the UK program does not have specific penalty clauses, there is strict enforcement and monitoring of the policy.)

Source: US Department of Commerce, Bureau of Export Administration.

4. Talk to business associates to learn the real rules, relationships, and dynamics of offset management within the customer country

Once official local guidelines have been obtained and digested, try to learn more about how official policy is translated into realistic practice. Find experienced people who have first-hand experience at managing offset in the customer country. Personal biases and current political moods can have a major impact on the structure of a workable offset program. A particular country, for example, might be promoting a political campaign to advance the domestic software capability, and political decision-makers might therefore be particularly interested in indirect offset projects that involve software development. Another country might have a politically backed policy to develop an aircraft assembly capability, in which case direct offset involving final assembly might be attractive.

A good source of first-hand information about offset practices in many countries is the *Defense Industries Offset Association*, a forum of offset managers that meets twice a year in conferences at which papers are presented on the subject of offset policies in many customer countries. Membership is primarily American, but international industry also participates.

Often the best sources of information about local offset practices, formal and informal, are the individual companies located within the customer country. These are the parties who stand to directly gain from the eventual offset program, and they have vital interest in cultivating positive relationships with the international firms that will be placing contracts in their country.

5. Do a preliminary survey of local industry to identify what capabilities, and attempt to identify opportunities and alternatives

Before a meaningful concept for an offset plan can be put together, a preliminary familiarity with the customer country's industrial capabilities is required. Gather information about the local firms that have an interest in working in the framework of an offset program, with valid industrial capability to offer. The customer offset administration officials can provide a list of firms that they know to be interested, and in many cases they will become actively involved in arranging appointments to visit industrial facilities and offices. Visits to the sites will entail meeting a few key contacts at the company, receiving a formal presentation of a company overview, engaging in general discussions of the offset opportunity, taking a plant tour, and receiving general brochures and references describing the company.

6. Attempt to form alliances with influential local industries that can affect the outcome of the government selection decision for the prime contract

As the company works to put together a winning offset proposal as part of its competitive effort, it should attempt to enlist the active support of industrial heavyweights in the customer country. The local industry will consider the prospective offset program as an important opportunity to acquire workload and technology, and will be disposed to support the foreign competitor who offers them the most advantageous program.

The marketers and the offset team should attempt to identify local industries having significant political power, cultivate personal relationships at the senior levels of the firms, and attempt to formulate offset projects attractive to those firms. In effect, the foreign competitors will be competing against each other to gain the support of local industry.

Generally, senior management of local industry will not publicly declare favoritism for a particular competitor, but these managers will often work aggressively behind the scenes to influence the outcome of the competition to favor their preferred candidate. In addition to lobbying government and military officials, the local firms will sometimes act as invaluable informal advisors to their preferred foreign competitors.

7. Convene a meeting of the entire domestic industrial team to tell them how they will be expected to support the offset initiative

When the full-scale marketing campaign is launched, the prime contractor's offset managers should convene an offset team consisting of all significant suppliers and industrial partners with an interest in the aircraft program. Representing the company at the meeting should be factory management and subcontract management specialists with longstanding relationships with supplier firms.

At this meeting, the participants should be given background material summarizing the industrial possibilities of the target customer country. This background material can be based upon brochures and information collected during preliminary visits by the marketing and offset team to industry sites in the country.

The message to the participants at the supplier conference is simple: *We have the opportunity for a significant aircraft sale that will result in additional revenues for all of us. In order to make the sale, we have to satisfy the customer's offset requirements. We, the prime contractor, expect every member of our industrial team to actively attempt to place offset work in the customer's country. Your future business relationship with us will be influenced by your efforts to support this common cause.*

The prime contractor's contracts department should take pains to ensure that all business agreements undertaken between members of the industrial team and the industry of the customer country include a standard clause stating that both parties agree that the transaction can be used to qualify for offset credit relating to the aircraft sale. This clause is important to prove *causality*, as described below. The best practice is to provide each member of the industrial team with a printed copy of the exact legal language that they should insert in the causality clause in their contracts.

8. Continuous contact with local offset administration authority

As the company's industrial team mobilizes to establish contact with industry in the customer country, maintain regular contact with the country's offset administration authority. The administrators will be reporting regularly to decision-makers in the government and military, who will be favorably impressed if they are aware of the serious effort the offset team is making.

9. Detailed survey of candidates

The outcome of the suppliers' conference will be that members of the industrial team identify potential subcontractors or partners in their fields of specialty in the customer country. The next step is to arrange direct visits by the team members to their potential business partners. At these visits, the visitors should have a prepared presentation to describe the type of work they are considering for placement in the customer country. The visitors' teams should include technical experts capable of accurately evaluating the capabilities of the foreign firms.

10. Development of offset plan

The offset managers will work closely with the individual members of the industrial team to develop concepts of industrial projects they think may be achievable and fit well with the overseas firms they have surveyed. If the customer has emphasized specific technology or industrial sectors that he wants to develop through the offset program, the marketing manager should ensure that the industrial team includes firms that have capabilities in the specified sectors. Following the surveys, write summary descriptions of the offset concepts, to include the identity of the local partner firm, a technical summary, a business outline, a timeframe, and an estimate of total value. Accumulate these summaries in a single volume, which will become the basis of the offset plan.

11. Submittal of the offset plan

Edit the volume of offset project summaries, add some introductory language to extol the technological and industrial benefits that your industrial team can offer to the local industry, put it in an attractive binding, and deliver it to the customer country offset administration authority. Ask the administrators to give feedback concerning the adequacy of the plan, and work to continuously improve it. Until the offset commitments are eventually formalized in a contractual agreement, the parties will have a continuing series of across-the-table discussions to resolve the details of the plan. Bear in mind that the individual projects in the plan are not firm commitments at this stage – they are credible projects that the industrial team has a reasonable chance to deliver. The final result is to some extent also dependent upon the capabilities of local industry to satisfactorily perform the work offered.

12. Work with firms in the customer country to get their political support for the aircraft sale

A major attribute of the offset program as a marketing tool is that offset can enable a deft competitor to gain the support of local industry. This local support is particularly powerful in peaceful countries that do not believe they face a realistic military threat, and who therefore do not put their primary focus on the comparative military effectiveness of the competing aircraft. The author recalls a marketing campaign in the 1980s in which he was part of a team attempting to sell jet fighters to Denmark. In an informal meeting with the president of a medium-sized Danish airframe subcontractor, the author was told that the proper way to sell military aircraft in Denmark was to gain the support of Danish industry by offering an overwhelmingly superior program of industrial benefits. Danish industrial leaders would then prevail on Danish politicians to select the aircraft linked to the industrial benefits package. In the author's years of subsequent experience selling in Denmark, this approach did indeed prove to be effective.

13. Negotiation of offset commitment at time of sale

The nature of the formal contractual commitment will depend upon specific national regulations, local industrial capability, and circumstances of the sale, but it will generally include a combination of specific firm commitments and expressions of intent. At a minimum, the agreement will include the following elements:

- *Amount of obligation*, expressed as either an absolute amount or as a percentage of contract value
- *Qualifying types of offset*, which may include some or all of a wide variety:
  - Direct procurements
  - Co-production
  - Marketing assistance
  - Investments
  - Export sales
  - Import substitutions
  - Transfer of technology
  - Joint ventures
  - Licensing agreements
- *Definition of parties eligible to qualify for offset credit.*
  This definition should be a straightforward enumeration of the specific parties who will be considered by the offset administration authority to be acting on behalf of the prime contractor to accomplish offset in the customer country. Examples are:
  - The company committing to the offset obligation (usually the prime contractor)
  - Subsidiaries
  - Subcontractors
  - Suppliers
  - Other parties directly influenced by the prime contractor
- *Causality.*
  Causality is the definition of the circumstances under which the prime contractor can claim to have caused a specific transaction to occur, so that it can qualify for offset credit. In some cases, for example, corporate subsidiaries

of the prime contractor might place manufacturing work in the customer country, but the work may not qualify for credit. This would be the case if the subsidiary were engaged in a longstanding production arrangement with the customer country that pre-dated the prime contractor's aircraft sale. Logically, the offset administration authority can claim that the subsidiary's work would have taken place in the customer country regardless of the prime contractor's aircraft sale to the customer.

- *Valuation of transactions.*
  How much of each transaction can be counted as offset credit? Will offset credit be based upon the total value of delivered goods, or upon the value added in local factories? Will training be counted in the total? Does technology transfer have a value?

- *Multipliers.*
  Individual offset transactions have big qualitative differences that have to be recognized in the offset accounting methodology. Multipliers are commonly used to adjust for these differences. Normally, in-country purchases of locally produced products are considered basic transactions without multipliers. Direct investment into local industry is considered more desirable, and will receive a multiplier of, for example, ten. In other words, one million dollars of direct investment will garner ten million dollars of offset credit. Other, more desirable, transactions can earn higher multipliers still. An outright grant of modern production equipment or technology, for example, might qualify for a multiplier of twenty. In all cases, guidelines for multipliers should be clearly defined in advance, and all transactions involving multipliers should be approved on a case-by-case basis before their individual implementation.

- *Period of performance.*
  The offset administration authority will require that the offset obligation be completed within a specified interval. This period should be clearly defined, and should include start date (or milestone event that will begin the period), length of the period, grace period for extension, and methods for mutually agreeing to changes in the period. The parties should also define the conditions that will formally complete the offset obligation. At fulfillment of the obligation, the authority should be required to issue a formal statement declaring that the prime contractor has met the conditions of his obligation.

- *Termination.*
  Because the offset agreement is often separate from the contractual sales document, the agreement needs to specify the conditions under which the offset program will be terminated. If the aircraft program is terminated or significantly curtailed, the offset program should be adjusted accordingly. The parties should agree in advance concerning disposition of offset credits in the event of termination of the offset program. The authority should be required to issue a contractual declaration of any termination-related changes to the offset agreement.

- *Performance milestones.*
  Offset agreements generally include intermediate milestones, often in the form of percentage-of-completion requirements. Such milestones ensure that the

prime contractor immediately shows good faith effort to fulfill his obligation. Because of the time required to get organized and to begin production, offset accomplishments begin slowly, and accelerate geometrically later in the program. However, the offset administration authority will prefer to see immediate accomplishments, so that he can satisfy expectations of national politicians and industry. Another consideration for the authority is that he has greater leverage over the prime contractor earlier in the program, before the prime contractor has received the bulk of payments for fulfillment of the aircraft delivery program. From the point of view of the contractor, it is important to avoid allowing aggressive milestones for unrealistic early accomplishment of the offset program.

- *Penalties and performance guarantees.*
  The offset agreement will provide for penalties to be incurred in the event that the prime contractor fails to fulfill his offset commitment in accordance with the conditions to which he has agreed. The most common form of penalty, and the easiest to administer, takes the form of liquidated damages. Liquidated damages are specific cash payments paid to the customer country. The size of the payment will depend on the magnitude of the offset shortfall, and the agreement should specify a formula for calculating the amount, and should establish timing for payment of the penalty. The agreement should specify that payment of liquidated damages relieves the contractor from all further offset obligations, and that no further contractual remedy is required.

  Customarily, the customer country will insist on financial guarantees that the offset obligation will be fulfilled. In its simplest form, a guarantee can take the form of a written corporate commitment to pay contractual penalties if commitments are not met. More common are third-party guarantees, in the form of letters of credit or surety bonds, provided by banks or insurance companies paid by the contractor.

- *Escalation factors.*
  Offset obligations are multi-year commitments, and sometimes the offset administration authority will suggest annual escalation of the obligation based on economic indices. This is undesirable because it introduces administrative complications and potential disagreements. The best policy for the contractor is to attempt to impose a fixed offset obligation at the time the agreement is signed.

- *Force majeure.*
  Events beyond the reasonable control of the prime contractor are subject to occur, and the agreement should have force majeure provisions that give relief to the contractor. Natural disasters, strikes, acts of war and terrorism should qualify as force majeure, and their occurrence should, at a minimum, result in the contractor being given a grace period in the term of his offset commitment.

- *Reporting requirements.*
  It is in the interest of both parties that the status of the offset program be summarized in frequent reports submitted by the contractor and approved by the authority. The format, intervals, and reporting periods should be defined

in advance. A procedure for negotiating and arbitrating disputed items should be established.

- *Confidentiality.*

  Within reasonable limits, the contractor is entitled to protect information about his offset program. Government transparency will require that most transactions be publicly reported, and that summary financial information about performance towards the offset obligation be disclosed. However, the contractor has a right to confidentiality when he is engaged in conceptual exploratory talks with potential partners, or when he is performing due diligence in view of local investment possibilities. The prime contractor should reserve the right to provide any information specifically requested by his own government.

- *Banked credits.*

  Once the offset program is under way and begins to gather momentum, there is a real possibility that the amount of offset realized within the period of performance will exceed the contractual commitments of the contractor. If there is any possibility that the prime contractor will compete for other business in the customer country, and will possibly incur future offset obligations, the company should attempt to include language in the offset agreement that will allow it to bank surplus credits to be used in the future. Most countries have policies concerning whether or not they will permit banked credits.

14. Claim credit. Keep score. Monitor internal efforts

As the offset program progresses through its implementation phase, the offset managers will exercise close and continuous surveillance over the activities of the industrial team and the local industry, to ensure that appropriate claims are submitted for all transactions initiated within the context of the offset program. In turn, the offset managers must carefully accumulate this information for inclusion in their periodic reports to the local authority. And, continuously, the offset managers must act as the internal advocates of the offset program by persistently searching for new offset opportunities and encouraging members of the industrial team to make a maximum effort to boost the volume of their offset transactions.

15. Do not forget to comply with legally imposed domestic reporting requirements.

Remember that several countries, notably the United States, require that domestic industry engaged in offset transactions with foreign countries must report the nature and size of all offset commitments and performance to the exporter's government. In the United States, the governing law is the Defense Offsets Disclosure Act of 1999. Under the conditions of this law, US exporters of defense goods and services are required to report to the Bureau of Export Administration of the US Department of Commerce any offset agreement greater than $5 million in size, and any offset transaction greater than $250,000 in value that they complete.

In addition to reports to customers and to the seller's national government, the offset manager will also be expected to prepare status reports for distribution within his own company. Summary reports generally contain key information such as the total value of the offset obligation in each individual customer country, the value of offset transactions approved by the customer's national authority, and the value of offset claimed by the company. An example of a summary report of this type is depicted below. More detailed reviews of offset management status, on a less frequent basis, normally involve detailed scrutiny of commitments in the individual countries, specific plans to fulfill commitments, and identification of known problems.

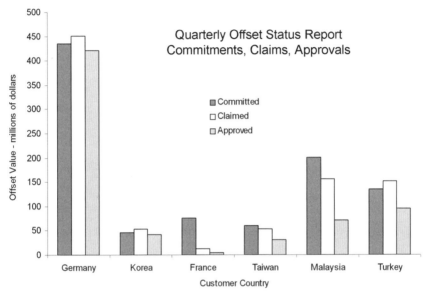

Figure 6.5 Internal reporting of offset performance status
Note: For their own internal management of offset obligations, companies monitor their commitments, claims, and approvals in customer countries.

Industrial offset, by its very nature, involves a political-military-industrial melange that tends to produce controversy and unpredictable results. It is a difficult aspect of aerospace marketing to manage. However, marketers should view offset as a valuable tool that potentially can have great influence upon customer decisions in the competitive selection process.

Chapter 7

Government Relations

Legal efforts by aerospace companies to influence governments are a normal and legitimate aspect of marketing in the industry.

The international aerospace business is profoundly affected by government policies and decisions. Although contemporary aerospace companies are predominately owned by the private sector, their welfare is inescapably linked to government actions that take place within many disparate administrative agencies and political offices of national governments and international organizations.

In most countries, the national government, as a buyer of military aircraft and services, is the single largest customer of the aerospace industry. This reality by itself is sufficient to justify a major effort by the industry to influence government policy and decision-making. However, aside from their roles as customers, governments affect companies' profitability by means of establishing tax policy, promulgating compliance requirements in a variety of domains, and determining official policy and practices pertaining to foreign policy and relations with international organizations. In some countries, governments are also involved in direct subsidies and loans to their national aerospace industries, and control programs of credit guarantees to international customers.

For the American aerospace industry, perhaps the best indication of the importance it attaches to influencing government policy is the magnitude of the industry's political contributions. In the 2004 national elections, political contributions from American aerospace companies (including US-based subsidiaries of overseas companies, such as BAE Systems, DaimlerChrysler, and Rolls-Royce) totaled $7,075,566. The twenty largest contributors were:

Table 7.1 Top aerospace political contributors

Rank	Organization	Amount	Dems	Repubs
1	Lockheed Martin	$2,074,118	33%	67%
2	General Dynamics	$1,336,877	44%	56%
3	United Technologies	$789,561	35%	64%
4	Honeywell International	$549,279	40%	60%
5	BAE Systems	$475,334	43%	57%
6	Boeing Co	$271,695	36%	64%
7	General Electric	$220,950	50%	50%
8	Spectrum Astro	$152,961	2%	98%
9	Teledyne Technologies	$117,120	41%	59%
10	Vought Aircraft	$108,500	45%	55%

11	Textron Inc	$96,650	34%	66%
12	GenCorp Inc	$77,881	18%	82%
13	Analytical Graphics Inc	$68,100	32%	68%
14	Daniels Manufacturing	$68,000	3%	97%
15	Rockwell Collins Inc	$65,257	30%	60%
16	Dynetics Inc	$57,150	19%	81%
17	Lau Technologies	$46,600	100%	0%
18	Northrop Grumman	$40,000	50%	50%
19	Orbital Sciences Corp	$37,500	3%	97%
20	Kaman Corp	$34,500	52%	48%

Note: Of the total contributions, 67 per cent came from corporate political action campaigns, and 33 per cent from individuals.
Source: The US Federal Election Commission, as reported by The Center for Responsive Politics.

What exactly are the benefits that accrue to the companies as a result of these large financial contributions? Answers to this question vary according to the perspective of the person who answers. The contributors normally respond that they are supporting re-election of enlightened politicians who promote policies that are favorable to the aerospace industry. Critics contend that the contributors are buying political influence. An example of these critics is William D. Hartung, whose Arms Trade Resource Center takes the view that contributions by arms-makers, and the aerospace industry in particular, are motivated by sinister intent:

Excerpt from New Data Reveals a Record $10.8 Million in Contributions by Arms Merchants During 1995/96 Election Cycle; Martin Remains Leader of the PACs' by William D. Hartung, Arms Trade Resource Center, April 1997.

Quid Pro Quos: Actions by Specific Lawmakers on Behalf of the Arms Industry

In addition to rewarding members who vote with them, arms exporters have cultivated a powerful grouping of individual members who take a leadership role in securing funding or favorable regulations, making it easier (and more profitable) to sell U.S. weaponry overseas. Industry contributions are heavily concentrated among key committee chairs and ranking members on armed services, appropriations, foreign relations, and budget committees; members in leadership positions (including House Speaker Newt Gingrich); and members from states with clusters of major weapons manufacturing facilities (most notably California and Texas). A few examples are presented below.

The Helms/McCollum letters and fighter plane sales to Latin America: Lockheed Martin and McDonnell Douglas have been vigorously lobbying to reverse a 25 year-old U.S. ban on exporting advanced fighter planes to Latin America, and the Clinton Administration took a giant step in that direction in late March when it authorized the firms to provide technical data for U.S. combat aircraft to the Chilean Air Force. At a pivotal point in their campaign to lift the fighter ban, in the spring of 1996 the companies prevailed upon Senate Foreign Relations Committee chairman Jesse Helms (R-NC) and Rep. Bill McCollum (R-FL) to send letters to Secretary of State Warren Christopher urging him to reverse U.S. policy and open the way for sales of U.S. combat aircraft to Latin America. Taken together, Helms and his 37 Senate co-signers and McCollum and his 77 Senate co-signers received over $1 million in campaign contributions by Lockheed Martin, McDonnell Douglas, and other major prime and subcontractors for the F-16 and F-18 aircraft.

Jane Harman (D-CA) and the $15 Billion Arms Export Loan Guarantee Fund: In June of 1995, Jane Harman led a successful fight in the House to preserve one of arms export industry's pet projects, a $15 billion government-backed loan fund. Harman received $66,750 in arms exporter PAC funds in 1995/96.

Norm Dicks (D-WA), Randy 'Duke' Cunningham (R-CA), Duncan Hunter (R-CA) and the B-2 Bomber brigade: These West coast lawmakers, whose districts are close by Northrop Grumman's B-2 facility in Southern California and Boeing's B-2 subcontracting work in Seattle, spearheaded the fight to keep the B-2 alive during 1995/96. All three made the top 10 list of arms exporter PAC recipients, and they were richly rewarded by B-2 contractors Northrop Grumman, Boeing, and General Electric: Dicks received $19,500 from the three firms during 1995/96, Cunningham got $18,211, and Hunter received $10,500.

In fact, the beneficiaries of these political contributions do tend to be elected officials who have the power to influence government policy and decisions that directly affect the aerospace industry. In the American democracy, voters (often acting through political action campaigns organized by their employers) have the legal right to contribute money to political candidates who promise to promote the voters' specific interests and points of view. These contributions by no means infer that the politicians are selling their votes. However, among the examples cited above, Congressman Randy 'Duke' Cunningham was later convicted and imprisoned for taking bribes from defense contractors.

Outside the United States, where political cultures are different, the phenomenon of cash flows from the aerospace and aviation industries to politicians remains an international constant. Since the dawn of the aviation age, cash contributions to influential politicians have been a fact of life within the aerospace industry in most countries. In order to compete and survive, aerospace companies traditionally have focused their government relationships in two specific areas: 1) marketing of aerospace equipment and services to government customers, particularly the military, and 2) lobbying elected officials and political candidates.

More recently, as the industry has evolved, and as government involvement in aerospace has become more multi-faceted and pervasive, the nature of relationships between the industry and governments has changed. Government regulators, policy-makers, and administrators have accepted the reality that industry is the principal repository of technical aerospace expertise, and have encouraged the development of direct working links between government and industry throughout the range of government involvement. Government offices routinely use industry representatives as sources of information and ideas, and as critics of preliminary drafts of government edicts circulated prior to final approval and release. This practice of industry review of government policy has often been beneficial to all concerned, but introduces a risk of undue influence by industry.

At the same time, the aerospace companies have expanded their interest in official entities beyond the Federal government. Increasingly, as the companies have come to recognize the importance of political support from their state and local governments, they have created lobbying entities dedicated to maintaining relationships with regional and local politicians.

In addition to efforts to directly influence government policy, the aerospace industry frequently uses third-party advocacy to communicate its point of view to governments. Commonly, research institutes, political foundations, and 'think tanks' are closely aligned with industry perspective, and receive much of their funding by means of paid study projects, consulting agreements, or direct donations from aerospace firms. Management of the institutes often have close relationships with elected officials and appointed government officials, and ensure that the results of analytical research are used to support views propagated by the industry. Depending on the outcome of national elections, senior government officials whose political parties are temporarily out of power often find temporary employment with research institutes and political foundations until they return to appointed office when their parties once again return to power. Consequently, the aerospace firms have the opportunity to earn favor with these politicians by indirectly supporting them during their out-of-office period, while at the same time providing themselves a degree of virtually unlimited personal access that will become impossible when the politicians return to official public office.

Other examples of third-party advocacy involve industry associations and trade groups that often have broad national constituencies and which consequently carry political weight that crosses regional and local boundaries. In the United States, the politically powerful Aerospace Industries Association (AIA) is the industry's primary trade group. The equivalent organization in the United Kingdom is the Society of British Aerospace Companies (SBAC). In France, the industry lobby organization is Groupement des Industries Françaises Aéronautiques et Spatiales (GIFAS), and the German aerospace industry's lobby organization is the Bundesverband der Deutschen Luft- und Raumfahrtindustrie (BDLI) e.V. The Japanese organization is the Society of Japanese Aerospace Companies (SJAC).

This kind of multi-level working relationship between government and industry has profoundly affected how modern aerospace companies throughout the world organize themselves to effectively influence the government. 'Government Relations' offices located in national capitals have multiplied in size, and have expanded to include organizational units specializing in affairs pertaining directly to specific government entities that they attempt to influence.

A representative government affairs office in Washington, D.C., for example, might be organized along the following model:

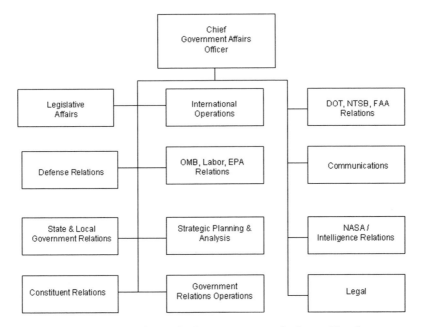

Figure 7.1 Organization of a typical government relations office for an aerospace corporation

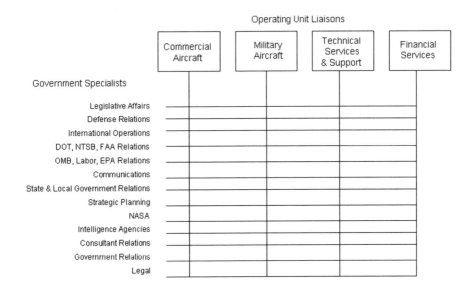

Figure 7.2 Matrix reporting for a government relations office

The government affairs organization acts as a conduit for communications between the various government entities and the operating units of the aerospace company. In order to do this effectively, it must be organized so that it has strong links with the operating units that it serves. Customary practice is that each of the operating units or product line groups assigns a representative to the government affairs office to act as a liaison between the two. When the operating unit wants the government affairs office to take action, the operating unit contacts its liaison in the office, who makes direct contact with the government affairs specialists who will make direct contact with appropriate government interlocutors. The liaison acts as a gatekeeper to prevent chaotic or uncoordinated communications between the operating units and individual specialists in the government affairs office.

US Government Entities of Importance to the Aerospace Industry

The quantity and diversity of US government entities regularly involved in matters of interest to the aerospace industry is impressive. In the Executive branch, the President's executive office is frequently involved in aerospace affairs, as are numerous departments and independent agencies and commissions. Following are a few of the most obvious examples. Although these descriptions apply specifically to the American Government, equivalent government agencies and offices exist in most other developed nations.

Cabinet Level Departments

Commerce The Commerce Department contains the Trade Export Administration agency, which has general authority for authorizing and controlling exports of civil aerospace products and technology. Commerce also represents the aerospace industry and aviation industry in overseas exhibitions and in industrial development initiatives.

Defense The US Defense Department is the world's largest customer for aerospace products and services. In addition to being a direct customer, DoD has a major role in defining technical requirements for defense aerospace in the present and the future.

State The State Department is the primary authority for providing export licenses for American international sales of military aerospace equipment and services. The State Department also has responsibility for negotiating international agreements with foreign governments on many subjects that relate to aerospace. In a general way, the State Department works to ensure that the overall interests of the United States are protected in its relationships with foreign governments. When important aerospace contracts overseas are at stake, the State Department and ministries of foreign affairs from competitor countries often become actively engaged in attempts to influence the purchasing decisions of the foreign customers. An excellent example of this type of diplomatic arm-twisting was the 2002 US State Department's effort, in collaboration with a spectrum of US Senators and Congressmen, to coerce Taiwan to purchase Boeing aircraft instead of Airbus planes. The message from the American officials to Taiwan was blunt: the USA expected pay-back for longstanding political and economic support of Taiwan.

Transportation The Transportation Department controls the all-important Federal Aviation Administration (FAA) that has responsibility for all civil airworthiness regulations and enforcement. Aerospace industry relationships with the FAA and with its international counterparts in other countries are of fundamental importance, and are the subject of a section of Chapter 16 in this book.

An example of the effects of FAA policy upon the aerospace market involved the Boeing effort to obtain extended-range twin-engine operations (ETOPS) for the soon-to-be introduced Boeing 777 in 1995. The 777 was developed as an extraordinarily large twin engine aircraft that took advantage of evolutionary jet engine technology that had enabled engines to grow dramatically in power, while simultaneously becoming so reliable that engine failures became very unusual events. Because twin-engine aircraft are more efficient than four-engine aircraft, and cost less to maintain, Boeing correctly foresaw that operators would chose the 777 to replace older four-engine aircraft types. However, FAA rules developed during the earlier epoch of relatively unreliable piston-engine aircraft stipulated that passenger-carrying twin-engine aircraft were required to fly within 120 minutes flight-time of an emergency landing runway. This regulation, known as the 120-ETOPS rule, had an adverse marketing impact upon the 777 because it prevented the aircraft from flying the fastest and most efficient routes across the Pacific Ocean. To eliminate this marketing handicap, Boeing approached the FAA with the recommendation that the new-generation jet engines of the 777 be tested to prove their increased reliability, and that the aircraft be considered for approval to fly routes that took the 777 180 minutes from the nearest emergency airport. This new rule, known as 180-ETOPS, was eventually approved by the FAA, thereby clearing the way for the 777 to compete effectively against four-engine aircraft.

Justice The size and complexity of the aerospace industry make it very likely that large companies will sooner or later have legal disputes with the government. The Justice Department represents the interests of the US Government in these disputes. Legal disputes can range from criminal issues such as violations of export control laws, to civil disagreements resulting from contractual terminations.

Labor The Labor Department is responsible for promulgating and enforcing regulations that apply to the aerospace industry workforce, with major cost implications for the industry.

Treasury Much of US financial policy is controlled within the Treasury Department, which includes the US Internal Revenue Service. International economic sanctions are managed by Treasury, and US Customs, an agency of the Treasury Department, manages tariff policy.

Executive Office of the President

National Security Council The NSC, which formulates overall security strategy for the US, has an interest in alternative technologies and military equipment available to support security policy.

United States Trade Representative The USTR represents the United States in negotiations concerning terms of trade with international partners, and therefore deals with issues concerning government subsidies provided to international aerospace producers, government loan guarantees, and tariffs on aerospace imports.

Office of Management and Budget OMB has overall responsibility for formulating the President's budget, including planned government expenditures on defense, space, intelligence-gathering, and civil aerospace infrastructure.

Office of Science & Technology Policy OSTP evaluates how technology affects US national interests, and makes recommendations to the President concerning how technology should be used, which new technologies should be developed, and how the US technology base should be fostered.

Council on Environmental Quality The Council's recommendations include policies that affect aircraft design, notably standards for noise and atmospheric emissions, and also affect environmental rules governing manufacturing facilities.

Independent Agencies and Commissions

Environmental Protection Agency The EPA is the primary Federal authority with responsibility for establishing and enforcing national regulations governing protection of the environment. Whereas the Council on Environmental Quality is limited to policy recommendations, the EPA has legal power of enforcement. It is concerned with noise, atmospheric emissions by aircraft, and toxic by-products of aerospace manufacturing.

Federal Communications Commission The FCC is notably responsible for control of the spectrum of wavelengths for wireless communications, and accordingly has immense influence over the satellite communications industry. It also regulates traditional air-to-air and air-to-ground communications involving aircraft in flight.

Federal Trade Commission The FTC, among other responsibilities, is responsible for enforcing US anti-trust legislation, which has particular significance in the modern era of large-scale aerospace mergers and acquisitions. Normal practice for the companies is to request FTC pre-approval prior to major mergers. In the case of ongoing business, the FTC is empowered to bring legal charges or seek injunctions if it perceives that US laws governing anti-trust and fair trade practices have been violated.

National Aeronautics and Space Administration NASA is a major customer for the space segment of the aerospace industry, and is a source of advanced aerospace technology throughout the industry.

Central Intelligence Agency The CIA is the source of specialized aerospace equipment relating to covert information-gathering. Examples are high-altitude surveillance aircraft such as the U-2 and SR-71, and, more recently, surveillance satellites.

International Trade Commission The ITC furnishes studies, reports, and recommendations involving international trade and tariffs to the President, the Congress, and other government agencies. In this capacity, the Commission conducts a variety of investigations, public hearings, and research projects pertaining to the international trade policies of the United States.

National Transportation Safety Board The NTSB works across the entire spectrum of transportation modes in the United States to investigate accidents and to recommend improvements, including design changes, to minimize risks of future mishaps. During investigation of aircraft accidents, the NTSB works in close collaboration with aerospace manufacturers, and accident reports often result in changes to aircraft design, manufacturing processes, or training.

Ex-Im Bank A government-chartered corporation funded by Congress, the Ex-Im Bank is the official export credit agency of the US Government, providing essential financial guarantees for aircraft exports to customers with imperfect credit ratings.

The Legislative Branch

In addition to the many agencies and departments of the Executive Branch, government affairs offices working with the American Government must also maintain close liaison with individual elected members of Congress, with Congressional support staff, and with the multiple Congressional committees and subcommittees that have influence over the aerospace business.

Some of the principal aerospace-related committees in the Senate are:

- Appropriations
- Armed Services
- Banking, Housing, and Urban Affairs
- Budget
- Commerce, Science & Transportation
- Environment & Public Works
- Finance
- Foreign Relations
- Government Affairs
- Health, Education, Labor & Pensions

- Rules & Administration
- Select Intelligence

In the House of Representatives, the equivalent committees are:

- Appropriations
- Armed Services
- Banking & Financial Services
- Budget
- Commerce
- Education & the Work Force
- Government Reform & Oversight
- International Relations
- Rules
- Science
- Small Business
- Transportation & Infrastructure
- Ways & Means
- Permanent Select Intelligence

Typical government affairs offices of the aerospace industry include a Legislative Affairs unit that has the responsibility for maintaining close contact with Congressmen and Senators, and particularly with the staffers that support them. The legislative affairs specialists are often drawn from the ranks of former Congressional staffers. This background enables them to draw on a familiarity with the workings of Congressional committees, and provides them with a network of staffers and elected officials. As the legislative affairs specialists become aware of legislative initiatives that can potentially affect their company's interest, the specialists report to company management, who make assessments concerning how company interests will benefit or suffer as a result of prospective legislation. Company policy concerning the legislative initiative is formulated, and the legislative specialists then go to work to influence the eventual legislation in a direction favorable to the company.

As the legislative specialists work with Congressional staffers, they draw upon the technical resources of their companies to provide expert analysis to support their recommendations. In the absence of strong analytical evidence to the contrary, the staffers and their elected officials often rely on information and recommendations promulgated by the industry. Industry commonly provides re-election support, in the form of cash campaign contributions, to legislators who support the industry point of view on specific legislation.

Governments, as presences in the international aerospace marketplace, are too important to be ignored. Apart from their weight in the marketplace as the largest individual customers, they have enormous effect upon the broader business environment in which the aerospace companies operate. Governments dictate the technical, financial, and industrial regulations pertaining to aerospace. Governments have powerful influence upon diplomatic relationships with other countries. In order to survive and prosper, the aerospace industry has a clear interest in attempting to influence government policies, decisions, and actions to the industry's benefit.

Chapter 8

Brand Management and Advertising

Corporations and their advertising agencies have always been aware of the importance and value of their brands. In recent years, perhaps as a result of improvements in mass communication and advertising media, the concepts of *brand identity* and *branding* have been the object of much attention from advertising professionals.

Brand identity is, in a very comprehensive sense, the overall image of the brand in the minds of consumers or customers of the product. Branding involves unifying the activities of an entire company in a way that will gain customer preference. To maximize the effectiveness of its brand, the company strives to link a formal corporate vision with brand values perceived by customers. Obviously, success in executing such a process requires the complete endorsement and support of a strong company leader.

Taken to its extreme, the *total branding* concept is that the brand drives the business, and that an integrated cross-functional emphasis by senior management is necessary for it to work.

Perhaps the branding movement is the twenty-first century's first messianic management fad, in the tradition of *Total Quality Management* or *World Class Competitiveness*. A minor industry has developed to provide consulting services to senior executives who want to inculcate their companies with a strong sense of vision and brand identity.

> …research and surveys repeatedly show that brands generate more trust than any institution – government, church, politicians all fall before the credibility of some brands. Many brands show a remarkable ability to bypass our cynicism; people have great affection and loyalty to them and will pay over the odds for the logo. The argument runs that a successful brand – Swatch or Calvin Klein – offers consistency of quality, a point of certainty in an uncertain world; insecure, we latch onto the familiar and the predictable. So we use brands and we decode other people's use of brands to establish their status. We no longer identify with churches, political parties or even our local community; we construct our sense of who we are through our association with brands – from football teams to TV channels, from designer jeans to the make of car, from coffee shop to cosmetics.[1]

Although brands are most commonly associated with consumer goods, brand identity is also considered to be essential for companies involved in business-to-business markets. In the aerospace market, where technical products can become commodities, brands help to define companies and differentiate them from competitors. Increasingly, the corporate brand is also thought of as a vehicle for building company identity in the minds of employees, who can potentially lose their sense of corporate culture as a result of continuous mergers, acquisitions, and

---

1 Madeleine Bunting (2001), 'The New Gods', *The Guardian*, 9 July.

reorganizations. Strong brand identity is also theoretically effective in conveying expectations to subcontractors, and for attracting stockholders.

Devices used by companies to convey brand identity include logos, trademarks, slogans, color schemes, and so on. To ensure protection of these tools, the companies maintain rigorous internal standards to regulate how brand symbols are used, and they use aggressive legal action to protect the brands against misuse by outsiders.

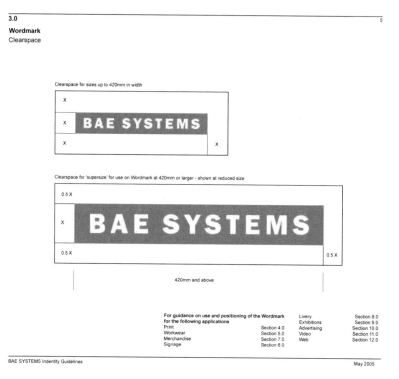

Figure 8.1 BAE Systems logo usage guidelines
Note: As BAE Systems becomes progressively more diverse and international in identity, the corporation pays special attention to maintaining a consistent and recognizable brand throughout the scope of its operations. Its logo, as the most widely recognizable symbol of that brand, is controlled with special care. The original color version of this guideline shows the BAE logo in its characteristic bright red.
Source: BAE Systems.

In recent years, most of the major international aerospace manufacturers have directed a great deal of management attention to defining and maximizing brand identity. Boeing, for example, entered the new millennium with a brand management campaign specifically intended to develop a company identity as a *category leader* in aerospace.

As part of the company's emphasis on its brand, former Boeing CEO Phil Condit personally led a corporation-wide initiative to identify Boeing's core values and to create a vision for the future. In Boeing's case, this view of the future was a projection to the year 2016, the 100th anniversary of the company's founding, and was designated Vision 2016. This vision, which was top management's perspective of what the company was and what it would become, was the subject of a broad effort to indoctrinate all employees. Vision 2016 then became the basis of a campaign of public relations and advertising to share the same perspective of the company's core values and attributes with customers, shareholders, suppliers, and the general public.

In Boeing's case, the brand managers felt a need to correct what they considered to be an inaccurate general perception of the company. The Boeing name was widely respected in connection with civil jet airliners, and in fact in local languages in many countries the word *Boeing* had become a common noun meaning a jet airliner. This association, positive though it was, did not recognize Boeing's activities as one of the world's largest makers of defense equipment and space launch systems, satellites, and communications systems. Boeing management believed that the company should be viewed not as an airliner manufacturer, but as a 'global aerospace company' possessing core competencies in the areas of large-scale systems integration, detailed knowledge of customers throughout the world, and efficient manufacturing technologies.

To promote brand identity, companies normally conduct multi-level advertising campaigns, targeting at least three distinct audiences, with three distinct types of message:

- Global advertising campaigns of the type often referred to as *image advertising* are intended to build a company's stature internationally and within its home country, to develop its brand as a significant player in the market, and to attract the interest of potential investors. Ads of this type are placed in mass media such as popular magazines, television, and major national newspapers.
- *Product advertising*, in the conventional Business-to-Business genre, or as Business-to-Government when military equipment is involved, promotes specific products to specific customers. These ads generally appear in aerospace trade publications, in air show daily reports, and in limited circulation publications for aerospace and defense professionals. For the segment of the market in which general aviation aircraft, equipment, and services are sold directly to private aircraft operators, consumer advertising in flight magazines is commonplace.
- *Community advertising* is intended to build local public and political support for a company, and takes the form of local radio and television commercials, local newspaper ads, and billboard advertising.

Whenever communication is involved, the risk of miscommunication is present. Miscommunication can take the form of conveying an inaccurate or misleading message, presenting information that can be misunderstood or misinterpreted in a harmful way, or taking actions that can be offensive or otherwise reflect negatively on the company or the product.

A well-known example of miscommunication involved an ad developed by Bell Helicopter's agency in Texas for the V-22 tiltrotor. The ad was placed in the limited-circulation defense periodical *National Journal*, without having been subjected to the normal internal review process required by Bell and its V-22 partner Boeing prior to public release. In the ad, a V-22 is seen hovering over the ground in a Middle Eastern scene, with soldiers rappelling to a street in front of a mosque. The ad copy says that the aircraft 'descends from the heavens' and 'unleashes hell'. Predictably, the US Council on Islamic-American Relations complained about the ad, as did a number of Middle Eastern governments, some of which were customers of Bell and Boeing. Bell and Boeing immediately withdrew the ad, apologized for its offensive content, and declared that it had been released without internal approval by the companies.

A Boeing image advertising campaign of the early 2000s, initiated under the theme 'Forever New Frontiers', developed the theme that Boeing raised the quality of life of people throughout the world, in a variety of technology sectors in which Boeing was involved. The audience was presented with the message that Boeing space systems facilitated international communications; Boeing defense systems enabled effective protection of national ways of life; and Boeing airliners made life better by making air travel easier.

During the same period, Airbus was at work to develop its brand and to advertise its capabilities. Establishing a corporate identity was a particular problem, because no corporation existed – the aircraft were produced by a multinational consortium whose organization was not well understood, and the individual consortium members had diverse and sometimes conflicting individual identities. In the early period of its existence, Airbus emphasized its European identity, and promoted itself as a European response to American hegemony in the civil aerospace industry.

Consider this commentary by a European corporate identity specialist:

An interesting example is the Airbus brand. The original genesis of the worldwide famous aeroplane manufacturer gives an answer to the question, how to build up a brand in atypical conditions. The Airbus project was a response to the massive onset of Boeing, which quickly managed to overtake all domestic and foreign competitors. Traditional European rivals – smaller British, French, German, Dutch, and Spanish companies – decided to establish a syndicate, and their product was given the name Airbus. They never had any united corporate identity. The common organizational structure and organization is responsible for the final product, and it even has a very unusual and complicated corporate personality (so-called Groupment d'Interet Economique). Particular parts of the planes are designed and manufactured in various European countries and they are assembled at Toulouse in France. An advantage of this complicated status is easier identification of employees, customers, and the public with the brand – the French people consider Airbus to be French, and the German people believe that it is a German brand. It is difficult to find the ideological origin of this brand, and in fact it is not important anymore. Airbus was established as a European challenge to the American dominance in the sphere of civil aviation. The common European origin has surely played a key role in the marketing communication. Emotions are a significant part of this brand. In this respect, time has confirmed its soundness and consistency – Airbus now is a classical chapter in the history of brand identity creation.[2]

---

2   Matej Jasso (2002), 'Corporate Identity – Brand Identity', *Designum Design Quarterly*, 1/2002.

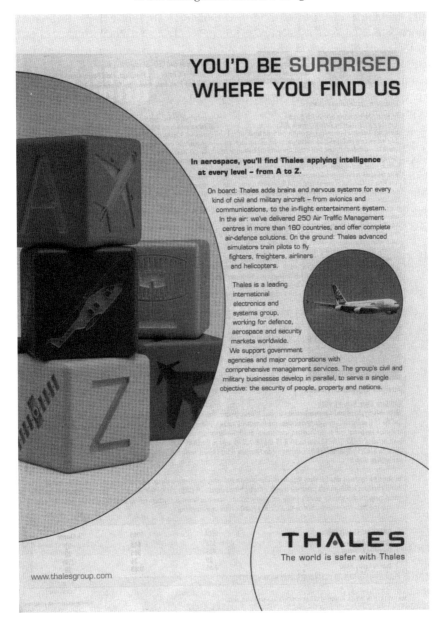

Figure 8.2 Thales image advertising
Note: In this well-executed sample of corporate image advertising, Thales conveys the message that their products make the world safer.
Source: Thales.

In fact, the Airbus brand identity has evolved and attained a level of sophistication. The Airbus consortium has legally metamorphosed into a multinational corporate entity, making it easier to establish a corporate identity. In Europe, the company continues to emphasize its identity as Europe's only manufacturer of large airliners, but in the rest of the world Airbus identifies itself as an international enterprise. In fact, American and international suppliers do provide much of the value of Airbus aircraft, and participate as limited risk-sharing partners, so Airbus has a valid claim to an international identity. According to John Leahy, Airbus' chief commercial officer, a key to Airbus' success in the American market was Airbus' claim that their aircraft contained 40 per cent US content, including General Electric engines, Honeywell avionics, and miscellaneous equipment and structure from 800 American suppliers.

A central aspect of the current Airbus brand is that the aircraft are the product of fine European design and the European tradition of quality and luxury. Airbus cockpits, we are told, are developed by the ergonometric specialists from the Porsche design bureau, and the business class cabins of Airbus are described as being exceptionally quiet and comfortable.

Figure 8.3 Airbus product advertising
Note: An example of an Airbus product advertisement. Although product advertising in business-to-business markets is normally directed to buyers (the airlines, in this case), Airbus chose to advertise directly to business flyers.
Source: Airbus.

In recent years, Boeing and Airbus have taken notably different approaches in defining the target audience of their advertising efforts. Boeing, as described above, has continued to focus its product marketing towards the direct customers for its civil products, the airlines and leasing companies. Airbus, in contrast, has persistently marketed to the traveling public, particularly the business traveler. Airbus' obvious expectation is that they will be able to shape the preferences of the travelers to the extent that the airlines will buy Airbus planes in order to satisfy their customers. Airbus says it is 'communicating with the customers of its customers'. This advertising strategy, based on a concept of derived demand, has recently been the object of extensive experimentation in the pharmaceuticals industry. Formerly, drug companies marketed controlled drugs to the doctors who had the authority to prescribe them. Recently, as advertising regulations have changed in the United States, the pharmaceutical companies have aggressively marketed drugs directly to the general public, in the expectation that patients who have seen the ads will ask their doctors to prescribe the medicine that they have seen on TV and in magazines. This strategy has shown some indications of success in the pharmaceutical industry.

Figure 8.4 Boeing community advertising

Note: In this example of community advertising, a billboard close to Boeing's helicopter factory in Philadelphia conveys the message that Boeing is a valuable local presence.

Source: Boeing.

Advertising, like all forms of business communication, can backfire if it is misused or managed improperly. Airbus, for example, was the object of negative attention from some members of the commercial air transport industry when it introduced ads in the late 1990s to promote the four-engined Airbus A340 against Boeing's new twin-engined 777. The Airbus ads inferred that four-engined aircraft were safer for long trips over water. These ads were viewed by some, particularly Boeing, as a violation of a longstanding tacit understanding within the civil aerospace industry that manufacturers will not make negative statements about competitors' safety standards. The reason for this understanding is the belief that the entire industry will suffer credibility problems if safety concerns are raised as in issue in the minds of consumers. After the outcry, Airbus denied that the twin-engines versus four-engines ads impugned the safety of the 777, but stopped publishing the ads.

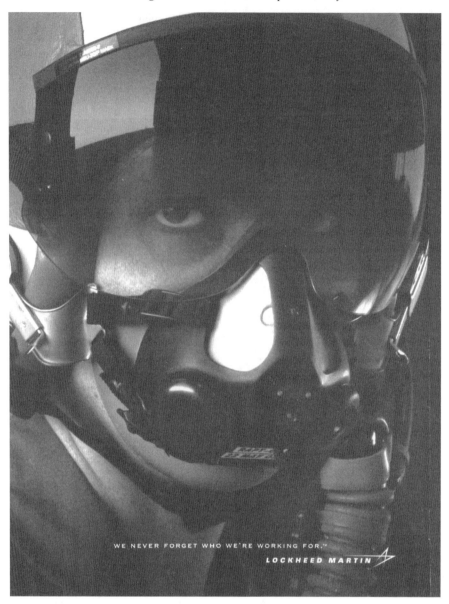

WE NEVER FORGET WHO WE'RE WORKING FOR."

LOCKHEED MARTIN

Figure 8.5 Image advertising for defense products
Note: This example of image advertising by Lockheed Martin, published during the Iraq war of 2003, is patriotic in tone but would be unlikely to offend international readers.
Source: Lockheed Martin.

Particularly in the case of sales of military aircraft to governments, advertising campaigns by competitors are not always welcomed by customers. Government procurement officials with responsibility for aircraft selection generally prefer to conduct their evaluation and selection without a great deal of public scrutiny and second-guessing. Public advertising campaigns increase public interest and often invite political meddling and investigative journalism. Government selection committees have been known to warn competitors informally that they will use the subjective evaluation process to penalize competitors that attempt to use advertising to influence the selection decision. Under these circumstances, each competitor is left with the decision of whether his overall competitive position will benefit or suffer as a result of the interplay of positive public reaction to ads, partially or entirely offset by negative reaction by the government evaluators.

Advertising military products poses special problems due to normal public sensitivities about military affairs. For this reason, advertising managers have to be selective about ad content, and must also carefully consider placement of ads. American defense contractors, for example, are generally safe in publishing overtly patriotic, flag-waving ads in the domestic American market, where such material is generally well received. However, the same ads would tend to be viewed askance in international markets or trade shows, where the viewers would have completely different national identities and geopolitical perspectives.

The size and variety of the international aerospace and aviation industries are demonstrated by the vast number of related publications. Virtually every country with a runway has at least a minor aviation magazine, and industrialized countries often have dozens of specialized aerospace publications. Existing side-by-side with commercial publications are private publications of aviation clubs, military institutions, aerospace manufacturers, technical societies, and so on. Most of these publications actively solicit paid advertisements. There is no shortage of available media.

The advertising message and target audience determines the choice of specific publications to carry advertising material. Widely read international publications such as *Aviation Week & Space Technology* and *Flight Magazine* are commonly chosen for corporate image advertising and for product advertising directed at general aerospace customers. Smaller local publications are often used when campaigns to market specific items of equipment to specific international customers are under way.

Most aerospace and aviation publications that solicit paid advertisements maintain circulation data obtained by surveys. The accuracy of the data varies dramatically. Customarily, circulation data is broken down into geographic regions and is divided into major categories of readers. Industry-oriented publications might use readership categories such as government, manufacturing, services, and air transport. General aviation magazines would include categories such as flight crews, hobbyists, private owners, and so on. Obviously the breakdown of readership is an important consideration in selecting a suitable publication for ad placement.

Chapter 9

Air Shows

Figure 9.1 Oshkosh Air Show
Note: Experimental Aircraft Association AirVenture Oshkosh is a unique show oriented to general aviation, private aircraft owners, experimental aircraft, antique aircraft, and stunt-flying.
Photo by Dennis Biela, www.dbiela.com.

It sounds like fun. Major international industry exhibits in places like Paris, Singapore, and Farnborough. Flying displays of high performance aircraft. Glitzy high-tech exhibits. Luxurious entertainment facilities. Personal appearances by famous people.

In reality, aerospace trade shows are hectic working environments. The large international shows generally involve long, grueling workdays for the participants, who have very little free time to enjoy the festivities seen by outsiders. The more common local air shows, away from major capitals and media attention, offer more opportunities for relaxation by professional participants, but they are often low-budget, short-duration visits to obscure locations.

What are aerospace shows, what is their purpose, and how do they function?

Aerospace shows are highly heterogeneous, but they can be classified into a few basic categories:

1. Major international air shows, generally biennial, have first-class permanent exhibit facilities, accommodations and logistic support for large numbers of flying aircraft, off-runway space for static display aircraft, well-equipped conference facilities, on-site luxury hospitality facilities, and extensive communications support for media and trade representatives. This type of show, the most prestigious of the genre, is invariably conceived as a business venue for industry interests. The well-known shows in Paris, Farnborough, Hamburg, and Singapore are examples. Less-established shows in Moscow, Berlin, Dubai, Langkawi (Malaysia), Seoul, Chile, and Zhuhai (China) are adding to the ranks of this category.
2. Major international aerospace exhibits are similar to air shows except that they do not have flying displays, and tend to be located in downtown convention facilities. Shows in Tokyo and Beijing are examples. These shows have the advantage of being less expensive for exhibitors because they do not require the presence of aircraft, and they are more accessible to customers because they are typically located in urban areas. Attendance by local customers is often excellent. Compared to air shows, indoor exhibits are less attractive to the general public, and therefore tend to have fewer distractions from business matters.
3. International defense shows are similar to aerospace exhibits, but often present a full range of defense equipment such as artillery, armor, communications, landmines, and so on. Aerospace companies often participate to market airborne military equipment. Examples of this type of show abound. Representative examples are IDEX (International Defense Exposition) in Abu Dhabi, DSA (Defence Services Asia) in Kuala Lumpur, IDEF (International Show of Defence, Aerospace and Naval Hardware) in Ankara, Eurosatory in Paris, and DSEI (Defence Systems and Equipment International) in London.
4. Aerospace sub-sector exhibits are narrowly focused on specialties such as aerospace avionics, intelligence-gathering systems, or maintenance-repair-overhaul (MRO).
5. Air shows limited to specific classifications of aircraft tend to be relatively small, but are highly focused. Examples are shows for helicopters, business jets, air ambulances, and unpiloted aircraft. An exception to the generality that this type of show is small is the Oshkosh Experimental Aircraft Association show in Oklahoma, which is perhaps the most widely attended of all international air shows. Other examples are the National Business Aviation Association (NBAA) show in Las Vegas, and the annual Helicopter Association International Heli-Expo show in various locations. These shows are fertile opportunities for contacts with customers with specific interests.
6. Air shows, exhibits, or open houses sponsored by local military units are customarily of short duration, generally over a single weekend. Located at military facilities, they sometimes display an impressive array of military aircraft, but have otherwise limited exhibits or amenities – sometimes only

tents. The events range from very large to very small. In the United States, they are often hosted by National Guard or Reserve units that have considerable political influence. Aerospace companies carefully cultivate relationships with these units, and reliably support locally organized military shows.

7. Locally sponsored air shows tend to be small scale, with little or no aerospace industry emphasis. Often they offer aerobatic flying displays, wing-walkers, sky-diving displays, and truck races. They are targeted at the general public, and have little marketing potential for major aerospace companies, but provide access to general aviation enthusiasts.

For the aerospace marketing department attempting to plan its participation at shows, there is a lot to choose from. Who goes to these shows, either as exhibitors or visitors, and what do they expect to accomplish?

These are questions that warrant reflection. Participation at aerospace shows can be very expensive. It requires a multimillion dollar budget to participate fully at an international show, with a flight demo aircraft, a hospitality chalet, a major exhibit, and a team of professional people. According to conventional wisdom, major companies cannot afford to skip major international shows because their absence would put them at a disadvantage relative to their competitors.

To obtain a general feel for the participation at major international air shows, it is worthwhile to compare attendance data at two of the major shows, Paris and Singapore. The Paris Air Show, formally known as Le Salon de L'Aéronautique et de l'Espace du Bourget, shares the honor with Farnborough of being Europe's premier show. The Singapore show, known as Asian Aerospace, has historically been Asia's premier show. (In 2006, following disagreements between the organizers of Asian Aerospace and the Singaporean Government, the organizers announced their intention to move future editions of their show to Hong Kong. Singaporean authorities, in turn, announced their intention to continue to host a biennial show in Singapore under a different name.)

At the 2001 Paris show, 71 per cent of the participants during the 'trade days' (the last two days of the show are open to the public, and are massively attended by non-professional aircraft enthusiasts of every ilk, including small children) were members of the aerospace and aviation industries, broadly defined. Approximately 15 per cent were members of the armed forces, and 14 per cent were from the government sector. At the Singapore show for 2000, military and government visitors constituted 32 per cent of the total, with the remainder being associated with the aviation or aerospace industries. A noteworthy difference between the two shows is their size. In contrast to the 121,119 reported visitors at Paris, Singapore reported 22,642 trade visitors – barely a sixth the volume of the larger show.

Table 9.1 Composition of visitors by principal sector of activity

Paris Air Show 2001		Asian Aerospace 2000 (Singapore)	
Aerospace Industry	71%	Air Transportation	34%
Armed Forces	15%	Military	32%
Government Officials	14%	Related Industries	18%
		Manufacturers	12%
		Corporate or Private Aircraft	4%

Source: Groupement des Industries Francaises Aéonautiques et Spatiales (GIFAS) and Reed Exhibitions.

Furthermore, the Paris organizers reported that of their total of 121,119 visitors, almost 63 per cent of the foreign visitors were from Western Europe, 20 per cent were from the Americas, and 8 per cent were from Asia. Looking at the national origins of the visitors to the Singapore show, we are not surprised to observe that the overwhelming majority come from regional Asian countries, although a solid 25 per cent are from Europe and the United States. Asian Aerospace clearly rates its reputation as an international show.

Table 9.2 Composition of visitors by geographic region of origin

Paris Air Show 2001		Asian Aerospace 2000 (Singapore)	
Western Europe (excl. France)	63%	Southeast Asia	37%
Americas	20%	North Asia	21%
Asia/Pacific	8%	Americas	14%
Eastern Europe	5%	Europe	11%
Africa	3%	Australia & Pacific Islands	8%
Middle East	1%	West Asia	7%
		Other	2%

Source: Groupement des Industries Francaises Aéonautiques et Spatiales (GIFAS) and Reed Exhibitions.

Let us look more closely at the type of industry representatives we are likely to see at a major international show. At the 2001 Singapore show, for example, we see that the air transportation sector is heavily represented, primarily by airline personnel, but also by visitors associated with government regulation, airport management, and ancillary services.

Table 9.3 Profile of air transport visitors Asian Aerospace 2000 (Singapore)

Airlines	53%
Civil Government Officials	23%
Airports	10%
Cargo & Freight Forwarders	7%
Passenger Services	7%

Source: Groupement des Industries Francaises Aéonautiques et Spatiales (GIFAS) and Reed Exhibitions.

The manufacturers generally are the principal exhibitors at the major trade shows. They present the equipment that is the most obvious attraction for the professional visitors. The largest, most dramatic exhibits and most opulent entertainment chalets belong to the relatively small number of major airframe, engine, and avionics manufacturers. Smaller suppliers of equipment, material, hardware, and miscellaneous items are more plentiful, and occupy modest exhibits throughout the halls.

A breakdown of professional disciplines of professional visitors to the 2001 Singapore show indicates a broad diversity, and also demonstrates an impressive participation by relatively senior executives. At the 2001 Paris Air Show, the profile of show visitors revealed a diversity of functional disciplines very similar to the Singapore show, with a similar relative abundance of senior management.

Table 9.4 Job function of visitors

Paris Air Show 2001		**Asian Aerospace 2000 (Singapore)**	
General Management	18%	Engineering	21%
Commercial Management	9%	General Management	15%
Marketing Management	7%	Sales & Marketing	12%
Government	6%	HQ Officer	12%
Purchasing Management	6%	Maintenance	11%
Administrative Management	5%	Planning	5%
Foreign Representatives	4%	Finance & Accounting	4%
Flight Personnel	3%	Field Officer	4%
After-Sales Management	2%	Production	3%
Others	40%	Consultant	3%
		Communications	3%
		Purchasing	3%
		Security	1%
		Other	3%

Source: Groupement des Industries Francaises Aéonautiques et Spatiales (GIFAS) and Reed Exhibitions.

And, finally, what do visitors at the major international shows come to see? Both Singapore and Paris have similar answers: the visitors come to see the aircraft, the equipment, the weapons, the avionics, and the variety of other aerospace-related items displayed by the manufacturers.

Table 9.5 Primary product interest of visitors

Paris Air Show 2001		Asian Aerospace 2000 (Singapore)	
Aircraft Manufacturers	21%	Fixed-Wing Aircraft	13%
Raw Material, Industrial Equip.	10%	Telecommunications	11%
Services	10%	Aircraft Components	8%
Components & Subassemblies	9%	Aircraft Maintenance Services	8%
Pilot & Navigational Aids	9%	Helicopters	7%
Airborne & Missile Propulsion	8%	Engines	7%
Airborne Weapons, Missiles	7%	Missiles & Weapons	7%
Space Systems	6%	Simulators & Training Equip.	6%
Aerospace R&D	5%	Airport/Terminal Systems	6%
Equip. for Maint., Training	5%	Ground Support Equipment	5%
Anti-Air Defense Systems	3%	Armament/Ordnance	5%
Airport Equipment	3%	Other	17%
No Response	4%		

Source: Groupement des Industries Francaises Aéonautiques et Spatiales (GIFAS) and Reed Exhibitions.

The kinds of activities that occur at the major international shows are not necessarily representative of the smaller, more local shows. Whereas a major exhibitor at Farnborough might have a multimillion dollar budget for the show, the same exhibitor at the Mississippi National Guard air show at Biloxi might have a $5,000 budget to cover a 3-meter by 6-meter portable display erected inside a tent over a weekend. Different shows entail different levels of commitment and different levels of support.

Participation at aerospace shows, even the smaller ones, is important because they give companies visible exposure to important customers and to the public. To make a positive impression, participants must ensure that their display materials and overall management of the event are commensurate with the professional standards they want to convey.

Major aerospace companies that are regular show participants will include, as part of their organization, a Special Events function that will have responsibility for planning and organizing the administrative and technical aspects of show participation. Special events managers working in this unit of the company have responsibility for ensuring that the company's participation is well organized. However, the actual marketing activities that take place at the show are the responsibility of the marketing unit, and a manager from this department is designated to lead the company's overall activities relating to the show. This person, colloquially known as the ringmaster, will hold periodic meetings to orchestrate all action. Throughout the period of the show, the special events manager will report to the ringmaster.

Trade shows are logistically complicated, and good planning is an essential element of success. Orchestrating a trade show presence is a form of program management, characterized by a multitude of interdependent events, irregular lead times, key milestones, fluctuating resources, and critical deadlines. So let us study trade show management from the point of view of an exhibitor acting like a program manager. Beginning with the tasks with the longest lead times, we shall examine the key tasks that have to be successfully managed.

Although the detailed planning and program management will be different for every show, a few fundamental requirements are part of the basic planning for any show:

- *Establish objectives.* Be specific concerning the target market, the geographical region of interest, the message to be conveyed, and the available budget.
- *Identify appropriate shows.* After objectives are articulated and understood, do the necessary research to identify the specific shows that will best accomplish objectives.
- *Design appropriate physical displays and accommodations.* Make sure that the exhibit and hospitality chalet are of the right size to receive the volume of expected visitors and to enable effective presentation of suitable display articles.
- *Do the necessary advance work.* Plan an advance program of advertisements, promotions, public events, and press conferences intended to attract the right kind of attention to the messages that the company is attempting to convey at the show.
- *Set up appointments with the right people.* Compile a list of target customers, send them invitations, and contact them directly to arrange appointments at the show. Make every possible effort to confirm specific meetings in advance.
- *Follow up after the show.* Make a consolidated record of every significant meeting at the show, with notes of specific subjects and action items. Send follow-up communication to customers. Maintain status of action to keep the promises that were made at the show.

Eighteen months lead time: Identify the show, designate a ringmaster, make a participation decision, register, make hotel reservations

In any given week of the year, probably at least one show of major or minor importance is scheduled, and it is a job in itself to maintain visibility of the calendar of shows. Some comprehensive published schedules exist, but they generally are incomplete or focused on specific market segments. The best source of information about the individual shows is the organizers themselves, who will eagerly make contact with potential exhibitors on their mailing lists. The marketing department should compile a complete week-by-week calendar with key information about each event in the entire year. An extracted sample is below:

Table 9.6 Preliminary planning for air shows

Show Event	Location	Dates	Exhibit Requirement
Utah National Guard	St. George, UT	April 27-29	Portable 10x10 Military Products Display
Mississippi National Guard	Biloxi, MS	April 28-29	Portable 10x10 Military Products Display
Naval Reserve Association Spring Conference	Honolulu, HI	April 28 - May 2	Portable 10x10 Military Products Display
Software Technology Conference	Salt Lake City, UT	April 29 - May 4	Portable 10x10 Corporate Tech Display
Space Control Conference	Lexington, MA	April 28-29	Portable 10x10 Space Products Display
Missouri National Guard	Jefferson City, MO	April 27-29	Portable 10x10 Military Products Display
Unmanned Underwater Vehicles Symposium	Newport, RI	April 27-29	Portable 10x10 Military Products Display
New Jersey National Guard	Atlantic City, NJ	April 28-29	Portable 10x10 Military Products Display
Washington National Guard	Tacoma, WA	April 28-29	Portable 10x10 Military Products Display

Note: An example of preliminary planning information for a variety of small local aerospace-related shows.

Major shows customarily occur on two-year cycles, but smaller ones may take place annually. Well in advance, the list of shows should be circulated within the company so that marketers and other interested parties can decide which shows warrant participation. As part of this decision, the level of participation will be chosen. Minimum participation would entail a small exhibit staffed by a single salesperson, whereas maximum participation might involve a large exhibit with elaborate electronic displays and model aircraft, supplemented by an entertainment chalet, possibly including an aircraft and crew for flight demonstrations. At this point, budgetary estimates should be made, and the sponsoring departments should obligate funds. The company's events planner should then send in required preliminary registration material to the organizers. Registration at this early stage may not be contractually binding, and planning changes will be possible as the date of the show approaches.

A word of caution: some major international aerospace shows with heavy demand commit their exhibit facilities years in advance. To avoid the risk of being involuntarily shut out, participants should maintain continuous contact with the organizers, long in advance of the opening date.

It may seem odd to reserve hotel rooms 18 months in advance, but it is necessary at the major international shows, which take place in cities where virtually all of the available first-class hotel rooms will be occupied due to the huge influx of visitors for the event. In some cases you will be required to commit to occupy a block of rooms for the entire period of the show, and will have to make a cash deposit.

Eight months lead time: Identify aircraft to be displayed, make arrangements to obtain them, and begin leasing discussions if necessary

The logistical arrangements for the show become dramatically more complicated if a flight demonstration is involved. Arrangements for a flight crew and ground support crew, with full accommodations, will have to be made. Aircraft parking space at the show will have to be arranged, with suitable security, and planning for flight programs will have to be coordinated.

Often the aircraft to be displayed will not be the property of the exhibitor. Particularly in the case of military aircraft and airliners, the aircraft in production are the property of the buyers, who have made substantial progress payments to finance the manufacturer's work-in-process. Consequently, the manufacturers are not free to use the aircraft for display purposes without the formal permission of the owner. Arrangements to borrow aircraft for display purposes take the form of short-term leases in which the exhibitor agrees to insure against all risk of damage to the aircraft and claims in the event of an accident. Often the exhibitor also has to pay an agreed amount per flight hour or per day of use.

When a military aircraft is being exhibited by a private company, obtaining a lease from a government can be complicated, particularly if the show is overseas. In the case of the US Government, approvals are required by the US State Department, the Department of Defense, the headquarters of the service branch that owns the aircraft, and the operational military unit where the aircraft is based.

Of great assistance in arranging aircraft leases are the national aerospace industry trade groups, which are lobbying organizations with close relationships with the government units involved in approving leases. Most significant aerospace companies are members of their respective national groups. In the USA, the UK, France, Germany, and Japan, the groups are, respectively, Aerospace Industries Association (AIA), the Society of British Aerospace Companies (SBAC), Groupement des Industries Françaises Aéonautiques et Spatiales (GIFAS), Bundesverband der Deutschen Luft- und Raumfahrtindustrie (BDLI), and the Society of Japanese Aerospace Companies (SJAC).

Formal policy of the US Department of Defense supports the use of military equipment for international shows, and provides specific rules for leasing aircraft. An extract of DoD Directive 7230.8, which governs these leases, is shown in Figure 9.2. Other major aerospace-producing countries have similar policies, with the exception of Japan, whose constitution prohibits export sales of military equipment.

Six months lead time: Define the show plan

By now, the overall plan for the show should be in place. The overall objective and theme of the company's participation should be defined and understood by all participants. The executives and supporting marketing representatives to attend should be tentatively identified, and a concept of messages to the press should be developed. This comprehensive plan should be endorsed by senior management and distributed to all concerned.

DoD Directive 7230.8 – Aircraft Leasing to Industry

4. POLICY

4.1. General

4.1.1. When it is determined to be in the national security interest, the DoD Components may participate directly in international trade shows and exhibitions. Consideration of direct participation will normally be on a case-by-case basis, using the following guidelines:

4.1.1.1. Participation shall be based on national security and foreign policy objectives, and will be reserved for events held in strategically important regions in which the Department of Defense wants to demonstrate continued U.S. interest and commitment.

4.1.1.2. Direct participation in a particular event must be supported by the relevant Military Departments, Unified Combatant Command, and U.S. Embassy before being considered.

4.1.2. When foreign sales of U.S.-manufactured defense equipment would contribute to U.S. national security and foreign policy interests, the Secretaries of the Military Departments or their designees may lease DoD equipment to a defense contractor or industrial association for demonstration to foreign governments or for display or demonstration at international trade shows and exhibitions. Equipment may be leased only if the equipment is not needed for the term of the lease by the Military Department, and can be made available without unduly impacting military readiness.

4.2. Leases of Equipment to Contractors or Associations for Sales Demonstrations to Foreign Governments

4.2.1. The Military Departments may lease DoD equipment to defense contractors or industrial associations for demonstration to foreign governments when that equipment is eligible for disclosure under NDP-1 (reference(d)), or an exception to reference (d) has been obtained. (See DoD Directive 5230.11, reference (e)).

4.2.2. The Military Departments may lease, under Section 2667 of 10 U.S.C. (reference (f)), or lend, under Section 2541(a)(2) of reference (f), equipment to contractors or industrial associations. Lease and lending agreements shall be approved by the Secretary of the Military Department involved, or a designated representative.

4.2.3. Charges for leased equipment shall normally be determined in accordance with DoD Instruction 7230.7 (reference (g)); however, lease charges on equipment that has undergone significant modifications at the lessee's expense may be adjusted to recognize the lessee's investment. Furthermore, in accordance with Section 2667 of reference (f), the Secretaries of the Military Departments or their designees may, in order to promote the national defense or serve the public interest, determine that no lease charge will be assessed for the leased equipment, or that a reduced charge (such as charging the contractor only for those hours that the equipment is operated in an aerial or live demonstration) will be assessed, notwithstanding paragraph 6.3.1. of reference (g). Examples of promoting the national defense or serving the public interest include, but are not limited to, helping preserve and broaden defense industrial base capabilities, and enhancing economies of scale for DoD procurement.

4.2.4. In addition to any charges assessed in accordance with paragraph 4.2.3., above, the lessee or the loan recipient shall pay other appropriate charges for any supplies or services provided by DoD personnel in connection with the lease. Such charges may include, but are not limited to, spare parts, maintenance services, fuel, crew pay, and crew per diem. The lease shall provide that the lessee shall not charge any costs assessed under this Directive, directly or indirectly, to any U.S. Government contract, except to the extent chargeable to contracts for foreign military sales under DFARS, Section 225.7303-2 (reference(h)).

4.2.5. The U.S. Government may assume the risk of loss or damage of the leased equipment when a U.S. Government pilot is the pilot-in-command during flights, or when U.S. Government personnel operate the equipment. The lessee shall assume the risk of loss or liability for damage in all cases except those in which the U.S. Government has chosen to assume the risk. That risk shall be covered by hull insurance or the posting of a surety bond on the depreciated value of the equipment being leased or, with the approval of the Military Department involved, the lessee may be self-insured. The Military Department involved shall review and approve the flight or operation plan to ensure that the risks are not inordinate to the need. In all cases, the lessee shall be required to hold the U.S. Government harmless against claims by third parties arising out of the lease or demonstration, and will be required to indemnify the U.S. Government against liability to third parties arising out of the lease or demonstration.

Figure 9.2 US DoD directive for leasing equipment for air shows
Note: Participation by military officials is an import element in many air shows. This document is the regulation that governs attendance by US military personnel.
Source: US DoD Directive 7230.8.

Fundamental agreements concerning leasing demonstrator aircraft should be in place, and planning for the flight demonstrations should have been fully coordinated with the show organizers.

A rigorous review of export licenses should be conducted at this time to ensure that all material to be exposed to customers is covered by valid export licenses. The export licenses must cover not only written material, but also display material such as simulators or demonstrator aircraft. If any lapses in license coverage are discovered, now is the time to submit license applications to the exporter's government licensing agency.

Four months lead time: Finalize the artistic design of the exhibit, define a detailed media plan, and begin production of any specialized literature for the show

At least four months prior to the show, the discussions between the exhibit specialists and marketers should have produced a final design concept for the display, and the artwork, models, electronic effects, signage, and furniture will now be sent to a subcontractor for production. Special brochures will be sent to the printer, and any program of press conferences and special announcements will be determined.

Three months lead time: Identify key customer meetings, tentative appointment agendas for senior executives, and an overall list of invitations for the chalet

Because of particular circumstances of individual marketing campaigns, certain visitors to the show will be considered to have special importance, and will be especially targeted for meetings with the company's senior executives. Preliminary coordination should begin to assure that necessary appointments are made. An extended tentative list of intended meetings for the senior company representatives should be prepared, and a longer complete list of invited guests should be compiled. Invitations should be ordered from the printer.

At larger air shows, big companies will normally have a technical display in the exhibit halls, and will have a chalet next to the runway. Although the exhibit halls are open to anyone who has a ticket to the air show, access to the chalets is restricted to guests with invitations. Standard practice is that companies will mail exhibit invitations to extended lists of supplier representatives and customers, but will send invitations to their chalets to more select lists of senior managers or other key customer representatives.

By three months before the show, arrangements with the show organizers for operating and parking demonstrator aircraft should be firm.

The company's security officials should be working with their government counterparts to assess the security environment at the show and to prepare guidelines for the complete team of show participants.

An important administrative detail at this point is to ensure that hardware import license applications have been submitted through the show organizers to the national authorities of the country hosting the show. For defense-related shows in particular, lack of appropriate import licenses can cause chaos in show arrangements. Most military gear, aircraft included, requires special customs authorization before it can cross international frontiers. Even dummy displays of inert or non-functional gear will require appropriate special documentation.

Two months lead time: Organize briefing materials for executives, mail invitations, begin scheduling appointments, schedule specific events such as interviews and media conferences. Confirm the final list of company participants

In order to ensure that participants are reasonably knowledgeable about the objectives and issues of marketing campaigns of the company's entire product line, a background book should be prepared for limited distribution within the company. The book should include basic background information about the company's product lines, a summary of the current status of programs, an analysis of issues that are likely to arise during discussions with visitors, and brief information about senior customer representatives who are likely to visit. The background book should be compiled from summaries written by the individual marketing leads for the individual campaigns.

The freshly printed invitations should be mailed to the guest list, and detailed appointment calendars should be maintained as acceptances are received.

As planned meetings with the media are identified, suitable conference facilities at the show should be arranged. Major shows will have special facilities available to exhibitors for press conferences, but the facilities must be reserved in advance. Special materials to be distributed at press conferences and interviews should be prepared. Detailed arrangements with local caterers should be in place. In locations where special religious dietary restrictions apply, be sure to take these into consideration. However, the best policy regarding food service is to offer guests dishes derived from your company's home culture, rather than engage in culinary competition with local firms. The Fort Worth division of Lockheed successfully followed this practice for years at the Paris Air Show by offering Angelo's Barbecue flown from Texas.

At this time, a final list of company participants should be available so that arrangements for hotel facilities and transportation can be finalized and security badges for the show can be obtained.

The flight demo routine should be defined, and a description should be sent to the show organizers for approval.

Marketing brochures for all product lines and promotional gifts should be accumulated and shipped to a holding point at the show location.

Ten days lead time: Update of background book and appointment schedules, re-confirmation of key customer meetings, and announcement of collective internal pre-briefing at hotel

In the days before the show begins, the advance special events team will arrive at the show location to set up the displays, make final arrangements at hotels, coordinate with local authorities, and so on. If a demonstrator aircraft is involved, maintenance facilities will be set up.

As the date of the show approaches, all preliminary schedules and background information should be updated a final time. A final organizational meeting at the show location should be planned. These meetings are usually held at the company-reserved hotel on the evening prior to the first day of the show. At this meeting, all participants will be briefed concerning detailed arrangements, including show schedules, security, and transportation between the hotel and the show facility. Individual people will be identified to represent the company at special events such as ambassadors' receptions, organizers' receptions, and customer functions.

In the days immediately prior to the show, the company pilots will be required to fly an example of their demonstration routine in order to be approved for qualification. The organizers will be particularly concerned that the routine meets safety standards and time limits. Normally the pilots will qualify for two routines – a 'high' routine for good weather, and a 'low' routine for overcast conditions.

Managing Daily Events at the Show

On each day of the show, the company's entire contingent of participants should convene for a breakfast meeting on the show premises. The company chalet, if one is available, is an ideal venue.

At this meeting, the ringmaster should review with the group the schedule of appointments for senior visits to the chalet, and should assign specific senior company hosts to welcome designated visitors. Critical subject matter for key meetings should be briefly reviewed among the group. In cases in which spouses are expected to accompany senior visitors, flexible arrangements should be made to entertain the spouses while the business discussions are in session. The conventional arrangement for entertaining spouses is to pair them with any spouses of senior company representatives who will be present in the chalet. If company spouses are not available, administrative staff at the chalet should discretely attend to the well-being of the visiting spouses, and assure that they are offered refreshments.

If the company has an aircraft performing flight demonstrations as part of the daily program, an alternate company pilot will provide narration of the routine, using a loudspeaker system. This narration consists of describing the nature of the maneuvers and the special capabilities of the aircraft. For marketing purposes, the period of the flight demo is prime time to entertain customers at the chalet.

Figure 9.3 Air show chalet
Note: A typical chalet at the Singapore Air Show. The glass wall to the right provides a view of the flying demonstrations (photo by the author).

If senior dignitaries are scheduled to visit the company's display in the exhibition hall, appropriate company executives should be assigned responsibility for being present at the display to welcome the visitor.

In general, movement of company representatives between the exhibition hall and the chalet will be fluid. The most senior company officials will be based in the chalet, but will make occasional visits to the display as their schedules allow. An adequate presence should be maintained at the display at all times, but company representatives will frequently invite desirable visitors at the display to go to the chalet for refreshments and discussions, and will accompany them from one location to the other.

Designated official spokespersons should be permanently stationed at the chalet and the exhibition hall. All media representatives who want information should be referred to these spokespersons.

In the case of large, diversified aerospace companies, the relatively small number of representatives at the show may receive detailed product inquiries to which they personally have insufficient knowledge to respond. To ensure that these inquiries are reliably relayed to the proper people within the company, a system of standard notecards should be maintained by the exhibit staff. The notecards will specify the nature of the inquiry and the business unit to which it was addressed, and will include the name, title, and address of the visitor who posed the question. Following the show, these cards will be appropriately distributed within the company.

Throughout the day, there will be continuous movement of people among the exhibition hall, the chalet, press conferences, and visits to facilities of other companies and customers. To assure availability of senior executives in the case of unexpected visits by key customer representatives, these representatives should be reachable by cell phone or pager at all times.

At daily closing time at the show, the entire company contingent should once again convene for an internal meeting at the chalet. The ringmaster should very quickly review the outcome of the most important events and meetings of the day in order to ensure that all participants have up-to-date information. Any problems of general interest should be identified, and solutions should be agreed upon. Evening events to follow that day's show should be identified, and specific representatives at each event should be reminded of their commitments. Necessary follow-up actions involving overnight discussions with the company's home offices should be assigned.

After the Show

Events after the show fall into three main categories: dismantling the physical show facilities, evaluating the way the show was conducted, and following up on marketing actions.

- *Dismantling.*
  Compared to the high-pressure events of previous weeks, this is easy. A crew dismantles the physical display materials and ships them to another show location or to storage. The special events manager settles administrative details and pays bills.
- *Evaluation.*
  The special events manager should circulate a questionnaire among all show participants, obtaining their opinions on subjects such as the quality of the show itself, the quality of the company's displays and chalet, hotel and transportation arrangements, overall company organization, and so on. The objective of the questionnaire is to ascertain if the show is worthwhile for future participation, and if the company's performance at the show can be improved.
- *Marketing follow-up.*
  As soon as possible after the show, when everyone has returned to their home offices, the ringmaster should convene a meeting of all show participants to discuss action to be taken as a result of events that occurred at the show. This meeting should include discussion of significant items of information obtained from customers, general impressions of customer attitudes and intentions, and development of plans intended to steer future events in a direction favorable to the company.

For better or worse, air shows are a fact of life in the business of marketing in the aerospace industry. At their worst, they can be a significant investment in time and money without commensurate returns in terms of marketing effectiveness. At their best, and if properly managed, they offer unique opportunities for access to many important customers in a brief but intense period of time.

U.S. GOVERNMENT INSTALLATION SECURITY SURVEY
LANGKAWI INTERNATIONAL AIRPORT, LANGKAWI, MALAYSIA

03 AUGUST 2001

4.2 Immediate Threat.
At this time, there is no specific threat to US personnel or facilities. Any threat to US personnel or facilities would be a peripheral threat based on the current political situation in Langkawi. For current terrorist threat, refer to Annex E. The criminal threat to US personnel is considered to be high, with a high frequency of petty theft, i.e. pick-pocketing and burglary. The local population consists of a high percentage of Muslim Malaysians. The local view of Americans, US military personnel specifically, is neutral with no specific dislike or distrust by the local populace. Americans are generally perceived to be Australian, unless personnel distinguish themselves as otherwise.

4.3 Airfield Security: The Langkawi International Airport is a closed civilian installation that is surrounded by mountains on three sides and ocean on the north side of airfield. Vehicle passes or authorized escort is required to enter the flight line area on a normal basis. During routine operations, maintenance, ground servicing, and Malaysian Airlines employees are permitted access to the flight line. Authorized individuals have numbered photo ID badges to control entry. Temporary escort badges are required by visitors for entry. All flight line badging issues are handled by the Airport Police. During LIMA 01, show staff, trade representatives, and aircrews will have access to the ramp via special photo ID badges during show hours. After hours, security staff and pre-announced persons will be allowed entry to the ramp. During LIMA, there will be four access points to the ramp during show hours and one access point after hours. The public will have access to the ramp during the weekend air show days from 0900-1600. There are no physical restrictions on movement on the flight line once access is obtained.

4.3.1 Airfield perimeter: There is one manned vehicle and pedestrian access gate near the main parking ramp. This is manned 24 hours by a civilian guard. There are two locked access gates along the perimeter fence; one at the north end, and another near the civilian homes opposite the main parking ramp. The perimeter fencing is approximately 8-gauge chain link fencing, six feet high with a three-foot outrigger holding 3 strands of standard barbed wire. There are no vegetation problems and there are adequate clear zones along the entire fence line. The perimeter is not lighted, and there is no Intrusion Detection System. There are many vantage points from which photos of the main ramp may be taken, including the high ground behind the civilian housing opposite the main ramp. A three-foot deep drainage ditch runs along most of the perimeter fence and provides an excellent vehicle barrier.

4.3.2 Airfield Lighting: There is no perimeter lighting. The main parking ramp has adequate area lighting (pole-mounted floodlights). No light-alls or light carts were apparent.

4.3.3 There are no portable barrier systems apparent, and no IDS system installed. There were no flight line security patrols observed during the visit. According to Maj Bakhtiar, RMAF, there will be a total of six patrols on duty during the show, divided between RMAF and PDRM assets inside the perimeter. During the show, barriers will be erected between the commercial operations area and the show area. Disembarking passengers will be marshaled into the terminal for added security.

4.3.4 The airfield uses standard international publications for emergency actions regarding natural disasters, mass casualties, and crashes. The survey team leader was unable to obtain a copy of the Airport Security Program manual, but was promised copies of the emergency publications prior to LIMA. An EOD special response team will be on alert during the show, provided by the Malaysian Army. This unit does NOT have trained Bomb Detector Dogs, but will provide disposal services for suspicious items. The lack of detection assets may require generation of a USAF BDD team for the airshow.

4.3.5 Dep Supt. Zakeri provided an excellent run down on the security force that will be available during LIMA. Approximately 1100 personnel, including regulars and augmentees, will be on hand for LIMA to provide security and rescue assistance. There will be 30-40 PDRM personnel at the airfield at all times. An additional 300 PDRM personnel will be in the area to provide increased security both to the airfield and the local community. Up to 200 additional rescue/response personnel will be brought to the island to augment the local hospital. Airport police will bring in an additional 70-80 personnel, and the RMAF will have detachments available for contingencies. The security layers will be: PDRM outside the ramp, RMAF on the ramp, Airport Police for all other actions. Security personnel use standard Motorola radios for communication, with telephone as a backup. Additional military response forces can be brought within 2-4 hours from RMAF Butterworth in Penang and possibly RMAF Subang in KL. Response time for additional PDRM forces is unknown.

4.3.6 The security for the event will be coordinated through the PDRM and will involve daily situation briefs with all involved security forces. We requested frequencies for pre-programming, but they would not entertain the idea. They asked us to provide a radio to them for coordination purposes from the central security office. The central security office will also act as the crisis management center in the even of an incident. Most if not all of the host nation personnel speak basic or advanced English. Our security forces are not expected to bring weapons and the issue was not cleared during our meetings. However, information on weapons storage may be coordinated with the USDAO office in KL.

4.3.7 The flight line and POL storage are restricted areas. During the air show, security will maintain a boundary between commercial and military operations. US Forces have been granted the right to detain any person seeking to cause damage to assets or personnel at the show, but we may not arrest or interrogate. All violators must be handed over to PDRM or RMAF forces once they arrive. We expect reaction time to any incident to be within 5 minutes due to the number of patrols planned. US security forces will be billeted at the Helang Hotel, approximately 300m from the main ramp, to increase security and eliminate transit requirements.

Figure 9.4 A typical pre-show security survey by the US Government, in Langkawi, Malaysia

Source: US Department of Defense.

Chapter 10

Operations Analysis

Relative Direct Operating Cost per seat %

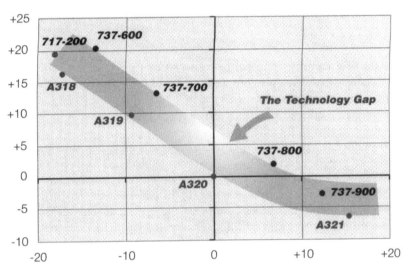

Relative Direct Operating Cost per trip %

Figure 10.1 Efficiency comparison of airliners
Note: Operations analysis in its most elemental form: Airbus claims its planes are more efficient than Boeing's. Boeing, of course, has analysis that gives different results.
Source: Airbus.

In the aerospace and aviation industries, *operations analysis*, as the words imply, is the application of quantitative analytical techniques to the operations of aircraft and equipment.

Aircraft operations in both civil and military service are complex, involving large numbers of variables that have a bearing upon costs, efficiency, and the ability of the aircraft to perform specific missions. The job of the analyst is to identify the many variables, quantify them, consolidate them into an abstract model of cost or performance, and use the model to predict outcome or to recommend mixes of variables that will result in optimal outcomes for the operator.

This is of fundamental importance to the marketer. In theory, aircraft customers want to buy the aircraft that will provide them with optimal outcomes. At the top level, airlines want to maximize their earnings and air forces want to field the most formidable national defense. The marketer who can convince them that his aircraft will enable them to achieve these desired outcomes has an excellent chance of selling the product.

The problem and the opportunity are that customers often do not have a precise definition of their desired outcome. An airline operator, for example, might be searching for the aircraft that can enable profit maximization on a specific route. A reliable projection of passenger volume and ticket price, combined with knowledge of the cost of ownership and operating costs of alternative aircraft, should provide sufficient information for the operator to create a simple analytical model to indicate which aircraft will deliver the best results.

However, the model can become infinitely more complex if other variables are introduced:

- If the new aircraft is from a different manufacturer than existing aircraft in the operator's fleet, the operator faces cost penalties because pilots qualified for one type cannot be easily reassigned to fly the other type.
- Aircraft of optimal efficiency for a specific route may be unsuitable as substitute aircraft for other routes.
- If an aircraft type with a lower reliability rate is used, purchase of additional aircraft may be necessary to assure service on the route.
- Better cargo-carrying capacity of one of the alternatives may outweigh marginal passenger-carrying capacity of the other alternative.
- Faster projected turn-around times on the ground of one alternative may enable the operator to use his limited airport gates more efficiently, or to fly additional flights.
- Differences in maximum range may allow desirable future expansion to possible longer routes and new markets.

And so on.

In the case of combat aircraft, the variables and the relationships among them are even more complex. Analysis of a fighter aircraft might consider factors such as sustained turn rates, rates of climb, range, armaments load, pilot workload, radar cross section, radar capability, survivability, maintainability, interoperability, and any number of other variables.

Operations analysis, colloquially called ops analysis, has many applications, both for the aircraft operator and the manufacturer. Both parties have an interest in understanding factors that determine the effectiveness of aircraft in the marketplace, and both utilize ops analysis to gain insight.

Because of its capability to relate customer desires, hardware, and the business case, ops analysis is of particular interest for strategic planners within the aviation industry. It is uniquely useful for identifying target markets, calibrating market size, evaluating alternative aircraft configuration to serve the markets (including competitor aircraft), and for assessing economic factors relating to hypothetical new product lines. When management decisions concerning strategic planning are made, ops analysis can be used as a tool to justify and explain the decisions to stockholders, governments, creditors, and the media.

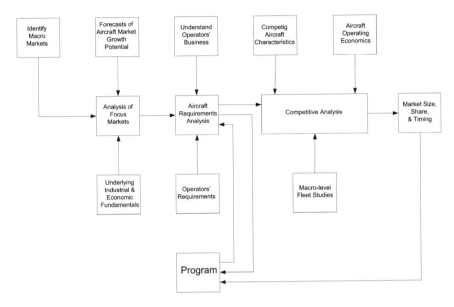

Figure 10.2 Aerospace market assessment process
Note: Reliable market assessments are based upon systematic gathering of relevant data, analysis of the data, and formulation of logical conclusions.

Apart from marketing applications, ops analysis is used in an important way during the design process for new aircraft. As the customer defines his operational needs and missions, it is the job of analysts to define operational characteristics of the aircraft. For example, if a detailed survey of a specific market segment for passenger transport aircraft identifies a variety of size and range requirements, operations analysts should be able to reach theoretical conclusions concerning optimal payload and range capabilities that should be designed into an aircraft targeted at the market segment. It then becomes the job of the design engineers to translate the required capabilities into a detailed aircraft design.

Logically, one would assume that the operator would understand his own business better than anyone else. This is not necessarily the case. The experience, competence, and management capability of operators vary enormously. As in most business sectors, aviation operators span the entire continuum from the highly knowledgeable to the complete neophytes. Often relatively unsophisticated customers rely upon aircraft manufacturers to provide extensive guidance and recommendations pertaining to the appropriate utilization of aircraft and equipment. In contrast, technically sophisticated customers typically have highly specific ideas concerning the operational characteristics of the aircraft they desire.

The nature of the technical dialogue between the marketer and the customer is affected by the level of technical sophistication of the customer. In the case of customers without extensive analytical experience, the analysts on the marketing team often provide the customer with tutorials that show how analytical methods can be applied to the customer's operational needs. Needless to say, customers are generally shrewd enough to recognize that analytical methods can be manipulated to produce outcomes favorable to the marketers. Although customers do not blindly accept the conclusions of operations analysis performed by the marketing team, they are usually interested in understanding the factors and variables used in the analysis.

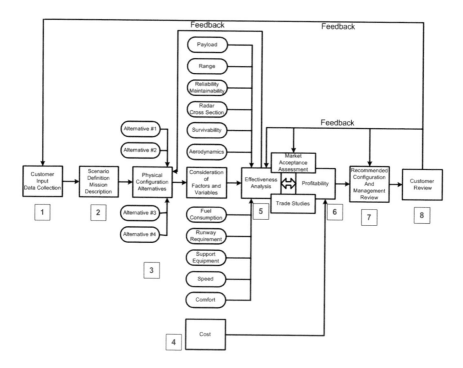

Figure 10.3 Methodology of aerospace operations analysis
Note: The nature of analysis varies according to circumstances and objectives, but the process generally involves identifying requirements and alternatives; evaluating factors; assessing effectiveness; and identifying an optimal outcome.

Apart from its role as a common language between customers and marketers, ops analysis is of fundamental importance to both the customer and the marketer, for several reasons:

•   It provides quantitative identification of missions, objectives, economic factors, and operational environments of the customer.

- As operational factors and variables are defined, it enables technical definition of specific customer requirements.
- It provides a bridge between technologies and market requirements, and provides a means for illustrating relationships between the two.
- Of particular interest to the marketer is that ops analysis provides a quantifiable means for marketers to support sales efforts for existing products to domestic and international customers.
- It enables the marketer and the customer to compare the operational qualities of competing aircraft.

The nature of the operations analysis process varies, depending upon the nature of the customer, the product, and the objective of the analysis. However, the process normally passes through a sequence of standard stages that yield a final conclusion concerning the suitability of the product for the customer's operations. Like all theoretical analysis, it is limited by the quality of the raw data, the validity of the underlying hypotheses, and the robustness of the analytical model. The fundamental process is similar for both civil and military operators, although the nature of their equipment and their operations obviously differ enormously.

1. Almost all ops analysis begins with *customer input*, which often takes the form of meetings with the customer to discuss operational needs and desires. During these discussions, the analysts attempt to reach an understanding of the customer's immediate requirements and his longer-term objectives. For use in subsequent studies, the analysts attempt to elicit as much detailed technical information as possible, including customer expectations concerning costs and budgets.

2. After gathering initial information, the analysts and marketers develop a specific description of the *customer's operating scenarios and missions*. This describes the job the customer wants to accomplish, the time he expects to have available, the prevailing environmental conditions, anticipated enemy capabilities, ground facilities available, and so on.

3. When the operating scenarios are understood, the analysts work with engineering project offices and design engineers to develop *physical configuration alternatives*. These alternatives are different engineering concepts that would theoretically enable the customer to attain his objectives. The alternatives could include, for example, designs for aircraft layouts for two engines versus four engines, or aluminum structure versus composite structure, or twin aisle versus single aisle. If a major new design is not envisioned, the alternatives may be more modest, involving competitive avionics equipment or minor airframe modifications.

4. When the alternatives are defined, their specifications are routed to technical offices that specialize in operational characteristics of the aircraft or equipment under consideration. Within these offices, *evaluation of factors and variables* pertaining to each of the alternatives is performed, assuming that each of the designs will be used for the operational scenarios defined earlier. Depending on the nature of the scenarios, evaluations include flight characteristics,

weapons effectiveness, inter-operability, survivability, stealth characteristics, range, takeoff and landing constraints, payload, ground handling constraints, loading and unloading characteristics, reliability, maintainability, operating costs, expected sales price, and any number of other factors.

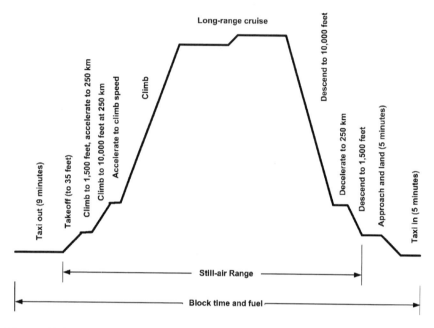

Figure 10.4 Mission profile factors
Note: Data elements relating to operating scenarios are ascent profiles, required fuel reserves, cruise altitude, distance, and taxi time.
Source: Boeing.

5. Upon completion of their analysis, the technical specialists forward their evaluation to the operational analysts, who perform *effectiveness analysis*. This analysis is generally based upon a computer model that calculates final scores for each of the alternatives by ascribing weighted coefficients to each of the operational variables. Obviously, the validity of the overall outcome is entirely dependent upon the formulas used to calculate the scores.
6. As effectiveness analysis is being performed, financial analysts are calculating projected *profitability* of each of the alternative configurations. Profitability assessments consider factors such as projections of development costs, sales price, manufacturing cost, risk, sales quantities, and investment required.

   During the overall operations analysis process, there typically exists an inherent conflict between objectives involving effectiveness and profitability. Effectiveness generally entails higher levels of investment, technological risk, customized engineering, and various expensive improvements. Maximum profitability, on the other hand, infers minimum investment and low levels of technological risk.

The process of evaluation and analysis recognizes these inherent conflicts and includes an iterative mechanism for resolution. As the physical design alternatives of new aircraft emerge, *trade studies* are conducted by engineers, financial managers, marketers, ops analysts, and maintenance specialists. Because aircraft design always involves compromise among conflicting priorities, the trade studies are intended to evaluate the overall effect if marginal capability of one type is sacrificed in order to boost capability of another type. The entire design concept is based on resolution and optimization of these trade-offs, such as size versus cost, speed versus efficiency, big wing (more lift, more internal fuel) versus small wing (less drag, less weight), and so on. Many aspects of the trade studies are performed by the ops analysts.

Because changes of this sort will affect customer acceptance of the product, marketers are involved to provide their judgment as part of *market acceptance assessments*. At the culmination of the trade studies, the result is the selection of an aircraft configuration that theoretically is the best combination of effectiveness and projected profitability.

7. After the thorough iterative process of optimizing performance, cost, and anticipated customer acceptance, the recommended configuration is formally defined, and is submitted for *management review*.

8. Following acceptance by management, the configuration is formally presented for *customer review* and further discussion. If the customer has an active requirement to acquire aircraft, the marketer's objective is to elicit a request for further information, eventually leading to contracting activity.

Operations analysis is commonly used in the marketing battleground between competitors. Analysis is an effective tool for marketers to demonstrate the superiority of their products to customers. The analysis is tailored to fit the circumstances, but certain types of comparisons have become industry standards.

Cost per passenger mile is a relatively simple metric of primary interest to passenger lines. For cargo airlines, the equivalent metric is cost per revenue ton. The math is more complex than it appears at first glance, because the calculations consider factors such as flight profiles, distances, load factors, and other variables. Sometimes the calculations are based on only direct operating costs, which include primarily fuel and maintenance costs. For other purposes, total operating costs, which include additional factors such as cost of ownership, crew salaries, insurance, overheads,and so on, are included.

A commercial airline's calculation of the value of an aircraft is straightforward. Financial analysts calculate the cost per flight hour of aircraft utilization, based upon the airline's internal costs and aircraft operating costs specified by the manufacturer. These cost calculations include cost of ownership of the aircraft, which relates directly to the purchase price. The analysts then calculate the revenue the aircraft will generate, based on projections of quantities of passengers flown, multiplied by ticket prices, multiplied by the number of times the aircraft will provide service over the route. If the difference between revenues and costs is sufficient to meet the airline's standards for profitability and return on investment, the aircraft is theoretically a good investment. However, the airline financial analysts can be expected to perform the same financial analysis of all competing aircraft. When the analysis is complete, the aircraft that theoretically will generate the highest profit has a competitive advantage.

Table 10.1 Estimated operating costs worksheet

A. Investment Cost
- Basic Aircraft $_____
- Options $_____
- Initial Spares $_____

Total Investment Cost $_____

B. Direct Operating Costs
1. Fuel at $_____per gallon times ____G/FH $_____

Oil at 1.5% of fuel cost $_____

2. Aircraft maintenance at $____per manhour $_____
   times ____MMH/FH
3. Reserve for major dynamics overhaul and repair $_____
4. Reserve for engine and APU overhaul and repair $_____
5. Reserve for airframe consumable spares $_____
6. Reserve for airframe reparable spares $_____
7. Reserve for rotor blades $_____

Total Direct Hourly Costs $ per flight hour

C. Fixed Annual Operating Costs
1. Depreciation: total investment cost minus $_____
   residual value divided by years of service
2. Interest on investment $_____
3. Hull insurance $_____
4. Liability insurance $_____
5. Flight crews salaries and costs $_____
6. Maintenance overhead $_____
7. General and administrative overhead $_____
8. Non-revenue flights $_____

Total Fixed Annual Costs $ per year

Total Hourly Operating Costs
- Total Direct Cost per Hour $ per flight hour
- Total Fixed Cost per Hour (total annual fixed $ per flight hour
  costs divided by flight hours per year)

Total Cost per Flight Hour $ per flight hour

Note: This worksheet depicts the relationships between investment costs, direct operating costs, and fixed operating costs.

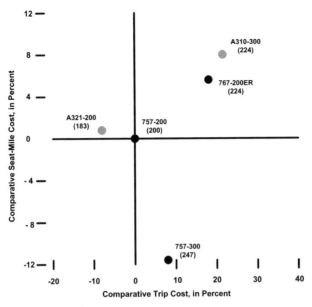

Figure 10.5 Comparative cost data for larger airliners
Source: Boeing.

Because time has a dramatic impact on airline economics, *route block times* are routinely used as a basis for estimating aircraft schedules and revenues to be earned. The block times are developed by applying aircraft flight capabilities to the specific routes to be flown. The final results depend upon factors such as rates of climb, cruise speed, takeoff and landing distances, noise footprint, avionics equipment, and ground-handling characteristics.

For transport aircraft, perhaps the most basic of all analysis is the *payload and range graph*. For fixed atmospheric conditions, it depicts the relationship between payload that the aircraft can carry and the distance that it can be carried. Greater payload entails shorter range. These graphs are often used for comparisons between competitive aircraft.

Maintenance costs are generally considered to be an element of direct operating costs. For civil operators, they have a significant impact upon profitability. For military users, they represent a major component of operating costs over the lifetime of any aircraft. To some extent, maintenance costs can be extrapolated from accumulated data from aircraft in service. However, these costs vary significantly depending upon the age of the aircraft, the quality of the maintenance it receives, and the conditions under which it operates. Aircraft operated in the salt air of coastal environments, or in desert areas where sand infiltration is a problem, tend to experience much higher maintenance costs than aircraft operating in benign environments such as inland areas of Western Europe.

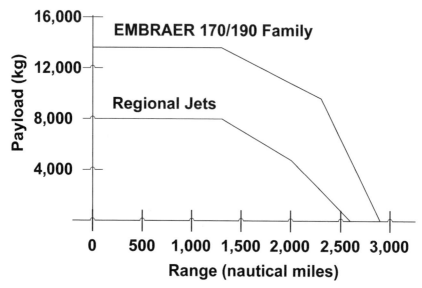

Figure 10.6 Payload-range analysis
Note: Payload-range analysis is a staple of transport aircraft analysis.
Source: Embraer.

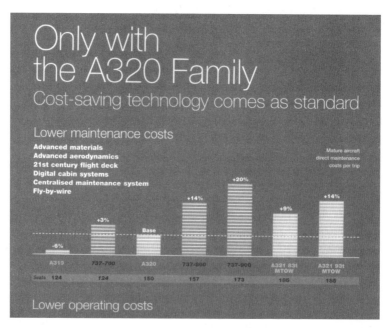

Figure 10.7 Maintenance cost comparison
Note: Analysis provided by Airbus projects lower maintenance costs than for competing aircraft. Perhaps Boeing analysis would yield conflicting conclusions.
Source: Airbus.

Cargo capacity is a primary consideration for freighter aircraft and military transports, but is also important for passenger airlines, which earn important revenue from freight carried in the lower cargo hold. Air freight is transported in a vast variety of physical shapes and sizes, including many standard and non-standard container types, open pallets of various shapes, unpalletized crates, and roll-on-roll-off vehicles. Cargo analysis attempts to show how the dimensions and weight limits of the cargo bay can best accommodate the variety of expected freight.

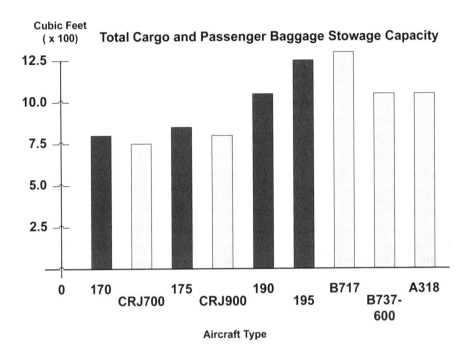

Figure 10.8 Cargo capacity representation
Note: For passenger transports, capability to carry cargo and baggage is also important.
Source: Embraer.

Passenger cabin dimensions, directly related to passenger comfort, are of fundamental interest to airlines. Historically, airlines have considered dual-aisle wide-bodied aircraft to be more appealing to passengers than narrower single-aisle layouts. Internal space is appealing because it permits greater headroom, accommodates greater storage area, and conveys an overall impression of spaciousness. However, as wide-bodied aircraft have become commonplace, analysts have concluded that larger fuselage cross section does not always infer greater passenger comfort. Marketers of smaller aircraft have sometimes produced analysis supporting the view that big aircraft have problematic features such as difficult access to aisles or delayed loading and unloading.

The 777 Offers Superior Comfort and Spaciousness
Cross-Section Comparison

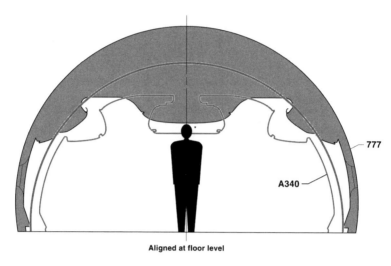

Aligned at floor level

* 97.5-percentile man: 6 ft 2 in (188 cm) tall

Figure 10.9 Depiction of interior dimensions
Note: Interior space is generally considered to be desirable for passenger aircraft.
Source: Boeing.

Crew training and cross-training are important to airlines that operate mixed fleets of aircraft that require air crews to be transferred from one type to another. Because flight training is expensive, and because crews occupied in training are unavailable to generate revenue, airlines prefer to minimize training time. The major civil aircraft manufacturers commonly promote their 'families of aircraft' with common cockpit designs that facilitate cross-training of crews between types.

Mission radius is a standard basis of analysis for military aircraft. The aircraft is given a specific configuration of weapons load or cargo, and is assumed to fly a combat mission of a specific profile in terms of speed, altitude, loiter times, and so on. Based on these parameters, maximum mission radius can be defined and used for comparison with competitors.

Maneuvering capability and general flight performance are of particular interest to military operators, for whom speed and agility are often associated with lethality or survivability. Analysts and engineers apply aircraft characteristics to fixed scenarios to calculate maximum speeds, turn rates, rates of climb, g-forces, and so on. The results of the calculations can be used to predict survivability or capability to perform specific missions.

Table 10.2 Comparative pilot transition times

Boeing Comparative Analysis of Pilot Transition Time Boeing 757 versus Airbus A321 (number of days required for transition between other airplanes and the 757 and the A321-200)		
Existing Aircraft Fleet	Transition Time to 757	Transition Time to A321
L-1011	21 days typical	25 days typical
DC-10	21 days typical	25 days typical
A300	21 days typical	25 days typical
A310	21 days typical	25 days typical
747-100/-200/-300	21 days typical	25 days typical
767-200ER/-300ER	4 hours	25 days typical
767-400ER	2-4 days	25 days typical
777	14 days typical	25 days typical
747-400	14 days typical	25 days typical
737-300 through -900	14 days typical	25 days typical
A330	21 days typical	8 days
A340	21 days typical	9 days

Note: Analysis of training time for pilot transition between aircraft types can build an economic argument in support of aircraft that require shortest transition periods.
Source: Boeing.

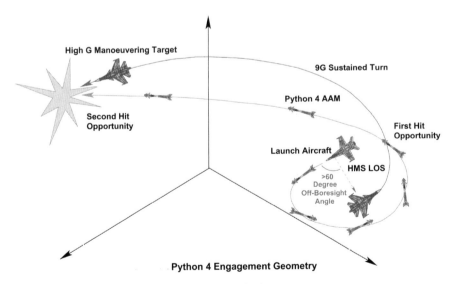

Figure 10.10 Missile maneuverability analysis
Note: Analysis of comparative maneuverability can demonstrate outcomes of hypothetical military engagements.
Source: Carlo Kopp (1997), 'Fourth Generation AAMs – The Rafael Python 4', *Australian Aviation*, April.

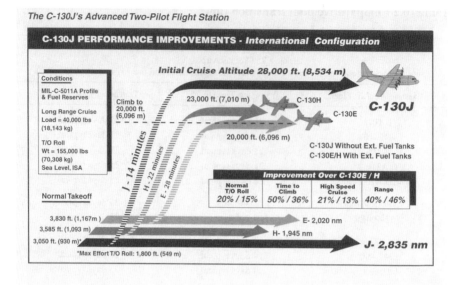

The C-130J's Advanced Two-Pilot Flight Station

Figure 10.11 Takeoff and rate of climb analysis
Note: Basic analysis of flight performance depicts takeoff distances, time-to-climb, and cruising altitude.
Source: Lockheed Martin.

Operations analysis is an indispensable part of the aerospace marketing process. It provides operators, manufacturers, and designers with a common vernacular to discuss requirements, capabilities, efficiencies, and costs. For the marketer, it offers a means of understanding the customer's needs, and furnishes a way of communicating how those needs can be met by the product being offered. It is the common international language of the aerospace marketplace.

Chapter 11

International Cooperation, Joint Ventures, and Teaming

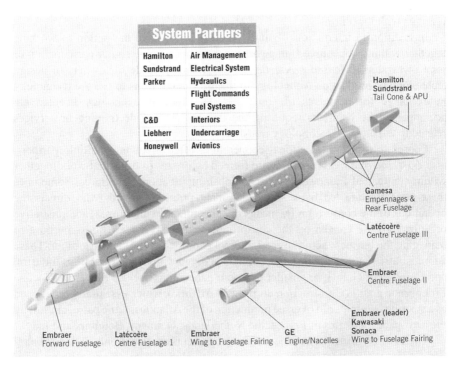

Figure 11.1 Risk-sharing partners in an international program
Note: The Embraer ERJ-170 is in many ways a typical contemporary joint international program, involving a pooling of resources of many risk-sharing partners.
Source: Embraer.

In the age of antiquity of the aerospace industry (that is, prior to the 1950s), programs involving cooperation among several companies or governments were unusual. Joint programs were not often necessary. Aerospace technology was accessible to large numbers of medium-sized companies. Development costs of new aircraft and equipment were low enough to be affordable by independent business entities. The pan-nationalism trend of the late twentieth century had not yet taken hold, and cooperative international industrial programs had not yet become a normal way of doing business.

By the end of the century, developmental costs for new aircraft had risen to staggering levels as technological content had increased geometrically. Only a comparatively small number of major aerospace firms were still in business, and governments actively promoted joint programs involving multiple firms, often of multiple nationalities. Economic and political factors had evolved in directions that created circumstances favorable for the emergence of the joint program as a dominant life form.

International cooperative programs take many forms. The strongest form of international commitment is the acquisition or creation of a *wholly-owned subsidiary* overseas. Partially owned subsidiaries are another alternative, including *joint ventures* with local firms.

In addition to international equity ventures, firms have the option of working together within cooperative frameworks that do not involve equity participation or joint ownership. *Licensed production* arrangements provide for owners of design technology or production technology to license foreign firms to use the technology in exchange for payments of some sort. Often these technology licenses are accompanied by contracts requiring the licensor to provide training or services related to the physical technology transfer.

Looser forms of international cooperation, often involving multiple partners, also exist. *International consortia* are formed by groups of firms that work together within contractual frameworks to accomplish multinational programs. Sometimes these consortia are led by a single dominant prime contractor who directs the operations of the consortium by means of subcontracts. Other times, administrative organizations are created by the consortium members for the express purpose of managing the business activities and internal coordination of the consortium. These administrative entities can be large, permanent organizations such as Airbus Industrie and Eurofighter GmbH, or smaller ad hoc organizations such as SECBAT (Société Européenne pour la Construction du Breguet Atlantic), which essentially functioned as a steering committee to oversee production of the Atlantic marine patrol aircraft by the aerospace industries of France, the Netherlands, Germany, Belgium, and Italy.

The least permanent of cooperative arrangements are commonly called *teaming agreements*, an imprecise categorization that includes joint efforts ranging from cooperative marketing teams to international manufacturing networks.

A comprehensive 1986 study by the author of a broad sample of major international cooperative aerospace programs found that virtually all of the programs were initiated because their participants believed that international cooperation would enable them to accomplish specific objectives. These objectives, which were not mutually exclusive, fit into eleven discrete categories.

The eleven identified objectives were diverse. Market factors were a prominent consideration, but other factors related to economics, technology, and military issues:

1. *International diplomatic factors.* Governments have repeatedly attempted to use cooperative aerospace projects as symbols of friendship and common economic interests. In many respects aerospace projects are suitable for this symbolic role, due to their monumental nature in terms of size, visibility, and

cost. Joint projects entail close, long-term relationships among industries of the participating countries. Concorde, as an example, is generally viewed as the consequence of a desire by the French and British governments of the 1960s to demonstrate Franco-British unity in the early days of the European Community.

2. *Regional or national pride.* Because the aerospace industry is generally associated with advanced economic development and sophistication, national governments sometimes promote the creation of international programs that they believe will provide prestige. Of course, this motive is also a factor in national programs. In the view of many, the development of space industry sectors in the USSR and the United States was largely attributable to the 'space race', financed by the two governments for reasons of national pride. On an international scale, the European Space Agency and the Ariane rocket were created by the European governments as a means of demonstrating an active European participation in space technology.

3. *Military standardization.* In an age of international military alliances that involve joint operations by armed forces of different nationalities, standardization of equipment has become a necessity. A major motive behind NATO government efforts to establish cooperative production of military aircraft is to increase joint effectiveness by standardizing warplanes, thus theoretically lowering unit production costs and rationalizing logistical arrangements necessary to support the aircraft. Standardization was widely cited as a driving force in the creation of the Atlantic marine patrol aircraft of the late 1950s, a joint production of France, Germany, Italy, the Netherlands, and Belgium.

4. *Balance of payments considerations.* In virtually every international cooperative aircraft program in which governments participate, balance of payments considerations are cited by governments as a significant positive factor in support of the program. Particularly in the case of the European economies in the period following World War II, governments insisted on coproduction of military aircraft as part of broader strategies to minimize trade deficits with the United States. European licensed production of the Lockheed F-104G Starfighter by Germany, Italy, the Netherlands, and Belgium was established in the context of these balance of payment strategies.

5. *Job creation.* Governments often utilize cooperative programs as a vehicle to create jobs. Considerations of employment in the German aerospace industry were a major political factor at the time of the governmental discussions that led to the creation of the French-German Transall program in the early 1960s. At the time, German aerospace factories were principally engaged in licensed production of the F-104G and the Noratlas transport. Production workload associated with both of these programs was scheduled to drop abruptly in the mid-1960s, and the German Government actively began to consider alternative aircraft coproduction projects that would ensure continuity of production and employment in the industry. The Transall was selected in large part because it was the best available alternative for maintaining continuity in German factories, although the Transall design in many ways did not correspond to

the transport requirements specified by the German military, and was not necessarily the least expensive technical solution.

6. *Suppression of competition.* Prior to the advent of Airbus Industrie, a major barrier to success of the European civil aircraft industry was that many small firms chronically introduced multiple similar aircraft that competed with each other for a limited market. One of the reasons for the success of Airbus was that it provided a means for European manufacturers to work together rather than complete against themselves. Likewise, international military programs are often viewed as a means of avoiding harmful internecine competition.

7. *Pooling of resources.* In some cases cooperative aerospace projects are formed because the individual participating firms do not independently have the necessary capital, engineering resources, or manufacturing capacity to design and manufacture complex aircraft. As the cost and complexity of modern aircraft have spiraled to extraordinary levels, even the giant firms of the industry have found the need to seek domestic and international partners. The manufacturing program for Boeing's 777 airliner, for example, comprises major participation by Japanese risk-sharing industrial partners, who produce approximately 25 per cent of the aircraft.

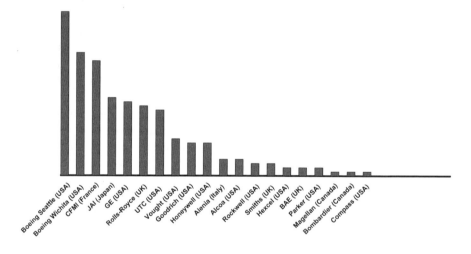

Figure 11.2 International aerospace subcontractors
Note: Major prime contractors such as Boeing typically work closely with multiple teammates, national and international.
Source: Boeing international subcontractors in 2001.

8. *Enlargement of prospective sales markets.* Marketing prospects for aircraft are improved if they are manufactured within the national boundaries of the target market. A preference to purchase locally manufactured aircraft is especially strong in the case of military aircraft. Competitive advantage for domestic firms is often institutionalized by law or government regulations such as

the Buy American Act in the United States. Consequently, manufacturers of military aircraft recognize that their prospects of selling to foreign customers will be enhanced if they have a local industrial partner.

9. *Profits.* Sometimes international cooperation makes sense strictly for conventional business reasons, as company managers put together business plans that involve participation of international partners. The Saab-Fairchild SF-340 commuter turboprop launched in the 1970s was a representative example. Both Saab, of Sweden, and Fairchild, of the United States, were privately owned companies that initiated the program without significant government intervention or support. Program launch was preceded by rigorous market surveys and break-even projections, and the program was approved by stockholders on the basis of its expected future earnings. Throughout the SF-340 development program the companies maintained severe financial controls, and business decisions affecting the program were made in the context of their impact on stockholder value.

10. *Technology transfer.* Customers who seek to gain access to technology often engage in coproduction as a means of attaining the technology. Technology transfer associated with cooperative aircraft programs can usually be categorized as either production technology or aerospace design technology. Sharing of design technology tends to be limited unless the partnership is initiated during the initial design phase of the aircraft's life cycle. Production technology, on the other hand, is shared whenever joint manufacturing is undertaken. European coproduction of the F-16 fighter, for example, was initiated after design had been mostly completed by General Dynamics in the United States. European firms were generally satisfied with production technology the F-16 program gave them in fields such as electronics fabrication, miniaturization, gas turbines, gyroscopes, automatic test equipment, forging of high strength aluminum, 5-axis numerically controlled milling, and so on. However, some participating firms were dissatisfied with their lack of access to F-16 design technology. Later, when European governments considered the Joint Strike Fighter as a replacement for the F-16, they successfully insisted on meaningful participation by their national aerospace industries in the JSF design process.

11. *Government emphasis of aerospace as a leading technology sector.* An article of faith among government economic planners is that high-technology industrial activities should be encouraged for economic reasons. The landmark Plowden Report issued by the British Ministry of Aviation in 1965 cited numerous examples of technologies that had been developed by the aerospace industry, but which had found important applications in other industries. The conclusion was that the national economy as a whole benefited from technological leadership of sectors such as aerospace. This credo has been widely accepted, for better or worse, by government leaders internationally. The Suharto government of Indonesia in the 1980s and 1990s attempted a particularly aggressive national experiment in technology leadership by the aerospace sector. Indonesia engaged in numerous international coproduction programs to develop a significant aerospace industry intended to promote

technology development for the rest of the country. Unfortunately, the effort ultimately proved unsuccessful as the industry collapsed following widespread political and economic turmoil in the late 1990s.

Table 11.1 Joint Strike Fighter partners

Partner Country	Partner Level	System Development and Demonstration		Production	
		Financial Contributions (in $ millions)	Percentage of Total Costs	Projected Quantities	Percentage of Total Quantities
United Kingdom	Level I	$2,056	6.2	150	4.7
Italy	Level II	$1.028	3.1	131	4.1
Netherlands	Level II	$800	2.4	85	2.7
Turkey	Level III	$175	0.5	100	3.2
Australia	Level III	$144	0.4	100	3.2
Norway	Level III	$122	0.4	48	1.5
Denmark	Level III	$110	0.3	48	1.5
Canada	Level III	$100	0.3	60	1.9
Total Partner		$4,535	13.7	722	22.8
United States		$28,565	86.3	2,443	77.2

Percentages do not add due to rounding.
Chart values do not reflect non-financial contributions from partners.
Note: The US-led Joint Strike Fighter program offered international partners access to technology in direct proportion to their financial contributions to the program.
Source: US Government Accountability Office, 'Joint Strike Fighter Acquisition', 21 July 2003.

The objectives and motivations on the foregoing list are by no means mutually exclusive, and often customers or firms are influenced by multiple factors. A firm that aspires to penetrate a new foreign market may seek a local partner who can provide an insider's access to the market, but who can also contribute financial resources and specialized technology. A government customer is likely to insist upon international collaboration involving local industry in order to secure jobs, technology, and prestige for his national aerospace sector.

The essential message for marketers is that their companies must be receptive to participation in cooperative international programs as a means to effectively market and sell their products. If the customer insists upon international industrial cooperation, or if access to the market is possible only through cooperative strategies with other partners, the marketer should move aggressively to develop cooperative concepts to respond to market requirements.

Whenever information is shared with international interlocutors, it is always important to take care that applicable government controls governing restrictions on export of technical data and hardware are observed. No restricted data can legally be shared unless export licenses are obtained. Licensing requirements and processes are discussed in more detail in Chapter 16 of this book.

Cooperative international agreements between companies are serious commitments, often with major financial and strategic implications for the companies involved. Consequently, companies generally impose rigorous controls over the process of establishing joint programs and cooperative arrangements.

Marketing considerations are often the driving force behind the creation of cooperative undertakings, but because commitments between firms have implications that extend beyond marketing, review and approval of joint agreements takes place at the senior management level. If the hypothetical joint agreement involves several firms, all the firms involved should simultaneously but separately work towards obtaining management approval.

Prior to any substantive discussions between companies, it is customary for both parties to sign a *non-disclosure agreement* that protects sensitive data shared by the companies. Non-disclosure agreements are explored in more detail in Chapter 15, dealing with contractual matters.

Normally the approval process begins as marketers identify a need for a joint undertaking, and prepare an internal recommendation that company management consider an agreement of a certain structure. This preliminary recommendation contains a statement of objectives of the joint undertaking, the business strategy, an assessment of the strengths and weaknesses of the prospective partners, financial requirements, distribution of profits, and an outline of responsibilities of both parties. The document is circulated for review among senior management, strategic planners, and among managers in other operating units that may have business interests involving the foreign firm that is a candidate for the joint undertaking.

If necessary approvals are obtained when the preliminary recommendation is circulated, the document is forwarded to the contracts department, where a draft formal agreement between parties is prepared and edited by the Legal department. The document should be as specific as possible, without being so rigid as to immobilize the decision-making process. Included in the terms specified by the document should be decision-making authority, procedures for modifying the agreement, and conditions for eventually dissolving the joint agreement. The completed legal document is routed once again for management review and approval, and is thereafter presented to the prospective partner for discussion and negotiation.

Once cooperative business relationships are established, they require careful maintenance, as is the case with any long-term relationships. A single point-of-contact should be identified within each company, and should be given primary responsibility for facilitating communications and business relationships with the partner. On a regular basis, several times per year, senior management of the companies should meet to discuss progress of the joint undertaking and to agree on future directions.

In addition to collaboration among companies that takes place in the framework of major international cooperative programs, firms often work together in less formal alliances known as *teaming agreements*. These agreements formalize intentions of the parties to work together towards a common objective of some kind. Teaming agreements may be framed in any of a wide spectrum of cooperative understandings among the parties, including MOUs, MOAs, Letters of Intent, Cooperation or Project Agreements, general declarations of strategic alliance or documents of some other title.

Cooperative agreements with other firms almost always entail complications that can be counterproductive. Examples of these undesirable complications are disputes over workshares; diminished speed and flexibility in program management decisions; entangling commitments to a teammate who may turn out to be less useful than originally thought; and limited flexibility to adapt to unforeseen changes in customer requirements. Recognizing these potential downsides, it is good business practice to avoid teaming agreements unless they offer clear business benefits. Examples of such potential benefits are:

- Although neither of the parties has sufficient internal resources to independently meet all program requirements, the team's resources are sufficient.
- In the eyes of the customer, a team would enhance credibility.
- Valuable alliances can be formed with partners that might be unwilling to accept clearly subordinate standard subcontracting relationships.

Likewise, the subordinate teammates can potentially benefit from the agreement in several ways:

- They are able to participate in a program that is beyond their reach as an independent competitor.
- They may be able to obtain commitments of guaranteed workshare if the competition is successful.
- They may be able to establish an exclusive relationship with a competitor more powerful than themselves.

From the vantage point of the dominant partner, who would prefer to avoid obligations such as exclusive relationships and guaranteed workshares for teammates, it is often preferable to obtain the resources of subcontractors through conventional contractual arrangements rather than through teaming agreements. However, if the potential teammate is considered to add critical value, and if he will not agree to lend support outside of a teaming agreement, the agreement may be a necessary means for proceeding.

By no means should a teaming agreement be established if the primary benefit is to avoid competition between the two team members. Agreements under such conditions are illegal in the United States and many other countries under antitrust laws and other regulations prohibiting restraints of trade. If an objective outside observer could conclude that the teaming agreement would dampen competition, the teaming agreement should be avoided. In fact, teaming agreements often enhance competition by creating joint entities that are able to offer credible proposals, even though none of the members acting alone would have sufficient resources to enter the competition.

Before entering into contractual teaming agreements with another company, rigorous due diligence should be performed to objectively assess the company's strengths, weaknesses, and general compatibility. The due diligence should attempt to evaluate:

- The prospective teammate's value in terms of access to technology, financial resources, management capability, prior experience in the market, and so on
- The teammate's current relationships and history with the customer
- Compatibility of the teammates in terms of company strategies, objectives, product lines, geographical focus, potential conflicts of interest, and general business practices and standards.

When teaming agreements involve international partners, special attention should be given to potential complications involving export licenses, international shipments, tariff duties, and legal jurisdiction for resolution of disputes.

In any cooperative agreement, it is often good policy to avoid overly-restrictive language concerning exclusivity, percentages of workshares, technological content of workshares, and other aspects that may require adaptability as time passes. Although all parties will want language sufficiently specific to protect their rights, the document must be sufficiently flexible to enable the teammates to respond quickly and easily to circumstances that are subject to change as time passes. However, the agreement must clearly assign responsibilities and roles of the teammates for the program and the competition that was the justification for creation of the team.

Any good agreement should also define the term of the agreement and conditions for termination or dissolution. Common reasons for termination involve circumstances such as cancellation of the competition, customer selection of a competitor's offer, disqualification of one of the team members, or major changes to the customer requirement. Team members who commit to work together on a program can expect to risk significant investments and professional credibility, and they will normally expect some protection against arbitrary withdrawal by other team members for capricious reasons.

As is the case with many legal commitments, circumstances may cause teaming agreements to become legally binding even though no formal document is signed by the parties. If the parties hold substantive discussions about teaming together, and if they inform external parties such as customers that they are teammates, then either of the parties probably has legal grounds to seek damages from the other if one party unilaterally repudiates the team concept. Prospective parties to teaming agreements should avoid announcements, formal or informal, of their intentions until the conditions of the agreement have been thoroughly defined, studied, approved, and signed.

Chapter 12

Working with the Customer

Ultimately, the crux of the marketing process becomes the challenge of convincing the customer to buy one's product. This chapter provides guidance on how to assess and respond to the peculiar requirements of aerospace customers. We will explore the progressive development of customer relationships, beginning with information gathering, progressing through the collaborative definition of technical requirements, continuing through the sales process, and culminating with protection of relationships after the sale.

In a conventional marketing environment, academic studies have identified eight more-or-less distinct steps in the selling process. These steps are 1) *prospecting*, 2) *qualifying the customer*, 3) *approach*, 4) *presentation*, 5) *demonstration*, 6) *overcoming obstacles*, 7) *closing*, and 8) *follow-up*. This model remains generally applicable to the special circumstances of the aerospace industry.

All customers are different, and the process of selling needs to reflect these differences. The fundamental concept of effective selling is that the salesperson should understand the needs and the psyche of the customer and, in response, should strive to convince the customer that the product offered responds to those needs and desires. No rigid formulaic approach to selling can take into account the infinite variations of customers. The artistry in the sales process comes into play when a technically proficient salesperson applies his personal knowledge, judgment, instinct, and creativity to tailor a sales strategy that corresponds to the peculiar circumstances of the opportunity at hand.

In the aerospace marketplace, military and civil customers are approached differently. Nevertheless, even considering these differences, sales campaigns generally pass through very similar generic stages. Bearing in mind that specific circumstances can cause one sales experience to be radically different from the next, we will identify these generic stages and will discuss effective ways to work towards sales goals in each stage. A successful marketing and sales campaign consists of attainment of the many intermediate goals and objectives associated with each of the stages.

Gathering Preliminary Market Intelligence

The first step in launching a marketing and sales effort is to identify prospective customers and opportunities. Preliminary information about customers comes from diverse sources. In the case of large aerospace corporations with widespread ongoing operations and broad contacts, the information most often surfaces during the course of current business contacts. Company representatives working with current or potential customers learn about future requirements, and forward reports of sales opportunities to the marketing department. Often salespersons working with current customers learn of future requirements as part of their routine contact.

Companies not broadly established in potential markets have a more difficult task, but abundant information is available through many sources:

- *Consultants and sales agents.* Dealing with local sales representatives is a complex subject studied in Chapter 4. A major attribute of agents is that they are well informed about the local market and can provide good information about opportunities. On the other hand, they sometimes exaggerate opportunities in order to induce sellers to commit to agency contracts or to pay retainers. In the absence of an agent located in a potential market, a marketer can often gain insight into the market simply by interviewing agent candidates, although it is considered unethical to interview candidates if no serious intent to eventually engage one exists.

- *Embassies.* Companies based within one of the major aerospace nations will normally be able to get some level of useful support from their national embassies in the capital cities of the customer countries. This support principally comes in the form of market intelligence and local advice from the military attaché or economic attaché at the consular section. The quality of this support varies greatly, depending upon the capabilities and motivation of the local embassy staff. For military sales in particular, the level of embassy support can change dramatically as national political policies of the selling country evolve. Under the administration of Jimmy Carter in the late 1970s, for example, American ambassadors were directed to eliminate marketing assistance to American firms selling military aircraft abroad. Later, under the Reagan administration, this hands-off policy was reversed, and ambassadors and US embassy staff were directed to support aggressively American exports of military equipment.

- *Official government gazettes.* Governments in most developed economies are required to formally publish announcements of intent to purchase large items of capital equipment, including aircraft. In the United States, for example, these announcements were formerly published daily by the US Government Printing Office in the *Commerce Business Daily*. The *Commerce Business Daily* was replaced in 2002 by FedBizOpps, an online service that provides the same information. In Belgium, planned purchases are announced in the *Moniteur Belge*. Other countries have similar official gazettes.

- *The media.* An enormous volume of aerospace-related data is available through the popular press, specialized aerospace and aviation publications, and through online information services. English-speaking aerospace professionals should routinely read *Aviation Week & Space Technology* (published in the United States), *Flight International* (published in the UK), and national aerospace publications of their specific customer markets.

- Conventions and trade shows. Air shows and smaller aerospace industry conventions serve as vast clearing houses of formal and informal information about markets and products. Flows of information are enhanced by professional and personal relationships among the exhibitors, many of whom cross paths regularly at similar industry events in different regions.

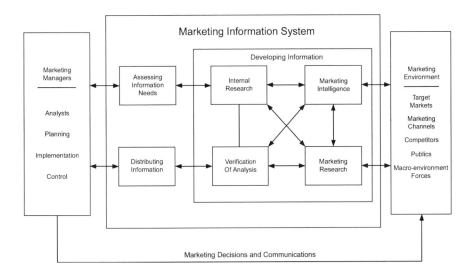

Figure 12.1 Marketing information system

Note: The marketing information system involves acquisition of information from many sources, processing the data, and acting upon it.

Source: Adapted from Philip Kotler (1984), *Marketing Management: Analysis, Planning and Control,* 5th ed., Prentice-Hall, Inc.,Englewood Cliffs, NJ.

Validating the Requirement

Following the identification of a potential opportunity, the next step is to determine if the requirement is genuine and realistic. An obvious way to begin verification of a requirement is to meet with the potential customer and ask him directly to provide information. In some cases, however, this direct approach is problematic. If military requirements are involved, government officials may be reluctant to have meaningful discussions about equipment needs unless formal requirements documents have been published. Sometimes, however, members of the military may be willing to have off-the-record exploratory talks with contractors about perceived national needs and requirements studies. When the potential opportunity involves a civil customer, it is generally easier to arrange face-to-face talks about future needs, although commercial operators are understandably reluctant to divulge information that has competitive sensitivity.

Defense & Aerospace Report
Annual Review 2002

Table of Contents

Figure 12.2 US-Taiwan Business Council report
Note: Published reports from government agencies or overseas business institutions, such as this report from the US-Taiwan Business Council, are often useful sources of information about aerospace sales opportunities.
Source: US-Taiwan Business Council.

Sometimes the marketer has to deal with a situation in which he is marketing a product or service that potentially could be very useful to a customer, but the customer is not aware that he needs it. This classical situation of *unarticulated demand* presents more of a marketing challenge than simply responding to published customer requirements. Unarticulated demand is common in the aerospace industry because the rapid advance of technology perpetually creates new products that are not part of existing business models. Airlines, for example, did not know that they had a requirement for broadband Internet access aboard passenger aircraft until the industry identified a technology and developed a product. Likewise, most worldwide military commanders did not realize that they had a requirement for unmanned aircraft until the aerospace industry demonstrated their capability.

When customer demand is unarticulated, the process of validating a requirement is less straightforward and more risky. Because the customer cannot express his need, the seller has to use his own judgment to assess the likelihood of an eventual purchase. Sometimes misguided anticipation of unarticulated demand can have catastrophic results. A legendary example was Motorola's Iridium program, a technological undertaking of monumental proportions that entailed a constellation of low-earth-orbiting satellites that provided capability for hand-phone communication from any spot on earth with a clear line-of-sight to a satellite. For various reasons, the product did not sell. The business failure was as monumental as the technological accomplishment.

Qualifying the Customer

As soon as an apparent sales opportunity is identified, the essential next step is verification of the credibility of the customer. The purpose of verification is to avoid wasting marketing resources on unrealistic sales prospects. Qualification of the customer entails determining that he is an established legal entity who is not proscribed by export restrictions, that he has a reputable business history, that he has sufficient financial resources to buy, and that he has authority to make valid purchase commitments.

In some cases, particularly when the customer is a sovereign government or an established airline, the qualification process is only a formality. But even sovereign governments can be ineligible customers because of export restrictions. Some, such as Nigeria, are highly risky because of historical patterns of corruption or failure to honor commitments incurred by authorized government officials. Others governments have prohibitive credit ratings, or might lack necessary technical sophistication to maintain and operate advanced equipment.

Qualifying a potential commercial customer in some ways is more complex. In the modern age of low-cost start-up airlines, entrepreneurs with very little experience in aviation might be credible customers for aircraft. On the other hand, the marketplace is rife with aspiring entrepreneurs who are captivated by the idea of aircraft ownership, but are clueless about the intricacies of the aviation industry. For commercial buyers, of course, credit worthiness and legality are the two factors of primary concern to the seller during the qualification process. However, at some point the seller has to make a judgment concerning whether the potential buyer is competent to operate aircraft. No one's reputation benefits from association with failed ventures.

Developing Relationships

Person-to-person buying and selling deals are sometimes divided into the two general categories of *transaction marketing* and *relationship marketing*. Some sales are single transactions in which the buyer and seller never expect to deal with each other again. However, many sales occur in the context of longstanding relationships between buyers and sellers. Customers prefer suppliers who are known to them, whom they trust, and who have a proven record of credibility and performance. In the aerospace industry, where both the customer and the supplier are mutually subject to complex circumstances, a knowledgeable, long-term relationship between buyer and seller is especially crucial.

Table 12.1 Time, account behavior, and marketing approach

Long-Time Horizon	*Short-Time Horizon*
Typified by lost-for-good customers	Typified by always-a-share customers
High switching costs	Lower switching costs
Substantial investment actions, especially in procedures and lasting assets	Smaller investment actions
High perceived exposure	Lower perceived exposure
Focus on a technology or on a vendor	Focus on a product or on a person
High importance: strategic, operational, and personal	Lower importance
Relationship Marketing	*Transaction Marketing*

Note: Relationship marketing prevails in the aerospace industry, with profound implications upon behavior of marketing professionals.
Source: Barbara Bund Jackson (1985), *Winning and Keeping Industrial Customers*, Lexington Books, Lexington, MA, p. 168.

According to studies of conventional marketing, personal contact between the seller and the buyer is particularly important if the product is expensive, is technically complex, and if the number of customers is relatively small. Certainly these conditions apply to most segments of the aerospace industry.

The notion that sales result from personal relationships is a timeworn cliché. Like most clichés, it resonates with our daily perceptions. Almost anyone who has been directly involved in face-to-face sales activities believes that relationships are important.

This is not to infer that relationships are necessarily the single most important factor in sales activities. Particularly in sales of high-value technical equipment such as aircraft, the technical characteristics of the product itself are generally the dominant considerations. However, the lack of workable human relationships between the buyer and the seller can be a serious obstacle to communications, with the result that the seller is prevented from effectively presenting critical information that would influence the buyer to purchase his product.

The process of developing relationships begins as soon as the opportunity is identified. Every step in the sales process, from qualifying the customer to eventually engaging in contract negotiations, depends upon human relationships. This is the age-old practice of salesmanship in its most basic form.

Regardless of information available through secondary sources, the marketer should work to develop his own personal contacts throughout the customer's organization. These relationships should not be limited to senior decision-makers. Most aircraft purchase decisions result from a consensus reached among a large number of operators, evaluators, advisors, and senior executives. Even the most junior participants in the consensus building, typically the operators, often have a clear understanding of how the decision will be made and how it can be influenced. It can be invaluable for a salesperson to have the friendship and support of a knowledgeable customer official of any level.

Relationships and trust are developed over time, and are more important in some cultures than in others. But even in the modern American business environment, where reorganizations, management mobility, and changes in ownership are common, and where businesspeople are accustomed to relatively short-term personal relationships, long-term relationships are especially valuable in industries in which trust and credibility are essential. In Europe and Asia, where business often is more personal than in the United States, potential buyers are perhaps less comfortable engaging in serious discussions with strangers.

The process of developing relationships involves more than simply arranging periodic meetings. Effective relationships are based on mutual trust and credibility. However, the relationships have no reason to exist unless they provide the parties with useful information, resources, influence, or advice. In other words, the marketer must contribute something useful if he wants to develop a relationship. Merely showing up is not enough.

From the customer's perspective, a valuable contribution of the marketer is detailed knowledge of his product. He is expected to communicate to the customer all necessary technical information about the product itself, the capabilities of the product, and operational experience with the product. In addition, he is expected to provide useful knowledge about the business operations and program management of his company, including possible delivery schedules, configuration changes, financing arrangements, and so on. He is also expected to serve as a communications conduit between the customer and all parts of the selling company, including senior management.

Well-executed relationship marketing can be extremely effective in the aerospace industry, where customers become committed to expensive, complex systems, and expect first class support and service over the long term. To win and retain customers of this sort, the marketer and his company will have to invest heavily in relationship marketing, but the final results will justify the investment.

In the words of former Boeing vice president of sales Toby Bright, 'Sales is about building relationships. Our organization doesn't just look at selling airplanes. We also provide a conduit for what our customers are saying.'[1]

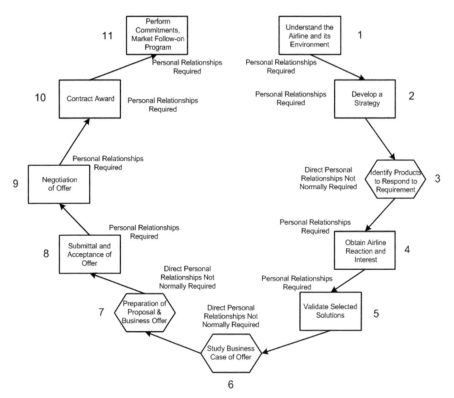

Figure 12.3 Personal relationships and aerospace marketing
Note: Contact and personal relationships with the customer are essential in most steps of the aerospace marketing process.

Assessing Customer Needs

To effectively promote his product as a means of satisfying customer needs, the marketer needs to understand these needs. Sometimes, it quickly becomes obvious that the potential customer has a requirement that cannot reasonably be met by the product line of the marketer's company. If, however, preliminary assessment indicates that the customer's need and the marketer's product may correspond, the effort to better understand the requirement continues.

In many cases, particularly when government procurements are involved, customers prepare and circulate detailed technical statements of the requirements

---

    1   Toby Bright, address to Boeing employees at Long Beach, California, 25 March 2003.

that competitors have to meet. These requirements documents become part of *requests for quotation* or *requests for proposal* furnished to competitors.

Often, however, customers identify a market they want to serve, or a mission they want to perform, but do not have a specific definition of the technical solution to their ambitions. In effect, the customers leave it to their competing suppliers to propose alternative solutions to their operational requirements. Sometimes the customer will be reluctant to publicize his requirement because the requirement itself reflects competitive strategic planning that he considers to be confidential. This might be the case, for example, with an airline that is considering entering a new geographical sector.

If these requirements are not formally defined, it is left to the marketer to attempt to find out what they are. Depending on the market segment involved, the marketer and his technical team attempt to gather information by all appropriate means available to them. Normally, the best sources of information would be direct discussions with strategic planners and operations managers of the customer, who theoretically should welcome the opportunity to open a dialogue with potential suppliers who will provide the customer with additional competitive choices and broader technical alternatives. If, however, formal access to the customer's planners is initially blocked for whatever reason, the marketer is left to obtain his information from secondary sources. These secondary sources might include informal contacts within the customer's organization, such as pilots or mid-level managers. Other sources would include consultants and other external professionals knowledgeable about the customer's operations and plans.

Understanding the Customer's Decision-making Process

The objective of marketing and selling is to influence the customer to buy the product that is being offered. In order to influence the customer, the marketer must have an understanding of how the customer's decision-making process works. As part of this understanding, the seller must identify the key decisions, the key decision-makers, and the advisors and evaluators who provide technical information and recommendations to the decision-makers.

For some customers, the decision-making process is clearly defined and is public information. For example, the processes of the US Department of Defense for selecting and procuring military aircraft are defined in detail by a series of directives and regulations published by the government. The directives stipulate key evaluation and approval events, and designate the individual government officials or military officers who have responsibility for each decision.

At the other extreme, many civil and military customers have organizations in which responsibility is not clearly defined, and operate under murky purchasing procedures that are poorly understood by outsiders. In between the two extremes is a wide range of more-or-less transparent processes that reflect peculiarities of individual customers.

To further complicate the problem for the marketer who is trying to understand it all, the customers who have formal procedures often depart from them. For example, aircraft procurement decisions of Air India and Indian Air Lines, approved by the boards of both companies, were in the process of implementation when they were cancelled in 2004 by the minister of transportation, who had personal views that differed from the senior management of the companies. In a similar example with opposite results, in the 1980s the US Congress appropriated millions of dollars for development of the V-22 tiltrotor transport aircraft, in spite of evaluations and recommendations by the US Navy that the aircraft was unsuitable for US Marine Corps requirements. In the United States, Congress and the Executive Branch can and frequently do override decisions and recommendations that result from the formal DoD selection process.

Often the best way to map the customer's decision-making process is to gather all the marketer's knowledgeable sources of information, such as experienced salespeople, agents, in-country office representatives, and consultants for a day of brainstorming with the specific objective of understanding how the customer can be influenced. The assembled group can share information and insight concerning the customer's process, and can identify by name the specific individuals who own the critical decisions. Such group efforts are useful ways of identifying key advisors to each of the key decision-makers and acquiring understanding of how each of the decision-makers and advisors can be influenced in favor of the marketer's product.

Offering Technical Assistance and Influencing User Requirements

A credo of aerospace marketing is that marketing activity should begin before user requirements are formally defined. One reason for this is that, once the requirements are written, the selection of the winning competitor will be based upon a judgment of which of the competitors best meets the requirements. Obviously, a competitor's chances of success will be enhanced if he can influence the requirements to favor his own product. When the customer is a government agency, evaluation of competitors is usually a highly structured process in which competitors are mathematically scored according to how well their product complies with each section of the requirements document. Civil buyers follow selection processes that are less bureaucratic, but they nonetheless score competitors against defined requirements.

Particularly in the case of relatively unsophisticated customers who are becoming involved in technology or business segments with which they are unfamiliar, outside assistance in writing requirements is often welcomed. The folklore of the industry is rich in stories of marketers who have arranged for their companies' engineers to write complete requirements documents that later became, verbatim, parts of the eventual request for proposal. Not all of these stories are apocryphal.

Small changes to requirements documents can have profound effects upon the outcome of competitions. By specifically defining parameters such as range, speed, payload, and operating efficiency, customers can easily exclude some potential competitors and favor others. Sometimes ostensibly unimportant parameters can eliminate most competitors. If a customer for helicopters requires an internal dimension of two meters height in the cabin, for example, he effectively reduces the field of competitors to a very small number.

The common strategy for influencing the customer's requirements document is to arrange early meetings between the seller's engineers and customer technical specialists and operators. If the competition is intended to be fair and legitimate, the customer specialists will want to take every opportunity to increase their technical knowledge of the equipment available in the marketplace, and to understand the relative advantages and disadvantages of alternative product design concepts and configurations.

This phase of the marketing cycle is an opportunity to gain a competitive edge. A seller whose aircraft has a unique six-wheel landing gear bogie will try to convince the customer's requirement writers that six-wheel bogies are so superior that they should be a mandatory requirement. If the aircraft has a unique emergency fire-suppression system, the marketers will try to get it included as a requirement. And so on.

Effective Marketing Literature

As marketing activities enter the phase conventionally known as *presentation*, the marketing team puts together specialized literature and electronic media that depict the advantages the product offers in the context of the customer's specific needs. All manufacturers have standard product literature describing the important technical considerations of their products. Literature of this type is useful as descriptive reference, but does not perform the essential marketing job of helping the customer visualize how the product can meet his own specific requirements.

In the current age of desktop computer graphics and publishing software, every marketing organization has the wherewithal to prepare easily and economically brochures that target the requirements of specific customers. As marketing campaigns advance, and as marketers gain improved knowledge and understanding of the customer's requirements, this literature should be refined and improved.

Continuous Customer Contact

Maintenance of relationships requires an investment in terms of time and energy. Throughout the marketing campaign, it is essential that the marketer remains continuously in touch with his network of customer contacts, and works to expand this network. Nurturing relationships involves regular face-to-face meetings where useful information is exchanged.

Marketing campaigns and aircraft purchase decisions usually involve a continuous cycle of 1) requirements communicated by the customer, 2) information provided by the seller, and 3) reaction by the customer, normally in the form of refined definition of the customer requirement or requests for supplementary information. The cycle repeats itself until the customer has a very clear definition of his requirement, and the seller has a clear definition of how his product can respond to those requirements. For this process to proceed, continuous contact between the customer and the seller is essential.

Flight Demonstrations

As part of most aircraft sales, the customer will undertake a formal technical *flight evaluation*, which measures performance of the aircraft against specific test parameters, and which is part of the competitive selection process if more than one aircraft type is under consideration. Somewhat different from the flight evaluation is the *flight demonstration*, a less technical flying display of the capabilities of the aircraft. A common variety of flight demonstration is the aerobatics routine that is a staple of air shows. Other demonstrations involve taking senior officials for rides in the aircraft. Although the demonstrations are of minimal technical value, they convey the usual emotion impact that accompanies close-up exposure to the noise, power, and visual effects of aircraft operations. Flight demonstrations are also effective in attracting media attention.

Hosting Customer Visits

Visiting a customer in his office is useful, but arranging a visit by the customer to the seller's facility is far more effective. This is because the customer is isolated from most of her workday distractions when she is away from her desk, and a visit to a production facility is likely to occupy more time than a typical sales call. In addition, a well-hosted visit will impart the visual impact of a factory tour and close-up inspection of the aircraft or equipment that is being marketed.

In the modern era, the nature of a customer visit will vary dramatically according to the conflict-of-interest rules to which the customer is subject. At one extreme, visits by US Government officials are rigorously austere. US Government officials are not permitted to accept contractor-provided transportation from the airport to the factory, nor can they accept free meals or entertainment of any sort. Many international government and commercial customers, at the other extreme, can accept airline tickets to transport them to the seller's facility, and can be treated to entertainment and gifts. To avoid embarrassment on both sides, it is important to understand in advance the rules to which the customer is subject. Obviously the customer is put in an awkward situation if she is obliged to decline a program of social activities that have been arranged in advance by the host.

Preliminary customer visits usually follow a basic routine common with other industries. The customer and her entourage arrive at the facility by means of transportation that may be provided by the host. They are introduced to appropriate members of senior management during either an office visit or group introductions in a conference room. In the conference room, the visitors are then given a presentation that provides a general overview of the company. The overview is followed by a more specific overview of the program in which the customer has an interest. If the visit spans the lunch hour, the group adjourns to the dining room or continues working in the conference room as sandwiches are served. After lunch, a plant tour is conducted, which gives the visitors an opportunity to walk around after their meals. Following the plant tour, the group returns to the conference room for wrap-up discussions to identify action items and to plan follow-up meetings.

In subsequent visits, as marketing discussions become more specific, the agenda dispenses with the formalities of the company overview and plant tour. Meetings focus on issues.

After business hours, if the visiting group will remain overnight in the host company's city, the host will arrange a dinner, if the visitors' conflict-of-interest rules permit. For initial visits, the host may also want to offer to arrange a guided tour of the city's shopping and tourism highlights, if the visitors are interested.

At the end of the visit, it is traditional to present the guests with a souvenir, usually of modest value. This custom is more important when Asian or Middle Eastern businesspeople are involved. It is best to avoid trinkets such as cheap pens. Model airplanes are always good. Fancier gifts, such as crystal or luxury leather goods, are appropriate for more senior visitors. Again, make sure that you are familiar with the rules to which the visitors are subject, so that you do not create a circumstance in which the guest has to publicly refuse a gift.

The best place to present the gifts is at the culmination of the business meetings, or following dinner. The gifts should be presented by the senior company representative in attendance.

Sales Calls by Senior Executives

In theory, sales calls by senior executives are desirable because they create more impact than routine visits by marketers. In practice, numerous factors can influence the practical usefulness of such visits.

Most aerospace companies are large and complex organizations filled with people with ambiguous job titles. Aerospace, like other industries, has followed the fashion of title inflation, which has resulted in numerous gradations of 'vice presidents' and 'general managers' who are in actuality department heads. This ambiguity, combined with complex matrix organizations in which responsibilities are often not clearly delineated, leaves the customer with a lack of understanding of the true identity of most company representatives with whom he comes into contact.

Sometimes marketers and their companies believe that the customer will be impressed by a visit from a personality in a position of power and respect within the company. In fact, unless the customer has some prior experience or familiarity with the person, he is likely to consider the visitor to be one in a series of ritual visitors of no special interest. This is particularly true if the visit is construed as a one-time affair that will not develop into a working relationship.

The customer has an interest in developing relationships with people who can be useful to him. Company executives of obvious power, such as CEOs and heads of major business units, are always welcome because their roles are clear and their authority imbues them with the power to produce results. Lower level executives are also of interest to the customer if they are expected to become continuously involved in the customer's business. Casual drop-in visits by other executives are of questionable value, and can be harmful if the executives appear to lack knowledge of the customer's circumstances.

The most effective executive visits involve individuals who are viewed by the customer to have power and authority, and who have a demonstrated personal interest in the customer's program. The customer will appreciate the symbolic gesture of the executive's travel to the customer's home ground, and will use the occasion of his visit to develop personal relationships between senior management of the two entities. Customers recognize that such relationships can be of critical value in working out thorny issues that may arise as marketing discussions lead towards a contract.

Promotional Events

Marketers are continuously looking for opportunities to earn customer goodwill. Sometimes these opportunities present themselves in the form of promotional activities in support of the customer, or events intended to attract positive attention of the customer.

Typical of this type of activity is sponsorship of golf tournaments organized by customers or military organizations, in countries where customer rules permit. The company makes a cash contribution to underwrite green fees and lunch for the participants, and often provides contestants with golf balls, shirts, or hats with a company logo, and may also furnish prizes. In return, the company receives the recognition and theoretically the appreciation of the players, and usually gets invitations for several executives to join the tournament in an honorary capacity. This type of event, and other similar goodwill-building events, have much in common with promotional initiatives in other business-to-business industries.

However, the aerospace industry has its own industry-specific forms of promotion. *Air shows* are lavish promotional events that are described and analyzed in Chapter 9 of this book.

Delivery ceremonies are important multi-phased events for both civil and government customers, and often involve the public and press. An initial *roll-out ceremony* occurs when the first aircraft is painted and is prepared to enter flight testing. The justification for the roll-out ceremony is that, because of the need for extensive flight testing of initial aircraft in a series, a long time interval often elapses between roll-out and actual delivery of an operational aircraft to the customer. When handover of the aircraft to the customer does occur, a first-delivery ceremony occurs at the manufacturer's factory. Often a separate delivery ceremony occurs shortly thereafter when the aircraft is delivered to the territory of the customer. Although these ceremonies occur at the end of the marketing cycle, they are important because they emphasize the productive results of collaboration between the buyer and the seller, and create a positive atmosphere for follow-on sales in the best traditions of relationship marketing. The customer likes them because they provide positive publicity for new capabilities.

World tours are commonly undertaken by manufacturers as promotional events to showcase new aircraft and features. Typically a newly introduced civil aircraft will be taken on an itinerary of visits to potential international customers. When the aircraft is on the ground at its international destinations, customer representatives are invited to come aboard for inspection. Often the visitors include a wide range of customer employees, including flight crews, maintenance crews, ticket agents, and reservations clerks as well as senior management. Members of the local press and travel agents are also invited to visit the aircraft. Receptions and news conferences are arranged. In some cases, if local customers have special operating considerations such as high altitude or short-runway performance, a test flight demonstration of specific performance parameters may be arranged. World tours by military aircraft are somewhat different in nature. They are less common, and generally target a smaller number of potential customers. Flight demonstrations or evaluations are almost always part of the visits. Although local press coverage may be invited, inspection of the aircraft is limited to a comparative small number of government officials, senior military officers and technical evaluators.

Using Government Support

Major aerospace competitions receive international government attention because they involve very large sums of money and pit high-technology flagship companies of several nationalities against one another. Because of this interest, competing companies can often enlist the active support of senior government officials of their countries. Such government support is of limited value for marketing commercial aircraft to private customers, but can be a powerful influence on government customers for military aircraft.

All major aerospace companies maintain government lobbying and liaison offices in their national capitals. The objectives and operations of these offices, described in Chapter 7 of this book, include enlisting national government officials to support international sales campaigns. Sometimes the extent of government support is impressive. During the 'deal of the century' fighter aircraft competition in Europe in the 1970s, US Secretary of Defense James Schlesinger led the American marketing efforts that eventually led to purchase of 348 F-16s by the governments of Belgium, Denmark, Norway, and the Netherlands. In the 1980s and 1990s, British Prime Minister Margaret Thatcher was closely identified with the international marketing efforts of British Aerospace, and was particularly involved with the sale of Tornado aircraft to Saudi Arabia under the Al Yamamah program.

International government customers generally react positively to courtesy visits by well-placed government officials, legislators, and senior military officers from the marketing company's home country. The official visitors should receive advance briefings and background papers from marketers to ensure that they deliver the desired messages and are sufficiently knowledgeable to be credible.

If mishandled, official visits can be detrimental. The most common negative side effects are that government officials in the buying country feel that they are being coerced, and the military feels that the marketers are attempting to circumvent the formal selection process by influencing the politicians. The marketer should be sensitive to these risks of negative reaction, and should plan political visits accordingly. As a general rule, the marketer has more flexibility if he believes that he is losing the competition. Under these circumstances, he has less to lose if he undertakes risky political strategies.

Assistance in Sales Financing

As the sales process advances, the marketer and the customer work together to explore financing arrangements to accommodate the customer's needs and financial constraints. Experienced and sophisticated customers will sometimes prefer to arrange financing independently of the seller, but many customers prefer to take advantage of the seller's influence and familiarity with financial markets. The marketer requires a working knowledge of aircraft financing practices, which are treated in detail in Chapter 5. At a minimum, the marketer should serve as an intermediary between the customer and the aircraft financing specialists within the selling company.

The Contracting and Pricing Process

The marketer has an essential role in the contracting process. Although contractual mechanics and pricing are the responsibility of technical experts in those areas, it is the responsibility of the marketer to ensure that the timing of the contracting steps proceed on a schedule that accommodates the customer's needs, and that the structure and content of the proposal reflect the customer's requirements.

Although some commercial and military customers have well-defined schedules and milestones for planned purchases, other customers take a comparatively unstructured approach. In this latter case, the marketer sometimes has the ability to influence the process in his favor.

The technical subject of contracting procedures and methods is addressed in Chapter 15 of this book. At this point, suffice it to say that the marketer can sometimes use the contracting process to elicit action from the customer. Customers normally have annual or multi-year cycles of planning, evaluating, and budgeting capital equipment investments. For the marketer, an important intermediate goal is to simply convince the customer to evaluate the seller's product as part of this planning and budgeting cycle. The challenge for the marketer is somehow or other to interject his product offer into the customer's evaluation process. Working informally with a familiar customer, he can sometimes elicit a request for tender that is not a binding commitment of the customer, but gives the seller an opportunity to present a formal offer. If a request for tender cannot be obtained, the marketer may recommend that his company submit an unsolicited proposal to give the customer something to evaluate.

As the formal proposal is eventually compiled, in a preliminary unsolicited form or as a best-and-final offer, the marketer will advise the contracts department concerning ways the offer can be tailored to maximize its appeal to the customer. When the proposal is formally presented, the presentation team should be led by the marketer, who coordinates the discussion agenda.

If the proposal leads to contract negotiations, the seller's negotiating team should be led by a representative of the contracts department, but the marketer will be present in all discussions. As negotiations progress and inevitably encounter sticking-points, the marketer will advise the seller's negotiators concerning the customer's attitudes and priorities, and will generally attempt to overcome obstacles.

Managing Sales Announcements

When major aircraft programs are involved, the style and timing of sales announcement are sensitive. Customarily, aircraft manufacturers delay any formal statements until after commercial customers have made their announcements. Depending upon the customer's preferences, the announcements are sometimes made in joint ceremonies, with the press in attendance, which senior executives of both companies attend.

Timing is affected by a number of factors. In many cases, the signed sales contract is contingent upon final approval of financing that will not become firm until some time afterwards, and none of the parties are eager to publicize a deal until it is certain. Other times, the parties will choose to time an announcement to maximize press coverage, and will delay the news until occasions such as major international air shows. Other common timing considerations involve anticipated reactions in stock markets and pending government approvals of new routes.

Sales announcements tend to follow a standard formula. The airline comments that the new aircraft are modern, safe, and comfortable, and will enable the airline to service new routes or raise the standard of service on older routes. The aircraft manufacturer makes positive comments about the airline, and notes that the quality and capability of the new aircraft will further enhance quality of service.

Announcements of sales of military aircraft are less exuberant. Some countries that are sensitive about military matters, such as Singapore, contractually prohibit suppliers from making public statements mentioning defense sales to the Republic. More commonly, an official spokesperson within the ministry of defense will make a standard announcement naming the winner of the competition, specifying the amount of the contract. In a tradition peculiar to the United States, the Congressional representative whose district includes the winning competitor is often given the privilege of making the first announcement of the outcome. The government announcements are then followed by an announcement from the winning company, in which the importance of the contract is emphasized.

Although the sales announcement occurs at the completion of the marketing campaign, it is an important event in the context of the enduring relationship between the buyer and the seller. Relationship marketing is based on the recognition that the long-term business interests of the customer and his supplier will continue well beyond the completion of any single transaction.

Managing Relationships After the Sale

The customer's decision to buy your aircraft or equipment was based on many considerations, including the belief that your company would support him in a long-term partnership that would continue to exist as long as he owns the equipment.

This post-delivery support is an essential element in relationship marketing, and will influence your prospects for future sales to this customer and to others.

In the period immediately following the sale, the marketer should make a special effort to visit the customer at regular, frequent, intervals, and should monitor continuously the progress of his company's performance of contractual obligations. The marketer should retain an identity as a principal point of contact that the customer can call upon to communicate concerns or problems. He should be a regular participant at program reviews and technical meetings that occur prior to delivery of the product, and should continue to function as an advocate of the customer's point of view.

A final menacing note: in the aerospace industry, an extraordinarily high percentage of announced sales are eventually cancelled or reversed afterwards. The company that has won an apparent sales victory should never presume that the competition is over. The correct attitude is that the competition has moved into a new phase in which the company's task is to protect its perishable victory. The art and science of protecting sales victories is the subject of Chapter 14 of this book.

PART 3
Managing the Marketing and Sales Process

Chapter 13

Managing the Marketing and Sales Process

In the international aerospace industry, marketing is different things to different people. The business acquisition processes of individual marketers depends upon whether they are selling commodity rivets or complete aircraft, whether their customer is a civil airline or a military organization, or whether the customer is located in Africa or North America.

However, regardless of the specific nature of individual organizations, their products, their markets, and their business environments, certain general practices apply to effective management of the marketing and sales process. These practices pertain to the marketing organization, to budgetary practices, and to management reviews and controls.

Organization

The marketing organization should be designed so that it effectively fulfills its most important priorities, which are:

- *Responsiveness to the customer.*

The customer should have a single primary contact within the seller's company, and that contact should be enabled to provide the customer with prompt responses to all customer requests.

As a consequence of the constant internal changes, increasing size and organizational complexity of modern aerospace firms, outsiders cannot realistically be expected to understand job assignments and organizational roles within the seller's company. Nor should they be expected to. Their account manager within the seller's marketing department should be empowered to act as their advocate within the seller's organization. The account manager should, in turn, be assigned direct points of contact with all of the functional departments that will be required to support marketing activities. This generally involves the creation of matrix organizations or integrated program teams to formalize working relationships across functional departments.

- *Management control and clear assignments of responsibility and reporting channels.*

The marketing organization should be designed so that reporting channels and responsibilities of its members are clearly defined, with management authority to control activities of individual campaign managers clearly delineated. Organizations in which campaign managers report to multiple bosses are to be avoided. An example of ambiguous control and responsibility is an organization in which an international campaign manager reports to a marketing manager at his local business unit, but also reports to a separate marketing manager, perhaps located at a group headquarters, with general marketing responsibility for the geographical region in which the campaign manager operates.

• *Incorporation of all essential marketing functions.*
The marketing department should include the individual campaign managers, but should also include essential related functions such as advertising, customer relations, proposal preparation, marketing graphics, and so on.

• *Clear interfaces with supporting organizations.*
Each functional organization should be required to designate a point of contact to provide response and support for activities of marketing campaign managers. Thus, when a campaign manager is developing a response to a customer inquiry concerning technical configuration options or financing, the campaign manager can work directly with the designated point of contact in engineering or finance.

• *Effective communication.*
Two-way communication within the organization should flow through both formal and informal channels on a continuous basis. Formal communications such as assignments of job responsibilities, program creation, or major changes in processes or procedures, should be published in the form of management directives. Less formal communications take place through relatively brief staff meetings that take place on a regular basis, through direct meetings between supervisors and members of their organizations, and by means of peer-to-peer discussions. For purposes of status reporting throughout the broader organization, marketing managers should prepare brief weekly written reports of significant developments in their active marketing campaigns.

• *Decision-making authority at the lowest appropriate levels.*
In aerospace marketing, important decisions are made by the individual campaign manager in the field. The campaign manager should have the experience, the judgment, and the detailed knowledge of the customer and her own company that qualify her to make valid decisions concerning action plans. Marketing management should review and adjust her plans, should assign her campaigns appropriate priorities, and should authorize resources in support of her efforts. The business unit senior manager should retain final control over strategies, resources, and commitments incurred by the seller's company.

Based on their own personalities, preferences, and interests, individual managers will choose the amount of detailed information they want to receive about sales campaigns, and will decide the extent to which they want to become involved in decision-making at all levels. As a general rule, it is helpful and positive for managers in all disciplines to be well informed about the sales process and ongoing marketing campaigns. However, it is distinctly counterproductive for senior managers to become personally involved in the routine daily details of sales activities. It is a mis-allocation of limited management resources, and it causes marketers to be less responsive to their customers if they must schedule meetings with senior management before they can proceed with routine tactical action that should be managed by marketers in the field.

Table 13.1 Marketing responsibilities

Management Level	Marketing Responsibilities
Senior Business Unit Management	• Approval of marketing budgets • Approval of key decisions at campaign milestone reviews • Approve contractual commitments • Perform direct marketing with senior customer representatives
Senior Marketing Management	• Endorse or reject strategy • Monitor status of campaign schedules • Prioritization and reconciliation of competing requirements • Mentoring and supervising front-line marketers • Evaluation and professional development of front-line marketers • Promulgation of departmental procedures • Management of consolidated departmental budgets
Front-line Marketer and Regional Manager	• Provide detailed customer knowledge • Gather critical customer information (processes, people, budgets, schedules, and so on) • Assess customer requirements • Develop recommended strategy • Develop customer relationships • Prepare and maintain campaign schedules • Estimate and request campaign budgets • Evaluate and acquire in-country agent • Lead and manage activities of campaign capture team • Monitor and report status of campaign • Perform detailed day-to-day management of campaign • Assure export license coverage

Note: A rough correlation of management levels and the types of marketing responsibilities they should have. Excessive management involvement in routine decisions is counterproductive to everyone, including the customer.

- *Minimal superfluous management levels.*

Marketing should generally be managed at the level of the business unit. In recognition of the organizational complexity of modern, large aerospace firms, marketing staff functions are often established at group headquarters to maintain consolidated status reporting and to coordinate marketing activities between separate business units. Group and corporate headquarters also have a need and a responsibility to review and approve major financial commitments, including sales contracts, made on behalf of the corporation. These are certainly legitimate functions.

The smooth and efficient functioning of the marketing organization depends upon assignment of appropriate decision-making responsibility to appropriate levels within the organization. Qualifications of individuals to make competent decisions will vary from company to company, but a rough correlation of the decision-making hierarchy and the decisions and responsibilities which they should be assigned is depicted in Table 13.1.

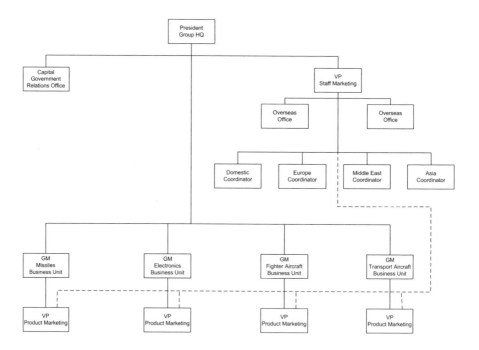

Figure 13.1 Aerospace corporate organization
Note: A typical aerospace corporate organizational chart depicting marketing relationships between Group Headquarters and individual business units.

The representative organization in Figure 13.1 shows the normal relationship between marketing functions at the corporate group headquarters and at the individual aerospace business units. Note that the government lobbying organization in the capital reports directly to the group president. This is because of the obvious importance of promoting a cohesive, unified corporate position in government relations.

Also at the group headquarters is a staff marketing organization responsible for preparing reports for the president based upon consolidation and distillation of information provided by the business units. The corporate staff marketing function additionally serves the purpose of coordinating activities of the business units in geographical markets to avoid conflicting activities and strategies.

International overseas marketing offices that support several business units should report administratively to the staff marketing function, although the offices should have clearly delineated accountability to the business units that they represent. In cases in which individual business units have sufficient regional business to support a dedicated full-time overseas office, it is common practice for the overseas office to report directly to the business unit.

The staff marketing function generally coordinates other miscellaneous activities that involve several of the business units. Examples are advertising and coordination of corporate participation at air shows.

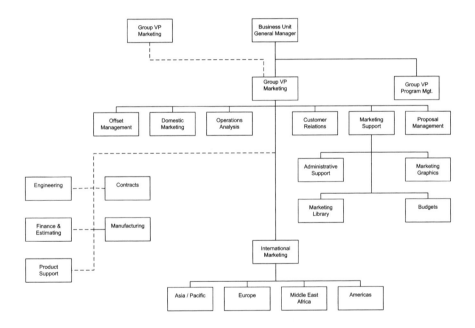

Figure 13.2 Marketing organization at the aerospace business unit
Note: A typical organization chart of the marketing function of the business unit demonstrates that primary responsibility remains within the unit.

At the level of the business unit, the senior executive with responsibility for marketing, usually the vice president of marketing, reports directly to the unit general manager, and also has a responsibility to coordinate as required with the staff VP for marketing at group headquarters, as described above.

Within an aerospace business unit, direct contact with the customer is principally handled by either Marketing or Program Management. The general rule is that Marketing is responsible for managing customer contact prior to the sale, and Program Management has primary responsibility afterwards. This dichotomy is, of course, an oversimplification. During the sales process, the marketer will put together a multi-functional sales team that will include a program manager, who will have regular contact with the customer. This mutual exposure will facilitate the transition of responsibility from Marketing to Program Management after the sale is complete. The primary responsibilities of the program manager are to ensure that a high-quality product is delivered to the customer on schedule and within planned cost, and that the product is well supported by the manufacturer following delivery. Further in the future, as the customer becomes a candidate for a follow-on purchase, Program Management remains the primary contact with the customer, but works jointly with Marketing to develop a sale. Continuous close cooperation between the two organizational units is essential.

At the business unit, the two essential line marketing functions are the domestic marketing and the international marketing operations. The relative size and importance of these two functions will depend upon the comparative importance of the two markets and the degree of intensity of ongoing marketing efforts. Whereas sustaining marketing of a mature product line to known customers can be handled with a relatively small front-line marketing staff, a greater effort and more people are required to market a newly introduced product line or to manage a major sales campaign that is in a period of intense activity immediately prior to competitive selection.

If possible, the same marketer should not handle marketing accounts for customers who are competitors. During the normal process of the marketer and the customer working together to identify technical and operational solutions suitable for the customer, it is inevitable that the marketer must have access to some degree of privileged information from the customer, whether it be sensitive military information or proprietary competitive information concerning business strategy. Customers rightly fear that this sensitive information is subject to leak to military or commercial competitors through marketers who are in regular contact with both sides of competitive pairings. If you are a marketer of commercial aircraft to American Airlines, for example, United Airlines may be reluctant to share strategic information with you. If you are marketing military aircraft to Israel, the Saudi Arabian military may feel that you should not be trusted with sensitive defense data.

The *Proposal Management* function is charged with responsibility for administrative tasks related to accumulating and formatting the proposal content, often voluminous and highly detailed, required to respond to customer requests for proposal. The details of the proposal process are discussed in Chapter 15 of this book. The proposal manager works closely with the lead marketer and program manager to collect assigned inputs from engineering, contracts, pricing, offset management, product support, and other functional departments whose contributions are required in the formulation of proposals.

Marketing Support handles miscellaneous administrative support of the marketing department. Often this section includes a small graphics support capability so that Marketing can respond immediately to small-scale requirements for marketing presentations and internal reports. Generally the business unit will have a larger centralized graphics department that will serve the entire unit, and which is utilized by Marketing for major graphics needs.

Customer Relations has responsibility for making detailed administrative arrangements for visits by customers, for buying promotional items, and for handling other local administrative matters related to dealings with customers.

The function and methods of *Operations Analysis* (OA) is discussed in Chapter 10 of this book. Because OA deals with analysis of performance of an aircraft or subsystem on specific routes or in specific missions, some companies consider that the analysts should be part of the engineering department rather than Marketing. Other companies believe that, because routes and missions are inherent customer requirements, Marketing is the best organizational home for the analysts. Certainly it is true that the analysts themselves should have technical and quantitative professional qualifications.

Qualifications of People

In any organization, the most important element is the quality of the people that constitute the organization. This truism applies unquestionably to aerospace marketing.

Because of the technical nature of aerospace products and business practices, a standard prerequisite for marketers is a sound professional background in a functional specialty of the industry. As in other industries, an aerospace marketer should have a basic technical competence and familiarity with his product line. Ideally, he should also understand industry practices pertaining to the program continuum, beginning at identification of requirements, and passing through engineering design, costing, financing, manufacture, contract negotiations, delivery, product support, and so on.

Because aerospace professionals tend to become specialized early in their careers, most candidates for marketing jobs do not have highly diverse work backgrounds and experience. This is particularly true when filling entry-level jobs with candidates that often are younger and have less time in the industry. So, by necessity, the hiring manager often selects beginning marketers with experience and skills that are strong in some areas, but comparatively weaker in other areas. Of course, personality attributes such as intelligence, drive, and common sense also weigh heavily in any overall evaluation of job candidates.

In the experience of most aerospace companies, the three most common sources for entry-level marketers are:

- From within other functional disciplines within the aerospace industry
- From companies outside the industry, but with some involvement with aerospace
- From the military (particularly in the case of defense aerospace).

Table 13.2 is a very general depiction of the theoretical strengths and weaknesses that candidates with prior experience in these three categories might offer.

Table 13.2 Hypothetical suitability of some backgrounds for aerospace marketers

	Background	Merits	Limitations
Prior Military	Military Pilot	Good fit for selling pilot-centric military aircraft such as fighters or attack helicopters	Very limited usefulness for commercial customers
	Non-pilot Military	Useful background for dealing with military customers	Very limited usefulness for commercial customers
Prior Aerospace Industry Experience	Engineering	Excellent background, brings strength to technical discussions; essential for marketing technical equipment such as avionics	Technical expertise must be combined with broader familiarity with other aspects of the industry
	Financial Management	Generally a good background, brings strength to pricing discussions	Financial background is insufficient unless combined with depth of hardware & operations knowledge
	Subcontract Management	Sometimes useful in selling to lower-tier equipment suppliers	Experience is not generally applicable for aircraft sales
	Product Support	Generally a good background, good customer focus & hardware knowledge	Sometimes have excessive fixation on operational details
	Quality Assurance	Less desirable background	Tends to be a relatively narrow specialization
	Program Management	Excellent background, breadth of experience is particularly valuable	Depends on individual characteristics and experience
	Operations Analysis	Excellent background	Analytical propensity needs to be combined with flexibility and business sense
	Manufacturing	Less desirable background, but useful for offset discussions	Often has to overcome tendency to focus inside the company rather than on customer
Outside the Aerospace Industry	Airline Industry	Excellent background for commercial sales, good empathy with customer	Needs to also have understanding of inner workings and culture of selling company
	Aircraft Leasing or Finance	Excellent background for commercial sales	Often of limited value in marketing of equipment items or military hardware
	Non-aerospace Marketing	Limited usefulness	Aerospace industry experience is generally indispensable
	Senior Government Service	Useful for narrow specialties involving government relations	With rare exceptions (such as FAA or Defense Ministry background), does not possess specific aerospace industry knowledge
	Specialized International Background	Useful for customer relations	Not generally useful for product marketing

Note: When evaluating candidates for aerospace marketing jobs, different backgrounds offer different strengths and weaknesses. Each individual case is different, and personality attributes are often more important than generalizations based on experience.

Another factor that should be weighed when evaluating candidates for international marketing jobs is familiarity with the specific culture and language of the overseas market. This consideration is often complex. It is desirable to have a marketer that can deal with his customers without an interpreter and who is at ease in the customer's cultural environment. Often companies attempt to find international marketers who are emigrants from the customer country, under the assumption that this background will facilitate dealings with the customer. However, this practice can sometimes have negative results. In some cultures, emigrants are considered disloyal, and are resented by citizens of the home country. Emigrants from poorer countries to richer industrialized countries may be resented when they return to their home countries and display a level of wealth beyond the reach of their former compatriots. Other potential problems occur when returning emigrants, who naturally retain emotional bonds with their countries of origin, feel that they have the right to speak critically about the perceived shortcomings of their former homeland. In this matter, as in many others, the overall qualifications and personal characteristics of the candidate should be weighed in their entirety. Language capability is one attribute among many others.

The Operating Plan

Establishment of sales objectives is an essential aspect of managing the marketing function. Management works with individual marketers to develop realistic sales projections over time for each active market. Development of these projections serves at least two important purposes: it provides working goals against which the performance of the individual marketers can be measured, and, in the aggregate, it provides an expectation of future business unit revenues that can be used for financial planning.

Common practice is that marketing projections undergo a thorough process of management review at least once a year, and that the baseline projections are subject to quarterly adjustments to incorporate new information. The marketing and sales projections become part of the business unit's *operating plan*, which contains comprehensive information about the unit's anticipated revenues, expenses, investments, employment levels, product deliveries, cash flow, profits, and other critical metrics for at least ten years into the future.

Marketing and sales projections are a particularly important element of the operating plan, because they form a basis used in calculations of many of the other metrics in the plan. Projected sales are translated into projected business base in the factory in future years. The size of this business base, in turn, is an important element in the calculations of future manufacturing costs, and the anticipated manufacturing costs are used as a major part of the build-up of product pricing for sales to customers. If sales projections are unrealistically high, and if actual factory business base is consequently lower than planned, manufacturing costs per unit will be higher than expected because fixed costs and overheads will have to spread over a smaller number of manufacturing hours. Higher-than-anticipated manufacturing costs have immediate negative impact upon cash flow and profits, causing the business unit to miss its financial targets. In short, missed sales projections cause business base reductions, which in turn cause hourly rates to increase, which degrades earnings.

The format of the sales projections in the operating plan is very straightforward. Expected customers are identified, and quantities of aircraft or products to be sold are depicted on a quarterly basis into the future. Normally the program office or financial management will convert the discrete sales quantities into monetary values, and will estimate profit margins, required investments, and other financial parameters related to sales.

Operational Control, Metrics, and Routine Recurring Reports

Perhaps the most perplexing challenge in managing aerospace marketing is devising meaningful ways to measure performance. Obviously, the ultimate measure of success of any marketing organization is the volume of sales. But in aerospace markets where the sales cycle is typically several years, and where exogenous factors such as political events and global economics have direct impact, it is often difficult to assess progress and performance of individual marketers and marketing campaigns.

For the marketing manager in need of a way to maintain visibility of individual campaigns and monitor progress, there is no substitute for detailed familiarity with the market, the customer, and the activities of the front-line marketer. Realistically, however, it is unlikely that more than one or two individuals, at most, will possess sufficient up-close familiarity to be able to meaningfully assess the marketing situation. In the absence of such familiarity, the next best tool for marketing assessment is the detailed schedule.

At best, a good schedule can identify and assign timing to detailed events relating to the customer's buying process, the seller's planned initiatives to support and influence that process, and known external events, such as competitor activities, that might influence the purchasing decision. To the extent that the schedule is accurate and complete, it provides a tactical roadmap against which marketing efforts and progress can be tracked. Schedules are familiar and comfortable management tools for aerospace executives, many of whom have professional backgrounds in program management and engineering development.

The problem with schedules for marketing campaigns is that often available information is insufficient to draft a meaningful roadmap. In some cases, particularly in the early stages of a campaign, the customer himself may not have a firm idea of the timing of the purchase, and may not have a well-defined formal purchasing process.

Under circumstances in which complete information about the buyer's purchasing plan is unavailable, the marketer attempts to fill in the information gaps, and proceeds to develop a schedule, speculative to some extent, based on the knowledge that is available. As more data is obtained, or as plans and events change, the schedule is revised.

Because of these circumstances, a schedule for a campaign involving, say, a sale to the US military, which publishes formal procurement schedules and follows a legally dictated procurement process, would be vastly more complete and precise than for a sale to a small African commercial airline with opaque purchasing processes and timing depending upon uncertain financing and political risks. Obviously, when using marketing schedules as a management tool, a manager must carefully weigh the degree of precision attributed to the schedule.

Routine marketing status briefings to management normally take the form of a review of the campaign schedule, discussion of schedule events that were accomplished or not accomplished, presentation of new information since the prior status briefing, and any recommended adjustments to tactics or strategy. Also included in the status summary should be a review of the *contact plan*, the specific agenda of planned meetings with customer representatives or other people having the capability to influence the outcome of the purchasing decision.

Budgeting and Cost Control

Almost every aspect of the aerospace industry involves complexity, and marketing and sales processes are no exception. Marketing campaigns are expensive and involve business decisions with important financial consequences for companies. This combination of complexity and financial impact implies that marketing activities must be carefully monitored and managed.

In order to identify and control marketing costs, budgets are established for individual campaigns, and all discrete costs incurred in support of those campaigns are accumulated by means of work order numbers and charge numbers. Annual budgets are established based on cost projections, and the marketing lead and program manager are assigned primary responsibility for controlling costs incurred against the individual campaign budgets.

Of course, some general costs cannot be easily or accurately allocated to individual campaigns. Separate budget lines and cost-accumulation accounts not associated with specific customers are established for general marketing-related expenses such as promotional give-aways, sales brochures, product advertising in wide-circulation media, support of regional air shows, and training of personnel. Costs for preliminary efforts to identify potential new customers and to gather information about them are collected in a general *market development* account.

Periodically, at least quarterly, budgets should be compared to accumulated actual costs to ensure that expenses are being incurred at projected rates. As new sales opportunities arise, or as prior opportunities change, budgets should be adjusted accordingly. This is normal cost control management as it applies to all aspects of a company's operations.

Phases in the Marketing and Sales Process

Distilled into its simplest elements, management of the sales process consists of a few simple steps:

1. Identify the objective
2. Understand the customer's process of selection and procurement
3. Establish a strategy
4. Continuously measure and monitor progress towards execution of the strategy.

International aerospace marketing is inherently difficult to manage because every sales campaign is different. Standardized metrics for measuring sales progress are often not effective because customers impose individualized processes for competitive selection, contracting, and procurement. Because customers follow different procurement roadmaps, they use different milestones.

This simple reality of customer differences is, surprisingly, a problem for experienced aerospace managers who do not have first hand experience in international marketing. Not everyone is accustomed to working within a framework that is externally imposed (by the customer), that changes on each project (as the customer changes), and that often is poorly defined or subject to re-definition at the whim of the customer. In many parts of the aerospace business, managers succeed by following a mantra of defining a repeatable process and following it with discipline. This is not always entirely possible in the sales and marketing part of the business.

Some customers facilitate the job of the marketing manager by establishing a detailed, clearly defined acquisition process, supplemented with detailed schedules for key competitive milestones and contractual events. The US Department of Defense, for example, publishes volumes of detailed procedures governing how its equipment acquisition selection process works, and DoD program managers for individual acquisition programs customarily provide all competitors with detailed program schedules covering all significant milestones. Consequently, marketing managers experienced in working with the DoD have an easy job of identifying major milestones in their marketing campaigns, and establishing dates for completion of the milestones. They know which individual offices of the DoD or the military branches will have responsibility for which task, and they know the procedures that the customer will follow to complete the milestone. It is relatively easy for a marketer to put together a detailed marketing plan that corresponds to the known DoD requirements, schedule milestones, and evaluation process. Once the plan is established, it is then fairly straightforward to manage the sales campaign by continually comparing actual progress to the marketing plan, taking corrective action whenever serious departures from the plan become apparent.

The marketing manager's job is not so easy when the customer has not publicly disclosed information about his acquisition process. Marketers may have to begin campaigns with no detailed knowledge about how the customer will evaluate competitors, which customer officials will make key decisions, and what schedule the customer will follow. Under these circumstances, it is difficult to prepare a meaningful marketing plan against which to measure accomplishments.

In any case, the job of the marketing manager is to boost sales by properly allocating marketing resources; applying discipline to the sales process by means of realistic plans and schedules; monitoring marketing performance by tracking status of plans and schedules; and intervening as appropriate when the marketing effort appears to be in trouble.

For management purposes, marketing campaigns are customarily divided into discrete phases that transpire more-or-less sequentially. Each of the individual phases represents an identifiable step in the marketing process, with the occurrence of characteristic events in the customer's acquisition process. Although these defining events are determined by the customer, they generally require corresponding activity on the part of the marketer's company.

As a marketing campaign advances from one phase to the next, formal management reviews are generally held to evaluate progress of the marketing campaign, to authorize action recommended by the marketing department, and to approve the budget required to support marketing activities through the next phase.

Phases are defined differently by individual companies, but a typical sequence might be as follows:

Phase A Prospecting, information gathering, and general customer development.

Phase B Recognition of a definable sales opportunity; definition of the requirement in more detail; formulation of a preliminary concept of a suitable offering; and projection of resources required to pursue the opportunity.

Phase C Development of a sales strategy, creation of an internal program capture team, and internal definition of a suitable program to offer the customer, including an engineering element, a financial element, a product support element, an offset element, and so on.

Phase D Formal offer of a contractual proposal to the customer.

Phase E Approval of negotiating positions and a final contractual settlement.

Phase F Development and approval of a keep-it-sold plan, if the marketing campaign has led to a sale.

Phase G Development and circulation of an internal critique of the marketing campaign, including lessons learned, whether or not the marketing campaign was successful.

As the marketing campaign proceeds in a more-or-less linear fashion through these successive phases, the company becomes progressively enmeshed in marketing activities, with increasing commitments in terms of time and resources that must be devoted to the campaign. As resources are required, management should take the responsibility of reviewing the status of the campaign and approving commitment of the resources. These management reviews, sometimes called *campaign milestone reviews*, are customarily established as the campaign advances from one phase to the next. The purpose of the reviews is to give management sufficient information upon which to base an intelligent decision to authorize expenditure of the resources required to sustain the campaign through its next phase. For marketing campaigns of financial or strategic importance, the management review should be chaired by the general manager of the business unit.

Here are examples of the relationships of typical campaign milestone reviews to campaign phases:

The *first campaign milestone review* takes place as the campaign passes from phase A to phase B. The general prospecting and information gathering activities in phase A have led the marketers to believe that an active marketing campaign is warranted. The purpose of this milestone review is to give the marketers a forum in which to justify their recommendation that resources be made available to support activities required in phase B. A major purpose of the review is the *qualification* of the customer as a viable and credit-worthy buyer. Accordingly, material presented and discussed at the milestone review includes the following subjects:

- A detailed description of the customer's perceived requirement
- Key background information about the customer, including historical context, key decision-makers, and financial factors
- A critical evaluation of the customer's overall qualifications to buy, particularly focusing on his ability to operate the equipment in a safe and profitable manner, his ability to pay, and the seriousness of his intent to buy
- A preliminary synopsis of the technical product that will be required to satisfy the requirement
- An estimated value of the sale
- A preliminary projection of the schedule of major events in the customer's schedule for making the purchase
- An assessment of how the selling company's capabilities and market presence fit with the customer's perceived requirement
- A preliminary assessment of significant capital investment that will be required if the campaign leads to a sale
- A listing and assessment of expected competitors
- An estimate of budget required to sustain the marketing campaign through the upcoming phase
- Initial estimates of probability that the purchase will actually occur (P_{go}) and that your company will win the competition (P_{win}).

From a budgetary point of view, this transition from phase A to phase B is particularly significant, because it marks the transition of the campaign from the general market development budget to an individual campaign budget, as described earlier in this chapter. A major conclusion of the first milestone review is that the opportunity under study has matured to the point that it can be recognized as a bona fide marketing campaign, with its own discrete budget and resources. If this conclusion is not reached, the sales prospect remains in the category of longer-range developmental opportunities.

The *second campaign milestone review* occurs as the campaign makes the transition from phase B to phase C. As the campaign enters phase C, activities that took place during phase B should have enabled the marketers to acquire a more profound insight into the customer and the factors that can be expected to affect the outcome of the competition. Because phase C will be largely devoted to establishing and executing a comprehensive campaign strategy, the second milestone review gives management an opportunity to evaluate the strategy.

The principal elements presented in this review are:

- A synopsis of circumstances that have changed since the first milestone review
- A detailed assessment of the customer's requirement
- A technical description of the product that the company should offer in response to the requirement
- A summary of the customer's procurement process and acquisition plan, including schedule and contracting characteristics, in as much detail as possible
- A detailed overview of the marketing strategy
- Identification of key customer decision-makers, and a plan for contact
- An overview of the business case for the program, including expectation of a winning sales price, investment required, time-phased cash flow, earnings, and the other customary financial metrics
- Time-phased projection of the budget that will be required to support the marketing campaign until its conclusion
- Identification of the capture team and leader
- Speculation concerning the offerings and marketing strategies of competitors
- Updated estimates of P_{go} and P_{win}.

The marketing strategy will include elements such as identification of the customer's highest priorities and principal objectives, followed by specific plans of action to convince customer decision-makers that your company's offering satisfies these objectives.

A critical part of the strategy involves analyzing the decision-making process within the customer's organization. A common practice is to assemble a working group of people with special knowledge of the customer, and to define the identity of all the individual executives within the customer's organization who will have authority to make specific decisions. This working group should also identify key individuals who are external to the customer, but who have the capability to affect the customer's decision. The most important advisors to these decision-makers are also identified. As the working group identifies decisions that are critical to making a sale, a strategy is developed to influence key decision-makers in a favorable direction.

This process of identifying and influencing key decision-makers has received much attention in the aerospace industry in recent years, and highly structured methodologies to analyze decisions have become a widespread practice. An early proponent of the process, Richard G. Hodapp, developed a structured methodology that he copyrighted as 'Decision Mapping', and which has been adopted by many major American aerospace companies since the early 1990s.

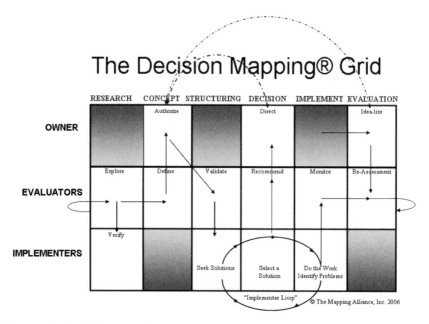

Figure 13.3 Decision mapping
Note: This element of Richard Hodapp's proprietary Decision Mapping® process is a well-known tool for identifying key decisions and decision-makers.
Source: The Mapping Alliance Inc. www.decisionmapping.com.

The capture team to be introduced in the second milestone review is a group representing functional disciplines such as marketing, contracts, engineering, manufacturing, estimating, offset management and program management. These team members have the responsibility for ensuring that their departments provide the support necessary to carry out the marketing strategy.

The *third campaign milestone review* is principally a senior management evaluation and approval of the formal priced proposal that will be forwarded to the customer, to begin phase D of the campaign. The review begins with a summary of significant changes that are known to have occurred since the second milestone review.

The focus of the review is on the content of the proposal: engineering configuration, pricing, contractual terms, delivery schedules, logistics support package, and industrial offsets if they are involved. Management will be particularly interested in cost estimates that were used as basis for the pricing, and will want to see the program financial projections represented in standard measurements such as cash flow, rate of return, net profit, and company investment. Program risks should be identified, their magnitude should be estimated, and the down-side projected negative impact on the program should be depicted.

At this review, the agenda should once again include a detailed overview of the customer's anticipated schedule and process for aircraft equipment selection and contract execution. The marketer should give an explanation of his latest assessment of P_{go} and P_{win}, and should give an overview of expected competitor strategies and offerings.

The *fourth campaign milestone review* occurs if the customer extends an invitation to negotiate a contract based upon the formal priced proposal submitted earlier. Procedurally, this step is the beginning of phase E.

An invitation for face-to-face discussions of the proposal can have vastly different significance, depending upon circumstances. In the most favorable scenario, the customer finds the offering to be attractive, and wants to conduct negotiations with the intent of moving promptly to a signed contract. In the least favorable scenario, the customer has no immediate intent to purchase, but simply wants to clarify pricing and other elements of the proposal.

However, any time a negotiating team is sent to a customer to discuss a proposal, the team should have clearly defined limits to its negotiating position, and the limits should be approved in advance by management. If the marketer and the capture team have gained an effective understanding of the customer, they will be able to anticipate the contractual concessions that the customer will seek. It is generally assumed that the customer will negotiate for a lower price. Other possible concessions will depend upon the customer's unique circumstances, but might involve special contractual terms and conditions, special post-delivery support, or favorable offset arrangements. Limits for the negotiating team must be established for all elements of the proposal that will be under discussion.

The presentation at this review should include a summary of expected customer issues at the negotiation, an overview of the customer's anticipated negotiating strategy, and a scenario of the path that the negotiations will follow. All of these factors are key pieces of information necessary to enable management to make an informed decision concerning an appropriate best and final offer (*BAFO*) that the negotiating team will be authorized to work towards.

It goes without saying that it is very difficult to accurately predict how major negotiations will unfold. Almost invariably, the customer will steer negotiations in a direction not anticipated by the offering company, and the negotiating team will have to request additional management approval for new negotiating limits in some area of the proposal. Approval for new negotiating limits, which often result from late-night telephone discussions between management and the negotiating team located in a hotel room near the customer's offices, are construed as a supplement to the fourth milestone review.

Once the proposal is formally presented to the customer, leadership in the business acquisition process transfers from the marketing department to the contracts department. The interplay between these two departments is important and complex, and is the subject of Chapter 15.

There are three main possible outcomes from the negotiations:

1. The customer buys your product
2. The customer buys the competitor's product, or spends his money to buy an unrelated system
3. The customer decides to buy nothing, or to postpone his decision.

Whichever of these three outcomes occurs, the *fifth campaign milestone review* is scheduled immediately after negotiations are completed or broken off. The purpose of the fifth milestone review is to obtain management approval for post-negotiation marketing action in the campaign. The period following negotiations is a particularly critical juncture in the marketing process, and the marketer should ensure that internal decisions are made quickly at this point.

If the outcome of negotiations is the first alternative, and the customer elects to buy your product (congratulations!), note that the milestone review should take place directly after the agreement to buy, and should not be delayed until the contract signature, which often follows the agreement by several months as financing, board of directors ratification, issuance of export licenses, and government regulatory approvals are finalized by the customer. In the case of government customers, delays may be even longer as various ministerial approvals, and sometimes parliamentary ratification, are obtained.

Suffice it to say at this point that a very significant percentage of sales agreements in the aerospace industry fail to convert into paid sales orders. If the negotiations culminate in an agreement to purchase your product, you can be assured that many forces will continue to work diligently to void the selection before the contract is awarded. These forces include your competitors, who will make desperate last-ditch offers and who will possibly file lawsuits protesting improper influence; government officials who have vested interests in alternative outcomes; industry interests who stand to benefit from selection of other competitors; and various other parties who are unhappy with the outcome.

If negotiations resulted in a sales agreement for your company, the primary purpose of the fifth milestone review is to approve a plan to ensure that the sales agreement does not unravel before the final contract signature and financial guarantees are in place. This is the *keep-it-sold (KIS)* plan. Keep-it-sold activity, which is of crucial importance and is the subject of Chapter 14 of this book, is phase F of the campaign.

The KIS plan should include anticipation of how competitors and other adversaries will attempt to void your company's selection. In response to each of these possible adversarial actions, counter-strategies should be developed to protect the sales agreement.

The best strategy for protecting a sales agreement is to move aggressively to convince supporters and doubters that your company will deliver an outstanding product and will comply with all aspects of the deal. Incorporated in the KIS plan should be a specific plan of action to immediately take visible, concrete steps to establish credibility concerning your company's commitment to the program. This action should include regular visits to the customer by senior executives of the selling company.

If, unfortunately, the negotiations resulted in alternative 2, a sales agreement with your competitor, the fifth milestone review has a completely different character and objective. Unless the marketer believes that the campaign has been definitively and irrevocably lost, he will use the fifth milestone review to justify his recommendation that he be allowed to develop a *spoiling strategy* intended to de-rail the competitor's sales agreement prior to actual contract award. The spoiling strategy will strive to draw attention to all the weak or questionable aspects of the competitor's offer, and will undermine the perception of the competitor's ability to perform.

The tenor of the spoiling strategy must be determined by the circumstances of the sale. If the losing company has a long-term relationship with the customer, and expects to obtain significant future business from him, any spoiling action should be sufficiently discrete to avoid antagonizing the customer. If, on the other hand, the losing competitor feels that he has nothing to lose by directly and publicly questioning the selection decision, the spoiling strategy can be brutal and direct.

If the marketer recommends a spoiling strategy during his fifth milestone review, his presentation to management will provide justification for that strategy, and will provide a tentative outline of specific approaches that should be considered. If management endorses the recommendation to mount a spoiling strategy, the campaign will be declared to have regressed to phase C, where the detailed new strategy will be developed. Thereafter, the campaign will undergo milestone reviews as it passes quickly through phases D and E, as new unsolicited proposals to the customer are developed and defined.

In the case of the third possible alternative outcome of negotiations, that the customer decides to do nothing or postpones his decision, the marketer must evaluate the meaning of the customer's action. If a future sale still appears to be likely, the marketer will probably attempt to re-open negotiations based upon the proposal that has been submitted. If, however, it seems that the customer has a serious problem with the proposal or the program concept upon which it was based, the marketer should question the fundamental soundness of his marketing strategy, and should consider revising it. Under these circumstances, the marketer would return the campaign to phase C, and would later develop a revised proposal based on a new strategy as he passed again through phases D and E.

The *sixth campaign milestone review* is the presentation to management of a frank internal after-the-fact critique of the marketing campaign. This review should be held as soon as the competition is considered to be definitively won or lost.

The emphasis of milestone review six is on finding ways to improve future results. An impartial senior editor should be temporarily assigned responsibility for compiling a report, and all parts of the company that were directly or indirectly involved in the marketing campaign should be invited to contribute comments and suggestions. The report should include:

- Identification of actions and strategies that were effective
- Identification of actions and strategies that were ineffective or counterproductive
- Reconstruction of the customer's decision-making process

- Review of competitor's actions, and analysis of their effectiveness
- After-the-fact speculation concerning alternative outcomes that might have resulted if alternative courses of action had been followed
- Specific suggestions concerning how procedures or management processes should be changed to improve future chances of success.

After the critique is presented to senior management at milestone review six, it should be presented and discussed in a bigger group of marketers and representatives of other functions normally involved in marketing and sales activity. The purpose of the critique is to disseminate lessons learned widely throughout the company. Copies of the report should be distributed, and a master library of critiques from successive marketing campaigns should be maintained for reference.

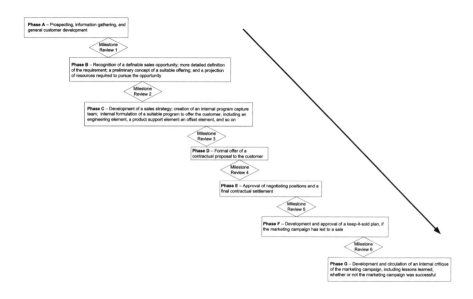

Figure 13.4 Phases and milestone reviews
Note: An orderly framework of milestone reviews is an effective tool for ensuring management control of important marketing decisions at critical junctures in the campaign. Over-emphasis on management reviews can cause harmful delays.

The purpose of the campaign milestone reviews is to give senior management control over major strategic decisions involving the marketing campaign and the expenditure of money to support it. The milestone reviews are not intended as tools for day-to-day or week-to-week management of the campaigns.

Marketing campaigns in the aerospace industry are complex undertakings that invariably involve unique factors and peculiar circumstances. Effective campaigns require knowledgeable management and coordination of diverse resources. Management of the effort is essential, and ultimately it is the front-line marketer who shoulders the greatest responsibility for managing the many factors that will determine the success or failure of the campaign. For this reason, aerospace marketers typically are aerospace professionals with prior management experience in disciplines such as engineering, manufacturing, subcontract management, business management, or program management.

Although aerospace is a technical industry, many aspects of the marketing process are based upon professional judgment and human instinct. Perhaps the most difficult aspect of effective management of aerospace marketing is arriving at a balance between, on one hand, enabling individual marketers to effectively use their personal judgment and, on the other hand, applying discipline and consistency to the process.

Table 13.3 Levels of marketing control

Type of Control	Primary Responsibility	Purpose of Control	Tools
Strategic control	Top Management	To examine whether the company is pursuing its best opportunities with respect to markets, products, and channels	• Marketing audit
Annual plan control	Top management, middle management	To examine whether the planned results are being achieved	• Sales analysis • Market-share analysis • Expense-to-sales ratios • Attitude tracking
Strategic component control	Middle management	To examine how well resources have been utilized in each element of the marketing strategy	• Expense ratios • Advertising effectiveness measures • Market potential • Contribution margin analysis
Profitability Control	Marketing controller	To examine where the company is making and losing money	Profitability by: • Product • Territory • Market segment • Trade channel • Order size

Note: Philip Kotler's classical depiction of levels of management controls applies reasonably well to the aerospace industry. Not all of his management tools are applicable.
Source: Philip Kotler (1984), *Marketing Management: Analysis, Planning and Control*, 5th ed., Prentice-Hall, Inc., Englewood Cliffs, NJ, p. 744.

Particularly in the case of marketing to international customers, which is often handled by solitary marketers out of sight of management, the company is, by necessity, compelled to rely on the judgment of the marketer. The marketer assesses the customers, gathers information from sources that he develops, selects agents and sales representatives, and develops personal relationships with representatives of the customers. There is no realistic way that a senior manager at company headquarters can effectively second-guess the day-to-day judgments of his marketer in the field. Either he has to trust the marketer's working judgments, within reasonable limits, or replace him. Appropriate management controls and milestone reviews will assure that senior management is given the prerogative to intervene whenever important decisions are made involving marketing budget, campaign strategies, pricing, or contractual commitments to customers.

Chapter 14

Protecting Sales Victories

Aerospace marketing campaigns are high-stress, high-stakes undertakings that require intensely concentrated energy over long periods of time. Everyone involved is focused on a single primary objective – to get the customer to select the product that the seller offers.

When the customer finally announces that a winner has been selected, there is a natural tendency for the successful marketing team to declare victory, open the champagne, and bask in the warm glow of appreciation and respect from their colleagues.

However, many aerospace companies have learned, to their chagrin, that the period following customer selection is a period of particular competitive vulnerability for the winner. The winner can be assured that, while he is enjoying the victory champagne, his competitors are making detailed plans to reverse the customer's selection decision and de-rail the program.

In fact, the sale is not entirely final until the product has been delivered and the money is in the bank. As we will see in Chapter 15, the aerospace contracting process is a long, time-consuming series of events, many of which must occur satisfactorily after the customer's selection has been made. If any of the events in this series are not successfully completed, the sale is subject to unravel. The tentative nature of the selection decision is further exacerbated by predictable actions by competitors to do everything they can to scuttle the original decision.

The history of the aerospace industry is rife with examples of major programs that have been lost by the declared winners of exhaustive competitions. We will examine a few noteworthy examples as we proceed through this chapter.

In the historical perspective of aerospace deals that have come apart after a selection decision has been made, we should recognize the true significance of the selection decision: it is a single milestone, albeit an important one, on the long and winding road to business acquisition, performance of obligations, and profitability.

In this context, the marketer and his colleagues in program management and functional departments should consider that the selection decision and subsequent contract signature are gateways that should lead to a continuous and orderly transition to the next phases of the program. Continuity is essential. In principle, the customer selected the product because he liked the offering that was presented. Obviously, he will want to be reasonably assured that the seller will fulfill the commitments contained in the offer. Nothing makes customers more nervous than to be abandoned immediately after selection by the marketers, who are sometimes replaced by seller's operational experts unknown to the buyer, who have no appreciation of the established relationships between the seller and the customer.

It is important to recognize that final signature on a formal contract does not ensure that the contract will be performed. Major aerospace contracts characteristically run for multiple years and involve large amounts of money. To protect both parties from unforeseen circumstances that might emerge during the period of performance, the contracts often include terms that permit the parties to unilaterally amend the contract or withdraw altogether. These provisions may entail specified penalty payments, forfeiture of advance payment, or bilateral negotiation of termination costs. Invariably, contracts include *force majeure* clauses, which protect both parties from damage claims if failure to perform is beyond the reasonable control of the non-performing party.

Because of the comparatively liberal escape clauses that typify many contracts, the seller is faced with the necessity of working closely and continuously with the customer throughout the period of performance of the contract, to enable the seller to anticipate the customer's problems well in advance, so that the seller can take joint action with the customer to reduce potential impact to the contract. This close cooperation over the life of the contract is part of the concept of relationship marketing discussed in Chapter 12.

Why do deals unravel? What are some of the most common reasons that deals do not hold together after they appear to be concluded? Let us look at some examples of problems that prevent conclusion of sales after the customer has made a selection decision.

Lack of Empowerment of One of the Parties

A surprisingly common reason for unconsummated aerospace deals is that one of the negotiating parties did not have genuine authority to make a commitment. Sometimes, in perfectly good faith, putative buyers engage with sellers and advance through the entire contracting process, only to discover that they ultimately do not have authority to spend the money they had intended to use for the purchase.

In China in the 1990s, a weakened Chinese central government was struggling to maintain administrative control over provincial governments that wanted to increase their autonomy, and regional airlines and aerospace firms attempted to make major business decisions without involving the Beijing bureaucracy that had historically approved such decisions. On some occasions, independent regional entities were able to successfully establish themselves and make major purchases and program commitments. In other cases, the breakaway attempts failed, as the regional entities discovered that they needed central government financial support or administrative approvals. During this period, stories abounded of Western aerospace firms that had laboriously concluded business negotiations with Chinese interlocutors in the provinces, only to learn eventually that the provincial firms were unable to obtain complete authority to make final commitments for the deals they had negotiated.

Similar issues arise within private entities. Executives of corporate business units occasionally make tentative purchase commitments that are subsequently repudiated when corporate officers determine that the commitments overstep the delegated authority of the individual who made the engagement.

In such cases, the best outcome the seller can hope for is that the purchase decision made by the unempowered buyer will be eventually approved and ratified by someone with legitimate authority to make a legal engagement. However, the actions by the unempowered buyer are likely to unleash internal rivalries and turf wars within the buyer's organization, and the legitimate authority is likely to repudiate the initial deal in order to exert his power and express his dissatisfaction with the attempt to usurp his responsibilities.

Example

In the late 1990s, Indian Airlines (IA) launched a major program to replace the old aircraft in its operating fleet with newer models. The company created an expert committee to solicit offers from Boeing and Airbus, to evaluate the technical proposals, negotiate pricing, and make a selection recommendation. The expert committee eventually recommended that IA buy a total of 42 new aircraft from Airbus, including 20 Airbus 321s, 19 Airbus 319s and four Airbus 320s. In 2002 the board of directors of Indian Airlines approved the recommendation of the expert committee, and notified Airbus of their intent to buy. Because Indian Airlines was a government-owned company, the board forwarded its recommendation to the Ministry of Civil Aviation, which also approved the purchase. As required by the notoriously burdensome Indian government bureaucracy, the Ministry of Aviation then forwarded the request to the Public Investment Board (PIB) for further approval. While the purchase request was under review by the PIB, national elections took place in 2004, a new parliamentary majority was elected, and the prime minister and his entire cabinet were replaced. Meanwhile, Boeing had submitted a new offer to Indian Airlines, at a price significantly lower than the original negotiated price for the Airbus planes. Taking pains to avoid any appearance of mismanagement or financial malfeasance, the new government then referred the aircraft purchase file to the Central Vigilance Commission (CVC), the Indian government watchdog agency with overall authority for identifying and preventing corruption and financial abuses. The effect of this action was to assure that the entire procurement process be returned to its initial starting point of inviting new proposals from the two competitors. In retrospect, a fundamental characteristic of the Indian Airlines procurement process was that commitment authority was not clearly assigned, and no single individual or organization was given final responsibility for the purchase decision.

Seller Bungles Execution

The contract is an agreement that commits both sides to perform, and the buyer has every right to expect that the seller will honor his obligations. If the seller does not perform to the buyer's expectations, the buyer's confidence in the business deal may be shaken to the extent that he seeks to end it.

The early days of an agreement, including the period between agreement in principle and a signed contract, are a period of particular vulnerability. The buyer, in the initial phase of engaging in a major financial commitment, will be understandably nervous. He will be sensitive to any signs that the agreement is going to turn sour or present problems during the implementation phase. Any indication that the seller is going to be difficult to work with or fail to perform commitments will cause the buyer to start thinking immediately of escape strategies before the contractual commitments become irrevocable.

Later, well into the implementation phase of the contract, cancellation of the agreement is messier, but most contracts offer the buyer a legal basis to discontinue the contract if the seller materially fails to perform. Even if an abrupt termination does not take place, many contracts are written so that the buyer is given a series of decision points as the contract progresses, in which the customer can elect to move to the next phase or end the agreement.

Example

In September 1987, the US Navy released a final Request for Proposal (RFP) for a marine patrol aircraft to replace the aging Lockheed P-3. Proposals were submitted by Lockheed, Boeing, and McDonnell Douglas. In October 1988, the Navy selected Lockheed as the winner of the competition. Lockheed's proposal was significantly lower in cost than proposals submitted by Boeing and McDonnell Douglas. It was also judged to be technically superior, with a less risky technical approach.

On 4 January 1989, the Defense Acquisition Board (DAB) recommended full-scale development of the program. The next day, the Navy awarded a fixed-price incentive contract to Lockheed to design, develop, fabricate, assemble, and test two prototype aircraft, designated the P-7A. The contract had a target cost of $600 million and a ceiling price of about $750 million. In March 1989, the Navy estimated acquisition of the planned 125 P-7A aircraft to be about $7.9 billion. Of this total, development cost was estimated at $915 million. Procurement of each production version aircraft was estimated at about $56.7 million.

In November 1989, Lockheed announced a $300-million cost overrun in its development contract, due primarily to schedule and design problems. In the following months, Navy and Lockheed officials held extensive but unsuccessful discussions in an attempt to address the contract issues.

By letter dated 20 July 1990, the Navy terminated the P-7A development contract for default, citing Lockheed's inability to make adequate progress toward completion of all contract phases.

Competitors and Enemies Undermine Decision

Competitors do not suddenly disappear after signature of the sales contract. They will remain active, taking every opportunity to convince the buyer to re-think his purchase decision. Allies of the competitor in industry and government will remain alert for problems that can be used to shake the customer's confidence in his purchase decision.

Particularly in the case of large government aerospace programs, where the approval process tends to be lengthy and where much public scrutiny is focused on the deal, losing competitors tend to organize very aggressive campaigns to discredit and de-rail the original selection decision.

Example

In May 2004, several months before a planned contract signature by the Czech Government to lease 14 Swedish Gripen fighter aircraft, news reports began to circulate in the Swedish press that the Gripen had serious operational shortcomings and would not be compatible with other NATO aircraft. Among problems cited in the reports were that the Gripen could not carry the AMRAAM medium-range missile, and would not be equipped with NATO-compatible IFF (Identify Friend or Foe) systems.

Earlier, a diplomatic row had erupted when the Swedish ambassador in Prague accused local US embassy staff members of providing Czech legislators with 'false and misleading information' about the Gripen fighter, including claims that the Gripen was not fully NATO-compatible.

In the original competition that had resulted in the Czech selection of the Gripen, unsuccessful bids for second-hand F-16 aircraft had been submitted by Belgium, the Netherlands, and the United States. Canada also submitted a bid for surplus aircraft.

When the anti-Gripen news reports surfaced in May 2004, a Czech Defense Ministry spokesman commented that a publicity campaign against the aircraft had been expected, and he speculated that one of the four losing bidders was behind the campaign.

Competitors Make Better Late Offer

Despite the announcement of a 'final' selection decision, experienced competitors recognize that the competition is not truly resolved at that point. The runners-up often have nothing to lose by submitting new sweetened offers to attempt to reopen the competition. If the buyer is not irrevocably bound by his initial selection decision, he may welcome the new offer, and may use it as a tool to elicit an improved offer from the original winner. If the original winner is unwilling to match the losing competitor's new offer, the customer may withdraw from his tentative commitments to buy.

Competitors who do not succeed in the initial competition sometimes become remorseful or desperate after their loss, and, faced with the prospect of loss of the business, abruptly become much more aggressive in offering pricing and terms attractive to the customer.

Example

In the 1980s the Indian Air Force (IAF) initiated a program to acquire a new jet trainer to replace its mixed fleet of obsolete trainers. In 1995, the IAF announced a decision to buy a quantity of 66 Hawk 100 aircraft from British Aerospace. Pricing negotiations between the parties began, and continued for more than seven years. Eventually BAe fixed a firm sales price of $21 million, while the Indian Government continued to demand a maximum price of $18 million. In 2002 the Ministry of Defence reluctantly accepted BAe's price, and requested final approval for the purchase from the cabinet. For two years the cabinet studied the acquisition request without acting on it.

During the period that the Hawk 100 procurement was under study by the Indian cabinet, a number of overseas defense companies offered competing advanced jet trainers at lower prices. Aero Vodochody of the Czech Republic offered its L-159B trainer at about half the price of the Hawk. Embraer of Brazil pushed its AMX-T trainer. Alenia Aeronautica of Italy resubmitted a proposal for its M 346 trainer, and Lockheed Martin proposed its T-50 advanced jet trainer built in cooperation with Korean industry.

To add further turmoil to the approval process, India's domestic manufacturer Hindustan Aeronautics Limited (HAL) proposed that it develop an indigenous advanced jet trainer at a price of $13 million each. HAL proposed to develop a single flying prototype at a price of $150 million, to be delivered in 30 months following go-ahead from the government.

In June 2003, Defense Minister George Fernandes announced that government action on the jet trainer procurement would be delayed by two to five years while the more recent competitive offers were evaluated.

Requirements Change

In the aerospace industry, years pass between a customer's identification of a requirement and delivery of the product. During that interval, the customer's requirements can change at any time. Airlines may enter new geographic sectors, or military customers may discover that they are dealing with new threats. If the product on order does not correspond to the customer's new requirements, he may attempt to end the order.

Example

Throughout much of the 1990s, Atlantic Coast Airlines (ACA) had operated turboprops and commuter jets as a feeder airline under contract to United Airlines. By 2003, more than 80 per cent of ACA's business involved operating feeder lines to provide traffic for United's larger transport aircraft. However, in December 2002 United Airlines declared bankruptcy. As it continued to operate under Chapter 11, management attempted to drive down contractual rates for feeder airlines such as Atlantic Coast Airlines. The new financial terms were unattractive to ACA management, who announced in July 2003 that they would discontinue their business relationship with United. ACA management announced a new business plan in which the airline would discontinue its historical emphasis on feeder operations and would begin to operate larger aircraft on longer routes.

As part of its new business plan, ACA notified Bombardier that it would terminate an outstanding order for 34 regional jets scheduled for delivery between 2004 and 2006. The regional jets were to be replaced by larger aircraft to be purchased from either Boeing or Airbus. The total value of the cancelled orders was estimated to be $1.08 billion. ACA noted that the terms of its purchase contract with Bombardier included an escape clause that permitted ACA to cancel aircraft orders if its business relationship with United ended for any reason.

Environment Changes

Changes in the broader environment can occur rapidly and with enormous impact. Terrorist attacks in the United States in 2001 had the overnight effect of drastically curtailing international air travel, with the collateral effect of causing widespread cancellation of purchases of civil transport aircraft that had been ordered earlier in anticipation of air travel growth. The end of the Cold War in the early 1990s resulted in cut-backs for certain types of military aircraft. Regulatory changes, such as international noise-abatement agreements, can result in abrupt lack of market interest in certain types of aircraft that do not comply.

Example

As a result of the precipitous drop-off in air travel following the September 11 terrorist attacks in 2001, American Airlines deferred 35 aircraft deliveries scheduled for 2002, and, according to a press release by the company on 13 August of that year, 'will seek every opportunity to defer or cancel new deliveries going forward'. By mid-2002, American had cut its fleet types from 14 to seven, and planned to immediately retire its 74-jet Fokker 100 fleet and nine Boeing 767s it had recently acquired from TWA.

Financial Problems

Except in cash sales to private individuals, virtually every significant purchase decision in the aerospace industry requires some kind of financial authorization by an entity independent of the buyer. In government and industry, normal internal financial controls dictate that the financial controller be distinct from the purchasing entity. Third parties are also commonly involved if outside financing through a bank or other financial institution is involved.

Failure to successfully negotiate the financial approval process is the cause of many unraveled deals. In many corporations and government agencies, the spending process involves at least four separate approval steps: *budgeting*, in which funds are set aside for a purchase; *authorization*, in which permission to proceed with the purchase is given; *commitment*, in which the budgeted funds are explicitly earmarked for the purchase; and *obligation*, in which a formal commitment is made to pay the funds to the seller. In each of these successive steps, there exists some risk that approval to move ahead will not be granted. Commitment and obligation of funding normally occurs following the source selection decision. If financial managers refuse to approve commitment or authorization, the designated winner of the competition will see his sales prospect evaporate.

Even after financial arrangements are in place and a contract is signed, customer financial issues can result in cancellation of the order, with appropriate termination costs to be paid to the seller. Because several years elapse between contract signature and delivery of aircraft, financial circumstances of the customer are apt to change significantly during the interval. When aircraft programs entail design and development as well as production, which is often the case with government military programs, the time interval is substantially longer, and therefore more subject to changes in financial circumstances and priorities of the buyer.

Example

On 9 December 1998 Trans World Airlines (TWA) became the third customer to order the Boeing 717 (designated the MD95 prior to the Boeing acquisition of McDonnell Douglas) when it placed an order for 50 firm aircraft with options for an additional 50 aircraft. The first aircraft was delivered on 17 February 2000. However, the financial situation of TWA, which had experienced a decade of financial turmoil, including bankruptcies and reorganizations in 1992 and 1995, continued to deteriorate, and in April 2001 TWA was bought by American Airlines. American management determined that the 717 did not fit in with future fleet plans of the combined airline, and announced that they would accept delivery of only 30 aircraft of the original 50 firm orders and cancel the 50 options.

Lack of Approval by Higher Authorities

The person or entity doing the purchasing within the customer's organization must obtain internal ratification for whatever purchasing decision is made. In corporations, this approval may be required by the CEO or board of directors. In government purchases, approval by a designated minister or by parliament may be necessary.

Even though the prchasing team and program manager may have been authorized to select a product and to negotiate a purchase contract, these selection and negotiation decisions are always subject to review and approval at higher levels. If approval is not forthcoming during this review process, the selection decision will not be formally ratified and the sale will not take place.

Example

In April 2003, Indonesian President Megawati Sukarnoputri signed an agreement with President Vladimir Putin during a visit to Russia to purchase four Sukhoi Su-30 fighters and two Rosvertol Mi-35 helicopters for an announced price of $197 million. The following month, an official Indonesian parliamentary commission demanded that the agreement be repudiated. According to the commission, Megawati did not have legal authority to sign the deal. According to the commission, Megawati had signed the contract based solely upon the recommendation of the Minister of Trade, whereas Indonesian laws required that purchases of defense articles be reviewed and approved by the Minister of Defense. Further, the commission concluded that the commitment was invalid because the expenditure had not been approved by the parliamentary budgetary committee, as legally required.

Upheaval in the Customer Organization or Political Scene

Sometimes the nature of the customer changes during the period that the deal is being developed. Management changes occur, strategic emphasis changes, and people are reassigned to new jobs. The seller can discover that the organizational unit that represented his customer has ceased to exist, or is populated by unfamiliar people in new jobs.

Because of their complexity and value, large aerospace purchases sometimes become the subject of controversy during political and corporate infighting. Challengers to incumbent decision-makers sometimes attack major purchase decisions as examples of poor financial management by the incumbents, and promise to reverse the decisions if a new management team or political party is given control.

Under such circumstances, cancellation of the program assumes the stature of a campaign promise by the insurgents, and, regardless of the inherent merits of the program, the seller is faced with an uphill struggle to protect it against emotional political attacks.

Example

In the early 1990s, the Canadian Defense Ministry of the Tory government of the period conducted an exhaustive selection process for a search and rescue helicopter to replace Sikorsky Sea Kings that had been in service for 30 years. In 1992, the Tories announced they would spend $4.8 billion to buy 50 EH-101 helicopters from the Anglo-Italian consortium European Helicopter Industries Ltd. The selection decision was followed immediately by the 1993 federal election campaign, in which Jean Chretien and other Liberal candidates attacked the Tory plan as wasteful, calling the EH-101 a 'Cadillac' helicopter. When the Liberals won and Chretien became prime minister, one of his first acts was to scrap the Tory deal, an act that cost the Canadian Government nearly $500 million in cancellation fees.

International Diplomatic Strong-arm Action

Sometimes selection decisions are overruled by domestic political authorities because of international diplomatic pressure brought to bear by important international allies. Aerospace competitions in which the buyer is an agency of the national government are particularly susceptible to influence of this sort. If the government of the losing competitor has an important strategic relationship with the government of the buyer, and if the competitor's government is willing to bring its influence to bear on the buying government, the selection decision may be reversed.

Example

In 1999, El Al, the Israeli national airline, made a preliminary announcement of a decision to buy a mixture of Boeing 777 and Airbus A330 aircraft as replacements for the airline's aging fleet of Boeing 747s. The competition for the sale had been particularly severe, as Airbus had sensed an opportunity to penetrate Boeing's exclusive historical relationship with El Al. Airbus' senior marketing executive had personally accompanied an A330 to Israel for flight demonstrations, and Airbus price concessions were reportedly extremely aggressive.

Release of news of the El Al purchase decision occurred in the midst of Middle East peace discussions that entailed an American commitment to provide $4 billion of annual financial aid to Israel. Upon learning of the El Al decision, US Secretary of State Madeleine Albright personally intervened, declaring, 'Our relations are excellent but there is a serious problem here.' Her concern was amplified by the official State Department spokesman, who commented, 'It would be extremely difficult for the American people to understand why Israel's official airline would look elsewhere and make a difficult task even more difficult.' The American Government continued to coerce their Israeli counterparts at a senior level until an order for Boeing aircraft was eventually signed in late 1999. The Airbus order was indefinitely postponed. Eventually El Al let the Airbus offer lapse and bought additional Boeing aircraft.

Export Licenses

Particularly when military products are involved, failure to obtain necessary export licenses is a potential deal-breaker. The subject of government export controls and licenses is addressed in Chapter 16 of this book. Under normal circumstances, the marketer should have obtained preliminary notification of exportability before the sale is consummated, but frequently technical details of the export raise export control issues. If the export license is not forthcoming, the sale cannot legally be made. Problems of this sort arise most frequently when the technology is particularly sensitive or when the buyer is politically controversial. Sometimes, however, changes in political relationships between the buying and selling countries cause export licenses to be denied after preliminary approval has been granted.

Example

In January 1989, a lengthy sales campaign by Boeing Helicopters culminated in a signed order by the People's Republic of China to buy six Boeing CH-47 Chinook heavy helicopters. The Chinese Government paid Boeing a down payment of $30 million. Prior to the order, Boeing had obtained US Government export licenses to market the Chinook in China and to provide the People's Liberation Army with technical information relating to the aircraft.

In June 1989, the Chinese Government suppressed the Tiananmen Square protests in Beijing, and the US Government responded by re-evaluating all aspects of its official relationship with China. As part of this re-evaluation, the US Congress passed legislation prohibiting most exports of defense equipment to China. As a result of this legislation, the US State Department denied Boeing's pending request for a final license to export the helicopter to China. Boeing refunded the $30 million down payment to the Chinese customer.

Irreconcilable Business Differences

After the selection decision, the parties work together to resolve all the detailed business issues that must be reconciled as part of writing the contract that will formalize the deal. Sometimes, the parties are simply unable to reach agreement on aspects of pivotal importance. Pricing is the most common irreconcilable issue. Others may be legal liability, delivery schedules, liquidated damages, performance bonds, control of intellectual property, or virtually any other element of the contract.

Example

In early 2004, the Turkish Government announced that its contract negotiations with Bell Helicopter Textron for a purchase of AH-1Z attack helicopters had broken down, and that the Turkish Ministry of Defense would begin contract negotiations with a Russian-Israeli industrial team that had earlier submitted a proposal for a competing helicopter based on the Kamov Ka-50 attack helicopter. The AH-1Z helicopter had been selected following an extended competition among a group of international competitors. During this competition, the Ka-50 variant and the AH-1Z had been short-listed as the two finalists before the ultimate selection of the AH-1Z as the winner.

At the time of the announcement that negotiations with Bell had broken down, the Turks declared that irreconcilable differences involved price, aircraft configuration, and conditions of industrial offset.

International Political Re-alignments

Large aerospace deals are financially important and often have special symbolic significance. Consequently, the programs are vulnerable if the vagaries of international affairs cause government-to-government relations between the buyer and the seller to suffer.

Example

In the 1980s, General Dynamics sold F-16s to Pakistan with the support of the US Government, which viewed Pakistan as an important element of military resistance again the Soviet occupation of Afghanistan. Later, in the 1990s, after the Soviets had withdrawn from Afghanistan, the US Government considered Pakistan to have less strategic importance as an ally. Displeased with apparent Pakistani development of nuclear weapons, the Americans ordered termination of the ongoing F-16 contract, and General Dynamics was compelled to abruptly stop deliveries.

Scandals Undermine the Credibility of the Decision-makers or the Process

Because of the inherent risk and controversy involved in major financial commitments to purchase aircraft, such purchases require the strong support and endorsement of influential backers such as senior executives, stockholders, government officials, and politicians. Public figures and industry leaders absolutely do not want to be embroiled in scandals. As soon as evidence arises that the decision-making process has been tainted by dishonest or improper behavior, the level of support for the transaction will drop precipitously as former sponsors flee from any further association with the project. This diminution of support frequently results in cancellation or termination of the planned acquisition.

Example

In November 2003, President Bush signed a defense authorization bill, approved by Congress, that provided an outline of a plan for the US Air Force to obtain 100 air-to-air refueling tankers from Boeing. Under the terms of the plan, which was criticized by some observers as corporate welfare for Boeing, the initial 20 tankers would be leased and the remaining 80 would be purchased outright.

On the day that President Bush signed the bill, Boeing announced the firing of its chief financial officer and another Boeing executive, a former US Air Force official involved in the tanker negotiations who later went to work for Boeing. The reason for the firing was that Boeing and the government had uncovered evidence that Boeing had illegally extended a job offer to the government official, during the period that the official was actively involved in negotiations with Boeing on the tanker deal.

The illegal arrangement between Boeing and the government official became the subject of extensive investigations by Congress and by government attorneys. The Secretary of Defense announced that the purchase would be suspended until the conclusions of the investigations became known. Resistance to the acquisition developed in Congress, and the transaction was indefinitely postponed. The two Boeing executives later were convicted of violations of Federal law and served prison terms.

Keep-It-Sold Planning

Every sales transaction is at risk until the product is delivered and the money is in the bank. In order to minimize the possibility of reversal of a customer's purchase decision, the seller should, as part of his overall marketing strategy, have a well-defined plan for protecting the sale. Because so many diverse factors can threaten the sale, the specific nature of the plan will depend upon prevailing circumstances, but a typical plan will consist of the following principal elements.

1. Maintain continuity while making the transition to the implementation phase. The seller's marketing team has been working with the customer throughout the customer's selection process, and these team members have developed meaningful relationships with the customer. The fact that the seller's team was victorious in the selection process indicates that the buyer probably trusts and respects the team members. The team members collectively understand the nuances of the customer requirements and know the evolution of the agreements that developed into the selection decision.

Do not abruptly replace the marketing team with a group of new people with responsibility for execution of the purchase agreement. Make sure that the customer continues to deal with familiar personalities, and progressively introduce new people as part of an orderly transition to the implementation phase. Protect the relationships between the buyer and the seller, and ensure that the new implementers have an appreciation of the nuances and importance of these relationships.

At the same time, it is essential for the customer to see visible signs that the program has passed from the marketing phase to the implementation phase. The customer will expect to see responsibility for successful implementation transfer to a knowledgeable program manager. The act of effecting this transfer is a critical but delicate process.

2. Map a detailed action plan to get to final contractual signature and down payment. Every phase in an aircraft program, including the customer's competitive selection decision, is merely an interim activity that leads to the next phase. As individual phases end, the seller must establish specific, detailed plans for successfully advancing to the next phase.

In the period leading up to the selection decision, identify the critical steps that will be necessary to move to formal contract signature and down payment, develop strategies for accomplishing those steps, and assign responsibility for execution. The nature of the steps will vary according to characteristics of the individual program, but will generally include formalities such as reaching agreement on contractual language, defining technical configuration, arranging financing and payment terms, negotiating price, establishing delivery schedules, and obtaining government export approvals.

If you are the prime contractor, remember that the survival of the program depends upon the successful performance of your subcontractors. Make sure that the critical activities and milestones of subcontractors are included in the comprehensive plan for concluding the contract.

In many aircraft programs, customers prefer to contract separately for engines, aircraft interiors, major avionics systems, and so on. The equipment items are then furnished to the prime contractor as *buyer furnished equipment*. Although the prime contractor has no formal responsibility for such equipment, serious problems caused by these equipment suppliers can place the overall program in jeopardy. The overall system prime contractor should maintain close communication with all associate contractors on the program and should attempt to work with them and the customer to resolve issues before they become harmful to the program.

3. Do not make early mistakes in execution. Buyer's remorse is a well-known reality of purchase decisions. Do not contribute to the seller's self-doubt about the decision by establishing an early pattern of failing to meet commitments. The seller should make a special effort to ensure that he accomplishes credibly his early commitments and milestones, thereby building customer confidence that the deal will work out as planned.

Unfortunately, initial phases of execution are particularly vulnerable to missteps by the seller, who is often in the midst of building a new implementation team and transferring management responsibility from Marketing to Program Management. In the warm glow of self-congratulation that follows a sales victory, there is sometimes a tendency to forget momentarily that the sales agreement contains a long list of promises that the seller is obligated to keep. Failure to honor these promises in the early days can cause the buyer to re-evaluate his entire selection decision. Strive to avoid any actions that will invite customer criticism. The period immediately after the selection or sales agreement is the worst possible time to announce schedule slips, price increases, or performance problems.

4. Open a visible office at the customer's location. Visible signs of the permanence of the relationship between the buyer and the seller are important. If the seller does not yet maintain an office at the customer location, an office should be opened and should be staffed by a person who has a relationship of trust with the customer. The existence of the office will facilitate communication and will be a visible symbol of the new customer relationship.

5. Be aware of likely spoiling strategies by your competitors, and plan specific counter-strategies to protect the program. Be prepared to deal with your competitor's onslaught after the selection decision is announced. It should be easy for the winning marketer to anticipate the spoiling strategy of his competitor. The winner knows what his program's weaknesses are, he is familiar with the behavior of his competitors, and he should anticipate that his victory will be attacked in the areas where it is most vulnerable. He should assume that the attacks will come, and he should develop specific strategies to forestall them.

6. Work quickly to finalize financial arrangements. Most failures of sales agreements are attributable to some form of financial problem. Make every effort to work with the customer to complete financial arrangements, even if the sales contract does not assign responsibility for financing to the seller. Recognize that the agreement cannot be consummated if the buyer is unable to align sufficient financial resources. At a minimum, the seller and the buyer should communicate frequently on an informal basis to discuss the status of the buyer's attempts to put together project financing, and the seller should be prepared to actively assist if the buyer encounters problems with the financial arrangements. In order to deal effectively with potential financial crises in the period following the sales agreement, it is essential that the seller have adequate information about the status of the buyer's financing.

7. Immediately start visible, concrete, work. Because of the nature of aerospace programs, the early phases are often the least dramatic. The manufacturer starts work on mundane tasks such as ordering long-led material, developing detailed planning schedules, revising engineering drawings, and so on. Because many of these tasks are not readily visible to the buyer, it is understandable that he may draw a false impression that the seller is not working to accomplish his commitments.

Look for ways to demonstrate to the customer that work is under way. Start work on aspects of the program that are visible to the customer, even if planning schedules indicate that these aspects should logically be performed at later dates. Arrange joint scheduling meetings with the customer's technical staff. Start preliminary customer training and familiarization meetings. Start engineering coordination meetings.

8. Provide regular formal status reports to the customer. To give the customer an understanding of the seller's internal activities to meet commitments, prepare regular status reports of internal program status, and present these reports to customer management in routine face-to-face meetings. An open flow of information will serve to dispel the buyer's doubts and suspicions about program status, and the buyer is more likely to feel involved in the seller's program activities if he has more information about them.

9. Broaden a support base by offering work to local industrial backers of losing competitors. In some competitions, individual industrial firms become closely aligned with specific competitors. Industrial allies of the losing competitors will continue to work against the selection decision after the fact, unless they are given some reason to support it.

Although the original industrial team of the winning competitor stands to enjoy the lion's share of industrial benefits, there is usually sufficient uncommitted industrial work available to offer meaningful consolation contracts to firms who supported the losing competitor. It serves no purpose to maintain an adversarial relationship with these firms. They are likely to retain significant political influence. It is worthwhile to attempt to find industrial roles for them so that they can be converted to industrial allies, or can at least be neutralized as political foes.

10. Attempt to replace the prevailing competitive climate with a more constructive atmosphere. Competitions can be bitter and can engender hard feeling among the parties involved. Once the selection decision has been made, it is in the seller's interest to replace the competitive stresses with a new mood of constructive cooperation with all the national parties that have an interest in the program. Try to be a gracious winner. A good start is to make contact with all disaffected parties, to listen to their concerns, and to try to convince them that you are genuinely interested in establishing a long-term relationship and will seek ways to work together in the future.

In the case of government contracts, it is particularly important to attempt to gain the allegiance of politicians who formerly supported the losing competitor. It is always a good idea to make courtesy visits to their offices to listen to their concerns and to attempt to agree on conciliatory gestures that can be made to encourage them to accept the selection decision.

11. Consider renegotiating the terms of the sales agreement if it appears that the sale will be lost otherwise. If the buyer is truly unhappy with the terms of his initial agreement, and if no ironclad contract prevents him from withdrawing from the initial agreement, the deal is probably doomed unless the buyer and the seller renegotiate the terms of the original understanding.

Renegotiation of the agreement is a nothing-to-lose strategy based on the assessment that the deal will be lost otherwise. This assessment should be made with caution. Many customers will continue to attempt to improve the conditions of the sales agreement after a handshake has occurred, and even after a signed contract is in place. Although the threat of cancellation may be a bluff, it is generally unlikely that a serious customer would make a direct threat to cancel unless he is genuinely dissatisfied with the terms. A well-informed marketer with intimate knowledge of the customer should be able to make an accurate judgment concerning the true degree of customer dissatisfaction.

12. If government sales are involved, maintain relationships with out-of-power political minorities, to the extent that this can be done without alienating incumbents. Newly elected governments like to repudiate decisions of their predecessors.

Sometimes political wrangling is so vociferous that the unfortunate contractor is realistically powerless to influence public decisions of politicians. However, if a change of government is anticipated soon after the selection decision, it is often worth a try to establish informal relationships with influential members of the opposition party. In theory, the new government may be induced to retain the program if they believe that the contractor's conciliatory attitude may permit a restructuring of the objectionable aspects of the deal.

In cases where program cancellation has become a campaign promise, consider action after the election to visibly create the illusion of improvements to sales terms of the contract, in order to enable new office holders to justify retaining the program.

The Last Resort: a *Pis-Aller* Strategy

If cancellation is inevitable, make the best of it.

Reversals of purchase decisions and program cancellations are an unfortunate fact of life in the aerospace industry. Sometimes even the most well-conceived keep-it-sold plan cannot overcome unfavorable circumstances that create insurmountable obstacles.

Of course, a marketer should never consider abandonment of his program until every available rescue strategy has been tried. When, however, defeat appears inevitable, it behooves the seller to fashion a last-ditch strategy to salvage the best possible result he can get, unsatisfactory though it may be.

As with much of the technical terminology in the aerospace industry, this last ditch strategy has over time acquired a French name: *Pis-Aller* (pis aller [French]

n. 'go worst'; last resort; something done or accepted for lack of anything better; less desirable alternative.) English speakers seem to feel that the resonance of the expression is apt for the circumstance.

If the customer is absolutely going to cancel, a popular and often effective *pis-aller* strategy is to induce him to transfer the order to another of the seller's product lines. This strategy may be attractive to the buyer under some circumstances because it offers several interesting advantages. First, it gives him a way to negotiate out of a purchase agreement that he no longer wants. Secondly, if handled properly, it may present an opportunity for the buyer to avoid termination costs or other penalties. And thirdly, it may provide the buyer with a means of engaging in a new purchase agreement under favorable terms.

A representative example of an imaginative *pis-aller* strategy involved overtures by United Parcel Service (UPS) to extricate itself from a commitment to purchase a large quantity of Airbus A300-600 freighters. UPS had contracted with Airbus to purchase 90 of the aircraft, but by early 2004, after 35 units had been delivered, UPS concluded that the short-range aircraft no longer fit its requirements. UPS opened discussions with Airbus to cancel part of the order.

Airbus raised contractual obstacles to outright cancellation of the order. However, Airbus proposed to UPS an alternative of converting the A300 orders to a smaller number of long-range high-capacity A380 transports. The 2004 discussions occurred after the A380 launch but prior to first delivery of the aircraft, at a time when Airbus was particularly eager to book additional new sales for the aircraft. The Airbus proposition to UPS was that Airbus would be happy to accommodate the UPS desire to be relieved of their obligation to buy the full quantity of short-range A300s, if UPS would agree to convert some of the orders to long-range A380 purchases. UPS accepted the offer and became a major early A380 buyer.

The Perspective of the Opposing Competitor

As a winning competitor, it is useful to know how to protect the customer's decision in your favor. As a losing competitor, it is equally useful to know how to undermine the winner's success.

Many of the defensive measures of a keep-it-sold strategy can be reversed and used as a strategy by the losing competitor to unravel the winner's victory. If, for example, a winning competitor can benefit by cultivating minority politicians to support his position, a losing competitor can possibly undermine the winner by working to influence the same minority politicians in other directions. This two-edged nature is true of many of the risks and countermeasures outlined in this chapter. Understanding keep-it-sold dynamics is a tool you can use to your benefit whether you are the winner or the loser of the initial competition.

Chapter 15

The Commercial Contracting Process

In order to accommodate the international nature of the aerospace industry, standardized contracting processes are necessary. Standardization has been the evolutionary result of buyers and sellers gradually adapting to each other's processes to facilitate business relationships. Buyers and sellers of virtually every nationality are able to communicate in contractual terms and transact aerospace business relatively smoothly within the framework of these standard processes. Because of the historical dominance of the United States and the United Kingdom in aerospace, many of the business practices are derived from those countries.

To complete a sale, the marketer has to successfully navigate the contracting process. A general knowledge of the process is an indispensable prerequisite for any sales or marketing professional.

The contract is the legal instrument that consummates the sale. It is a signed legal agreement between the buyer and the seller that defines all pertinent conditions relating to the sale. A contract consists of an offer by the seller and an acceptance of that offer by the buyer.

To maintain necessary internal checks and balances, the seller's contracts department is usually a separate organizational entity from Marketing. Despite this separation, the two organizational entities work closely together in the overall business acquisition process.

To maintain control over legally binding commitments, corporations rigidly restrict authority to sign documents or otherwise enter into formal agreements on behalf of the company. In most cases this authority is limited to senior executives of the corporation or to contracts managers that are provided specific company warrants to sign documents. Except in the rare companies that combine the marketing and contracts departments, marketers never hold such warrants, and thus are not authorized to sign commitments on behalf of their companies. Such commitments include letters of intent, memoranda of agreement, memoranda of understanding, and other agreements that seem to be relatively harmless in nature.

It frequently happens that a marketer far from home on a customer visit will receive an enthusiastic reaction from the customer, who will suggest that they conclude the day's discussions by signing a brief memorandum of understanding to formalize their mutual interest in proceeding. Much as he might want to sign the document, the marketer should refrain from doing so until he can get an authorized contracts person to read the document and approve it. Any marketer who signs contractual documents without approval can predictably expect to incur the wrath of his company's contractual managers and legal staff. If you are compelled to sign something in order to maintain credibility with the customer, jointly prepare formal minutes to the meetings, label them as such, and make sure that nothing in the minutes can be interpreted as a commitment.

Table 15.1 Contractual obligation and signature authority

(millions of dollars)					
	Proposals			**Contracts or Modifications**	
JobTitle	**B&P or ROM Estimates**	**Cost Type Proposals**	**Fixed Price Type Proposals**	**Cost Type Contracts**	**Fixed Price Type Contracts**
Contracts Director	Unlimited	Unlimited	Unlimited	Unlimited	Unlimited
Business Unit General Manager	Unlimited	Unlimited	Unlimited	Unlimited	Unlimited
Contracts Manager	$100M	$50 M	$25 M	$50 M	$25 M
Contracts Administrator	$50 M	$25 M	$15 M	$25 M	$15 M

Note: Specific limitation on authority to commit the company is an essential element of management control. Only senior management should be authorized to make major financial commitments.

Although the written sales contract is the culmination of the marketing process, the contracts department should be involved throughout the entire marketing campaign. Ultimately Contracts will have to find a way to package the sales agreement into a document acceptable to the executives and lawyers of both parties. During the marketing process, issues will arise that eventually will have implications bearing upon the content of final contract. To avoid thorny contractual obstacles that may arise as the sales process is reaching conclusion, it is preferable to have the benefit of contractual advice throughout the entire marketing process. Serious credibility problems and customer irritation result if the selling company is unwilling or unable to provide contractual coverage for terms that the marketers have implicitly promised. To avoid disastrous communication disconnects between Marketing and Contracts, both departments are represented in the program capture team, chaired by Marketing, as described in Chapter 13 of this book, dealing with management of the sales process.

Reduced to its basic elements, the contracting process is straightforward and easy to understand. The customer identifies a requirement. Based on the requirement, he invites suppliers to submit offers to sell. The buyer meets with the suppliers to analyze the offers. The buyer selects a winning supplier and negotiates a contract with the seller. The contract becomes a binding legal document when it is signed by both parties.

In reality, the process is much more complex. Each of the major steps can have numerous subsidiary steps, and additional steps can be added by the buyer or the seller if circumstances warrant. The buyer, particularly in the case of private-sector enterprises, ultimately has the flexibility to make the process as simple or as complicated as he wants.

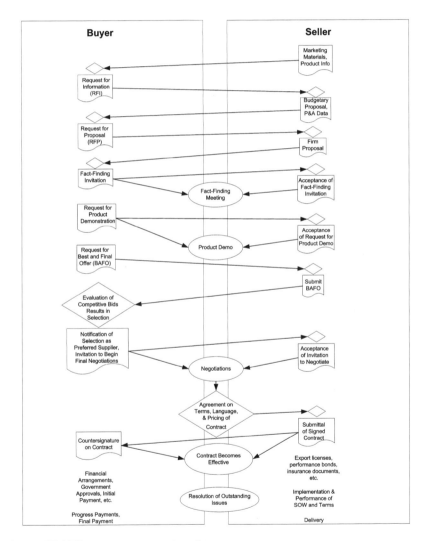

Figure 15.1 The aerospace contracting process
Note: Although aerospace contracts share many common processes, each contract is unique, and the process is often tailored to fit prevailing circumstances.

Recognizing that every aerospace contract reflects circumstances and developments that are unique in some ways, the following sequence describes typical contracting events and the activities associated with them.

1. *The customer issues a solicitation.*

As the marketing team has worked hard to develop a relationship with the customer and to provide the customer with detailed information about the product offered, hopefully the customer has considered the product information while requirements for new equipment have been prepared. The customer now wants to proceed to the preliminary phase of formally evaluating prices and performance of equipment available to satisfy the requirement.

REQUEST FOR INFORMATION
MEDIUM LIFT HELICOPTERS

1.	The Indian Air Force (IAF) is considering the acquisition of Medium Lift Helicopters in the 8-15 ton class along with simulators. The approximate number required is 80. The major requirements that have to be met are as follows:-

   a)	The Helicopter should be in the 8-15 ton class. The helicopter should be capable of all weather, day and night operations. The helicopters would be utilized in the troop transport, cargo helicopter, armed helicopter and utility helicopter roles.

   b)	The helicopter should be capable of carrying all contemporary weaponry that are fitted on helicopters including anti armour and air-to-air missiles.

   c)	The helicopter should be equipped with all required avionics and a comprehensive suite of sensors as determined by the role of the helicopter. It should also be equipped with a comprehensive self protection suite.

   d)	The helicopter should have high serviceability and the maintainability requirement should be minimum.

2.	In addition to the above, information regarding service ceiling, hover IGE, payload and max AUW at sea level may kindly be provided.

3.	In case your company is interested it is requested that ROM costs for working out the financial implications be indicated for the Govt. of India to make an assessment.

4.	You may send your replies to this office for onward submission to Air HQ, New Delhi, India.

Figure 15.2 Request for information
Note: An RFI can be a very general solicitation for information to enable preliminary planning and budgeting.

The customer has several alternative ways to request sales information from the seller. All of these diverse forms of request fall within the general terminology of *solicitation*.

- He can issue a document generally known as a *request for information*, or *RFI*, which generally requests non-binding preliminary data concerning prices, delivery schedules, and product performance. The RFI asks for preliminary selling data, but does not ask for a contractually binding offer to sell. If the buyer later wants to obtain a complete formal sales offer, he must request it from the seller. Usually the RFI is utilized when the customer wants to obtain planning and budgetary information prior to engaging in the actual purchasing process.
- If the purchase will involve a commodity item or a product with which the buyer already has technical familiarity, the purchaser may issue a *request for quotation*, or *RFQ*, which is sometimes nothing more than a request for a price.
- When the customer wants to purchase a complex aerospace product that entails broad program aspects such as training, logistics support, documentation, technical integration, and so on, a *request for proposal*, or *RFP*, is issued. Equivalent terminologies are the *request for tender*, or *RFT*, and the *invitation to tender*, or *ITT*. The requests specify the customer's essential needs, such as the number of aircraft required or the indispensable operational requirement, but give the seller considerable latitude to formulate a comprehensive program that he believes will best meet the customer's parameters.

The fundamental differences between a response to an RFI and a full-scale proposal are that the RFI response contains less detail and is generally not a contractually binding offer to sell. In theory, the pricing data provided in the RFI response is an approximate preliminary estimate. In fact, most sellers recognize that preliminary estimates sent to the customer will eventually have an effect upon final pricing negotiations, so the estimates are often prepared with the same precision and level of effort involved in formal proposals. This practice is sometimes a problem. Customers commonly utilize RFIs as a means of obtaining information quickly so that it can be used for planning and budgetary purposes. If the seller's process requires that even preliminary estimates must be the result of detailed cost build-up (generally requiring that quotes be obtained from second-tier suppliers), the estimating process takes a long time, potentially frustrating the customer's desire to complete the planning exercise quickly. On the other hand, if the seller produces quick rough estimates based upon data of questionable accuracy, he risks alienating the customer if the preliminary estimate turns out to be significantly different from the eventual formal proposal.

Although either an RFI or an RFP is normally the formal kick-off for contractual activities, sometimes the seller will proceed in the absence of a written request from the buyer. If the seller considers it important to provide the buyer with formal pricing data for the product, but if the buyer is not ready to issue a request, the seller has the option to offer an *unsolicited proposal*. More detail of the composition of proposals is below. The only significant difference between a conventional proposal and an unsolicited proposal is that the customer requests the former, whereas the latter is submitted at the seller's initiative.

2. *Formal face-to-face discussions between the buyer and suppliers occurs.*

When major contracts are at play, at some point prior to submission of the formal proposal the buyer and the competing suppliers meet to clarify the terms of the RFI or RFP. In the case of government purchases in industrialized countries with well-defined procurement systems, this meeting usually takes the form of a *bidders' conference* that is conducted within a framework of formal rules to ensure that all bidders are treated equally and are provided with exactly the same information. At the conference, a representative of the buyer will review the terms of the solicitation, and will publicly answer any questions posed by the audience of bidders.

In the case of non-governmental commercial sales that are less rigidly regulated, the buyer may elect to meet privately with competitors to explain the conditions of the solicitation.

3. *The seller makes the decision to bid or no-bid.*

Preparing a proposal or response to inquiries by the customer is expensive and consumes resources. Consequently, if the customer request is very unlikely to lead to a sale, the seller has the option of responding to the customer inquiry with a polite *no-bid* letter. This brief letter acknowledges receipt of the customer's inquiry and informs the customer that the seller does not intend to pursue the opportunity. No further explanation is necessary. Reasons for a no-bid decision may be that the customer is not considered to be qualified, that the required aircraft does not correspond with the seller's product line, that another competitor is considered to have an insurmountable advantage, or any number of other valid factors.

Receipt of an RFI or RFP from a serious customer should not come as a surprise. (If it does, it may indicate a significant breakdown in market intelligence in the relevant market.) In anticipation of the customer inquiry, the marketing department should obtain the necessary internal management approvals to authorize the expense and allocation of resources for preparation of the proposal or planning information. As described in Chapter 13 of this book, dedicated to management of the sales process, these approvals are usually the outcome of a formal campaign milestone review. In this case, the review would involve a request by Marketing to proceed to Phase C. Phase C includes development of a sales strategy, creation of an internal program capture team, internal formulation of a suitable program to offer to the customer, including an engineering element, a financial element, a product support element, an offset element, and so on.

4. *The seller manages internal resources to prepare information for the customer.*

Because the response to the customer inquiry will eventually be provided to the customer in a formal contractual document, the information must be prepared in accordance with approved processes, and must be appropriately reviewed and approved. To organize the effort of preparing the information, a proposal manager is appointed. This position is generally filled by a specialist within the marketing department who is dedicated to management of successive proposals for multiple customers. The proposal manager is responsible for ensuring that responsibility is assigned to all internal departments that will be required to contribute to the proposal. He defines the proposal tasks, establishes schedules for completion, and monitors interim status. The proposal manager is also responsible for overseeing the physical preparation of the proposal, including text editing, preparation of artwork and exhibits, and printing and binding.

Although the proposal manager performs the work of putting the proposal together, the definition of the proposal format and content is provided by others, primarily by the marketing campaign manager and by the contracts manager. The marketer, who is the customer expert, defines the format and elements of content that he believes will be most likely to sell the product. The contracts manager provides expert guidance concerning technical compliance with the contractual terms of the customer's request. The contracts department also has responsibility for ensuring that the language and content of the final proposal protect the seller's financial and legal interests.

Typically, the marketing campaign manager has advance notice that a solicitation from the customer is forthcoming. In preparation for receipt of the solicitation, he will convene a proposal management team consisting of representatives of all internal functional departments that will contribute to the proposal. At the first meeting of the proposal team, the proposal manager is designated. Assuming the content of the solicitation is known at this time, the solicitation is described and the basic outline of the proposal is defined. Responsibilities for input from individual departments are defined, and schedules for completion are established. An important purpose of the early team meetings is to allow informal give-and-take discussions among the team members to air different opinions and recommendations concerning the best ways to respond to the solicitation and to present the product most advantageously to the customer. The conclusions reached in these discussions become the basis for the proposal outline and the schedule of activities.

As soon as the formal RFI or RFP is received, the proposal team will undertake a systematic detailed analysis of the document. Paragraph by paragraph, the team will note the customer requirements contained in the document. Each of these requirements will be listed, and responsibility for preparing individual responses will be assigned to specific team members. As responses are submitted to the proposal manager by the team members, they are assigned paragraph numbers and are incorporated into the proposal document. This detailed list of data requirements and responses is known as a *compliance matrix*. It is a scorecard that tracks completion of all data items requested by the customer. In cases in which the seller cannot or does not want to supply specific elements of data requested by the customer, non-compliance is noted in the matrix. In addition to serving as a management tool for the proposal manager, the compliance matrix is also attached as part of the proposal to the customer, so that he can readily locate specific data within the overall document.

Table 15.2 A sample compliance matrix

RFP Pg #	RFP Sec #	RFP Requirement	Prop Sec #	Section Title
72	6.2	Proposal Documentations:		
		The proposal shall include:		
72		* Technical configuration/ specification document	6.2.1	Technical Configuration/ Specification Document
73		* Optional features listing/document	6.2.2	Optional Features Listing/Document
74		* Logistics support package	6.2.3	Logistics Support Package
76		* Separate commercial proposal	6.2.4	Commercial Proposal
78	6.3	Certifications:		
78		Aircraft must hold a current and valid Airworthiness Certificate.	6.3.1	Certifications
79		In addition, all Supplement Type Certificates (STC) for modified equipment, applicable ADs and Mandatory and Recommended Service Bulletins must be accomplished prior to the date of inspection and Technical Acceptance for the first aircraft.	6.3.2	Certifications, Supplemental
80		The manufacturer shall supply aircraft certification and documentations required to meet the registration requirements requested by Buyer.	6.3.4	Registration
81	6.4	Maintenance Inspection Program:		
83		The proposal should include a detailed manufacturer maintenance program.	6.4.1	Maintenance Inspection Program
85		It should also include a commitment for the development of a customized maintenance inspection program, if required, at no additional cost.	6.4.2	Maintenance Inspection Program
87	6.5	In-Service Technical and Logistical Support:		Maintenance Inspection Program
88		Bidders shall quote for a long term In-Service Technical and Logistical Support program.	6.5.1	Maintenance Inspection Program

5. The proposal is reviewed internally and approved for release.
When the work of compiling input for the proposal is complete, the content of the proposal is reviewed by senior management, including representatives of Program Management and all functional departments that will be involved in performance of an eventual contract. The rigorousness and level of detail of the management review will depend to some extent on the nature of the proposal. High value firm proposals for major programs will, of course, receive greater scrutiny than non-binding budgetary estimates for minor tasks.

The subject of management reviews of offerings to customers is discussed in detail in Chapter 13.

6. *The proposal is submitted to the customer.*

The manner of physical submission of the proposal depends upon circumstances surrounding the purchase. For minor purchases, the proposal is simply mailed or electronically transmitted to the customer. For major competitive purchases, the customer sometimes organizes formal ceremonies in which all competitors appear in person to officially present their proposals to a designated representative of the buyer.

A common practice is for the buyer to request or require that the proposal be submitted by a specific date, followed by an invitation to the seller to travel to the buyer to explain the proposal after the buyer's representatives have had sufficient time to perform an evaluation and analysis of the proposal. If the proposal is physically delivered by the seller to the buyer, it is not usually necessary to have a large team participate in the delivery, because the buyer will not be prepared for detailed discussions until he has had sufficient time to read and digest the proposal.

Every contractual offer should specify the period of its validity. Pricing information is perishable, and cannot normally be expected to remain valid without re-calculation for a period for more than six months. Remember that the total proposed price to the customer is based upon lower-tier proposals from subcontractors, and that the lower-tier proposals will also have expiration dates.

7. *A negotiating team is established, the fact-finding process begins.*

Generally the negotiating team consists of many of the same members who constituted the proposal team. Although the seller's team leader should be the member from the marketing department, the actual negotiations should be led by the representative from the contracts department.

After the customer has received the proposal, and as his specialists begin to study and evaluate it, they will inevitably have need of additional information and explanation of material in the proposal. The fact-finding process is intended to provide the clarification desired by the customer. Ideally, the customer will prepare a list of principal questions concerning the proposal, and will send the list to the seller in advance of the fact-finding meeting. The seller will then prepare requested explanations. As the fact-finding meeting takes place, discussions will prompt further questions from the seller.

Sometimes competitors are eliminated at the outset because their proposals are deemed by the customer to be *non-compliant*. A determination of non-compliance is to some extent based upon the subjective judgment of the customer. When competitors are responding to lengthy RFPs of a technically complex nature, it is highly probable that they will fail to respond appropriately to every detailed condition of the RFP. Customers tend to overlook minor instances of non-compliance, working under the assumption that the problems can be resolved during fact-finding or negotiations. In cases of gross non-compliance, however, where a competitor fails to comply with major elements of the RFP, the customer may exercise his right to dismiss the competitor from the competition.

Although theoretically fact-finding is not the same as negotiation, in fact all information and all statements provided by either side become part of the negotiation process. In order to justify and support their eventual negotiating positions, both sides will use any available fragments of information. Because the fact-finding process is a rich source of information, it can potentially have profound impact upon the outcome of the negotiations that occur later on.

Because of the wide-ranging nature of fact-finding discussions, it is unlikely that the seller's technical team will have with them sufficient reference material to answer all questions posed by the buyer team. To assure that questions can be answered promptly, each member of the seller's traveling team should have a designated support person at the seller's facility whose responsibility it is to obtain answers that are beyond the resources of the traveling team. For international fact-finding visits in different time zones, this means that the traveling team should expect to spend long hours in the evening or early morning in communication with their counterparts at home for the purpose of developing responses to customer questions.

8. *Product demonstration.* Sometimes, but not always, the customer will insist on a product demonstration, which sometimes will consist of full-fledged flight test programs. Such demonstrations can be expensive undertakings, particularly in the case of military aircraft that must be tested over a wide range of operational scenarios. In the case of competitive procurements, the customer normally defines a specific profile of performance characteristics that he wants to witness, and all competitors are asked to arrange identical demonstrations of these characteristics. The customer then scores the competing products based on their performance of the parameters.

9. *Best and final offer.* Following review and discussion of the initial proposal, competitors are usually invited to submit their *best and final offer*, or *BAFO*. This term is almost always a misnomer, because competitors often submit a succession of progressively more attractive BAFOs as the competition intensifies. In any case, competitors in major competitions are customarily given opportunities to submit revisions to their initial offers.

10. *Competitive selection.* The customer evaluation team generally has enough information to select a winner of the competition after the proposals have been reviewed, fact-finding has occurred, and a flight evaluation or product demonstration has taken place. Sometimes, especially when many competitors are involved, the customers will take the intermediate step of selecting a limited number of finalists for the competition, known as the *short list*. If a short list is selected, the customer then proceeds to a more rigorous evaluation to identify the overall winner.

The selection of the winner of the competition is conditional upon satisfactory completion of negotiations. In recognition of this conditional status, the winner is often declared to be the *preferred supplier*. If negotiations with the preferred supplier break down, the customer may return to other competitors to negotiate a satisfactory deal.

11. *Negotiations commence, proposal revisions occur, final language is agreed, contract is signed.* After the preferred supplier is identified, he is invited to begin negotiations. Almost always the central focus of negotiations is pricing, although it is likely that the parties will also have differences concerning other elements of the

RFP, notably payment terms, delivery schedules, technical factors, and any of the various terms and conditions.

Negotiating strategy and technique have themselves been the subject of much study, analysis, and folklore, and will not be studied in detail here. Individual companies and their negotiators have distinctive styles, and no single approach to negotiation is necessarily best under all circumstances. However, the lead negotiator should be given clearly defined objectives in advance. He should be given limits to his negotiating positions, and should have a well-defined process for requesting and obtaining management approval to change his negotiating limits if necessary.

At the completion of the successful negotiating process, which may involve multiple negotiating sessions and may require direct personal involvement by senior representatives from both sides, the lead negotiators initial an agreement between the parties. This agreement is prepared in final format, and is signed by officials designated by both parties to make binding contractual commitments on their behalf.

12. *Modalities (export license, bank guarantees, performance bonds, and so on) are completed.* The contract should provide very clear definition of the conditions that have to be met before the contract becomes effective. These conditions depend upon relevant circumstances, but generally include the requirement for the seller to obtain government export licenses, that financial arrangements be finalized, and that performance bonds, if required, be issued. In cases of major government purchases, legal approval by parliament or by the treasury is often required prior to expenditure of funds.

13. *Initial payment is made.* The single most significant event in the implementation of a new contract is the initial payment by the customer.

14. *The contract is implemented.* Once the necessary conditions for implementation of the contract are met, the seller's contracts department issues an internal *work authorization* notice within the company to notify other departments that the contract is officially in effect. The program office, which has primary authority for performing the terms of the contract and for spending the money necessary to do so, then issues a program directive, internally announcing the nature of the program and appointing a program manager. The program manager is given authority and control over budget for the program. Control of the budget is accomplished by establishing individual budgetary accounts and work orders for the specific tasks that are part of the program plan and program master schedule.

The contracts department has responsibility for formally communicating a list of contractual obligations to the program office, monitoring accomplishment of these obligations, and initiating action to collect payments as they become due from the customer.

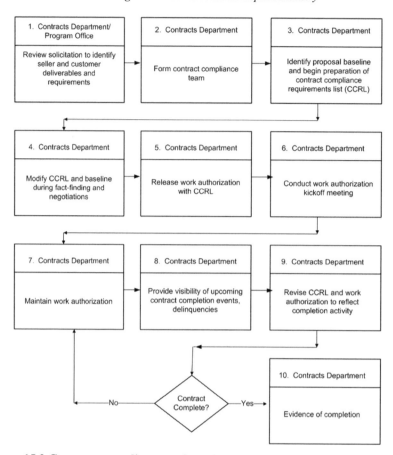

Figure 15.3 Contract compliance and work authorization process
Note: Marketing's primary responsibilities are met when the contract is signed, but Contracts and the program office take responsibility for ensuring that contractual requirements are met.

Content and Format of the Proposal

An RFP response, and even a smaller RFI response, is a sizable document when it involves a complex technical system such as an aircraft. The document contains numerous discrete sections, prepared by the seller's functional departments with responsibility for the subject matter. A major part of the proposal manager's job is to clearly assign responsibilities for input to the individual members of the proposal team, and to establish mandatory schedules for completion of tasks. When customers issue RFIs and RFPs, they invariably assign specific deadlines for submittals from competitors. Generally suppliers are disqualified from the competition if they miss the deadline. The period of proposal preparation is a stressful interval in which many people are working against short deadlines to prepare complex information that must be absolutely accurate, easy to understand, and professionally presented.

The specific nature of individual RFPs and RFIs depends upon a multitude of circumstances pertaining to the solicitation. Solicitations are used to buy virtually the full range of aerospace products, including complete aircraft, technical services, maintenance activities, or detail parts.

The proposal submitted by the seller should reflect the instructions contained in the buyer's solicitation. At one extreme, the buyer can request a single bottom line price for an off-the-shelf product. At the other extreme, the customer can request volumes of detailed data and supporting documents for comprehensive programs that involve equipment, R&D, training, and maintenance support.

1-AWD-005	Support Documentation for a Claim of Equivalent Safety	41
1-AWD-008	Type Certification Compliance Matrix (TCCM)	42
1-AWD-009	Airborne Electronic Subsystem Validation and Verification Summary	43
1-AWD-011	Airborne Electronic Subsystem Type Certification Summary	44
1-AWD-012	Type Certificate Data Sheet	45
1-AWD-013	Issue Papers	46
1-AWD-014	Certificate of Conformance	47
1-AWD-015	Flight Permit Documentation	48
1-AWD-017	MH Instructions for Continuing Airworthiness (ICA)	49
1-AWD-018	MH Flight Manual	50
1-AWD-019	Master Minimum Equipment List (MMEL)	51
1-AWD-026	MH Simulator Data Package	52
1-AWP-001	Airworthiness Program Plan (APP)	53
1-AWP-006	Type Certification Support Plan (TCSP)	54
1-AWP-007	Subsystem Type Certification Plan (STCP)	55
1-AWP-016	MH In-Service Support Plan	56
1-AWP-020	Plan for Hardware Aspects of Certification for Airborne Electronic Equipment (PHAC (AE))	57
1-AWP-023	Plan for Software Aspects of Certification (PSAC)	58
1-AWR-021	Hardware Accomplishment Summary for the Airborne Electronic Equipment (HAS (AE))	59
1-AWR-024	Software Accomplishment Summary	60
1-AWR-025	Subsystem Type Certification Report (STCR)	61
1-AWR-027	Airworthiness Standard Equivalence Justification Report	62
1-CMC-003	Engineering Release Record (ERR)	63
1-CMC-004	Engineering Change Proposal (ECP)	64
1-CMC-005	Request for Deviation (RFD)	65
1-CMC-006	Request for Waiver (RFW)	66
1-CMC-007	Notice of Revision (NOR)	67
1-CMD-002	Configuration Item and Documentation Recommendations (CIDR)	68
1-CMD-011	Configuration Management Data Summary	69
1-CMP-001	Configuration Management Plan	70
1-CMP-009	Configuration Audit Plans	71
1-CMR-008	Configuration Status Reports	72
1-CMR-010	Configuration Audit Reports	73
1-HSA-005	Human Engineering System Analysis Report (HESAR)	74
1-HSA-006	MH Critical Task Analysis Report (CTAR)	75
1-HSA-008	Human Engineering Design Approach Document - Operator (HEDAD-O)	76
1-HSA-009	Human Engineering Design Approach Document - Maintainer (HEDAD-M)	77
1-HSA-011	Preliminary Hazard Analysis (PHA)	78
1-HSA-012	Functional Hazard Assessment (FHA)	79
1-HSA-013	Preliminary System Safety Assessment (PSSA)	80
1-HSA-014	System Safety Assessment (SSA)	81
1-HSA-015	Operating and Support Hazard Analysis (O&SHA)	82
1-HSA-016	Health Hazard Assessment (HHA)	83
1-HSA-023	Workload Analysis Report	84

Figure 15.4 Request for proposal

Note: The customer's RFP defines the format of the seller's proposal. This example provides a highly structured format. This is a single page of a 668-page document.

For major aerospace proposals, the solicitation is likely to request information in the following primary categories, all of which are likely to be the subject of individual volumes submitted as part of the proposal:

Executive Summary

Because the proposal itself is often a massive document, a brief summary of a few pages is prepared to identify the most important aspects of the proposal. Because the summary is widely read by interested parties of all levels, it should be crafted with special attention so that it effectively conveys a perspective advantageous to the seller.

Technical Definition of the Product

The solicitation will require bidders to define their technical offerings in several ways. Certain physical characteristics are customarily specified by the customer, such as maximum gross weight, number of engines, interior volume, electrical power available, communications capabilities, and so on. In addition, the buyer may specify that the aircraft or product incorporate or conform to specific technical standards such as US MILSPECs, FAA airworthiness standards, ICAO noise standards, and material standards promulgated by international or national technical agencies. A comprehensive technical description of the aircraft, sometimes called an engineering statement of work, is invariably requested by the solicitation.

Required Operational Capabilities

In addition to physical technical characteristics of the product, the seller will also be requested to define his offering in terms of its performance capabilities, such as speed, fuel consumption, rates of climb, runway requirements, loading and unloading times, ballistic tolerance, and so on. Operational characteristics sometimes overlap post-delivery support considerations such as airframe service life, reliability of components, and corrosion resistance.

Most input for this section of the proposal is contributed by the Operations Analysis organization. The broad subject of operations analysis is the subject of Chapter 10 of this book.

Post-delivery Support

Because operational costs, including maintenance and spare parts, generally exceed purchase price over the lifetime of aircraft, the customer has a vital interest in understanding how the aircraft will be maintained. Modern aircraft are designed to be supported in accordance with specific maintenance concepts intended to reduce operating costs. The solicitation will request that the aircraft manufacturer describe the maintenance concept. The most common concept involves three levels of support:

- Flight-line maintenance for removal and replacement of light equipment such as avionics
- Intermediate maintenance, which involves back-shop repair of failed equipment, utilizing special test equipment and replacement of individual parts
- Depot maintenance, involving total overhaul and heavy maintenance of major equipment items such as engines or the aircraft structure.

PERFORMANCE AND TECHNICAL PARAMETERS FOR RFP: CHETAK/CHEETAH REPLACEMENT

Ser No	Parameter	Essential/ Desirable	Remarks	GSQR Para Ref
	Conditions of Use			For internal use
1.	Max All Up Weight must be below 3500 Kg.	Essential		7a
2.	Performance requirements to be in relation to Indian Reference Atmosphere (IRA).	Essential		8a
3.	Helicopter & its systems must be fully tropicalised and cleared to operate under following conditions:- <ul><li>Operate in temperature range of - 40 to + 50 ⁰ C. (Desirable + 55⁰ C).</li><li>Operate in relative humidity 85 % (desirable 100%).</li><li>Operate in saline environment without undue additional maintenance activity.</li></ul>	Essential		8b
4.	Must be cleared to operate from surface covered with snow, sleet, sand, dust, water & slush.	Essential		8 c i
5.	Must be capable of Landing and taking-off from upslope of up to 10 ⁰, down slope of up to 5 ⁰ and lateral slopes of up to 6⁰.	Essential		8 c ii
6.	Must be possible to carry the helicopter in IL-76 aircraft. Dismantling and preparation of the helicopter for transportation must be possible in 24 hrs. Similarly re-assembling the helicopter must be possible in 24 hrs.	Essential		8d i
7.	It is desirable to carry the helicopter in IL-76 aircraft by merely folding the blades.	Desirable		8 d ii
	Basic Design Feature			
8.	Must be of sturdy and robust design, capable of sustained operations from remote places with minimum of logistic and maintenance requirements.	Essential		9a i
9.	Must be easy to control & manoeuvre, to be able to fly 'nap-of-the-earth' missions, in plains as also in hilly terrain.	Essential		9a ii

Figure 15.5 RFP technical requirements
Note: This extract from an RFP depicts requirements for technical performance data for a helicopter competition.

This section will also describe ground support equipment and special test equipment required to operate the aircraft, incorporation of built-in test equipment, mandatory intervals between maintenance or overhaul of equipment, historical mean times between failure for equipment, reliability rates, and so on.

MIDN/DGAED *Public Tender no.2 DGAED/97*

PART II

LOGISTICAL ASPECTS

1. **Integrated Logistics Support (ILS)**

a. Description of stipulated ILS system .

2. **Mean Costs**

The mean costs can be calculated using the parameters indicated in 1.a. of the Logistical Requisites. Costs shall be submitted in U.S. dollars.

a. **Direct labour.**

Number of man-hours of direct labour per flight hour for maintenance levels O and I.

b. **Cost of consumable materials.**

Consumable material costs per flight hour.

c. **Reparable material cost.**

General service and repair costs of aircraft and the engine reparable items, per flight hour.

d. **Fuel cost**

Fuel cost per flight hour.

e. **Oil and lubricant cost**

Oil and lubricant cost per flight hour.

f. **Level D maintenance cost**

Aircraft and engine maintenance costs at level D, per flight hour.

The bidder shall present a detailed cost calculation method for this item including the figures used for labour costs per flight hour and mean fuel and oil cost.

3. **Documentation and data systems**

a. Indication of the documentation to be supplied in conjunction with the aircraft.

b. Supply the list of steps to be taken and the costs entailed to finalise the mid-air refuelling system installation.

DSCPCIE/DAPEC **204/232**

Figure 15.6 RFP product support requirements

Note: An example of RFP requirements for product support information.

Operational Cost Factors

This section will include a comprehensive summary of all costs projected for operation of the aircraft. Projected costs include salaries for flight crews and maintenance mechanics, fuel costs, spare parts, overhaul and heavy maintenance, and so on. Because some costs, such as salaries, will depend upon specific circumstances that apply to the operator, the solicitation will sometimes include instructions for competitors to use hypothetical data for some parts of the cost calculation formulas.

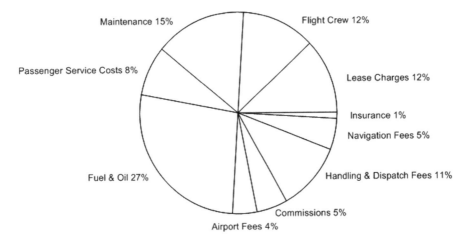

Figure 15.7 Airliner cost breakdown
Note: This cost breakdown is an average of data accumulated for a broad group of passenger transport aircraft. To comply with RFP requirements, sellers often provide analogous operational cost data that applies specifically to their own aircraft.
Source: International Civil Aviation Organization.

Program Management Plan

Particularly when military programs are involved, the customer will require competitors to show how the program will be managed by the supplier. To respond to this requirement, the competitors will propose program management plans that show what resources will be used to manage the program, how the resources will be organized, and how program management will be integrated into the supplier's other business activities.

At a minimum, the program management plan will describe the authority of the program manager and will depict his position in the seller's overall organization. The program management organization will be described and explained. The program management plan itself, and the explanation that accompanies it in the proposal, should be formulated with the specific purpose of providing assurance to the customer that the seller will put into place a management system that will ensure that the seller's contractual commitments will be met and that the execution of the program will be successful.

In addition to organizational structure, the program management plan describes other key elements of management of the program, such as management controls, financial controls, security management, quality assurance, procurement management, management of buyer-furnished property, production controls, configuration management, and so on.

Industrial Benefits Plan

Government customers for aerospace equipment generally require that foreign suppliers commit to provide industrial benefits for the domestic industry of the buyer. These arrangements, commonly referred to as offsets, were described in detail in Chapter 6.

Common practice is for national governments to publish written guidelines for offset commitments to which suppliers will be obligated. Competitors are expected to engage in discussions with local industry and to prepare a comprehensive plan for meeting the government's requirements. At the time of contract signature, the winning competitor will be required to make a contractual commitment to meet specific offset targets, with damages and penalties to be imposed in the event of failure to perform. Sometimes the government customer will prefer to handle the offset agreement in a document separate from the basic contract for sale of aerospace equipment. In this case, the basic sales contract may contain a stipulation that its validity is conditional upon the satisfactory execution of the companion offset agreement.

Price Proposal and Cost Data

A major part of any proposal is pricing information, and whatever price is originally proposed will be vigorously negotiated during discussions that follow initial submittal of the proposal.

Customers request pricing information in a wide variety of formats. In early requests for planning information, such as RFIs, customers may simply request a nominal unit price for an aircraft. This figure, traditionally called the *fly-away price*, is a price for the product itself, without any of the ancillaries such as training, documentation, spare parts, support equipment, and other elements required to operate aircraft. RFPs leading to negotiations of firm contracts typically request detailed pricing breakdown.

Price is important to all buyers, and they request pricing information in a format that will enable them to understand and analyze it. Even if the aircraft itself is offered at a standard catalogue price, the customer will want to see detailed itemized pricing for installed optional equipment and related equipment and services that go beyond the basic fly-away price.

ANNEX "A"
TO: PART III

Contract Line Item Number (CLIN)	Contract Line Item Description	Unit of Issue	Quantity	Unit Price	Extended Price
0017	Maintenance manuals, paper or IETM, (English), in accordance with the SOW.	Each	30	$_____	$_____
0018	Technical Publications Revision Service in accordance with the SOW.	Lot	1	$_____	$_____
0019	Interim Product Support Services, in accordance with the SOW.	Lot	1	$_____	$_____
0020	Interim Repair and Overhaul Program, in accordance with the SOW.	Lot	1	$_____	$_____
0021	Training, in accordance with the SOW.	Lot	1	$_____	$_____
0022	ILS-CDRLs in accordance with Section 5 of the SOW.	Lot	1	$_____	
0023	Royalty payments in accordance with Article 8.1.5 of the Contract.	Lot	1	$_____	$_____

GST $_____

TOTAL CONTACT PRICE $_____

pt(iii)a.fnl   18 November 1996   BB.M8475-7-IN301/000/A

4/4

Figure 15.8 RFP pricing template

Note: An example of a pricing template for the product support SOW in an RFP.

Major government customers in the United States and Europe often insist that major contracts be priced on the basis of audited costs plus negotiated profit rates. In this case, government auditors are given virtually unrestricted access to proprietary company cost data from their suppliers. For major defense contracts that require extensive investments in development, contractors are often paid separately for development tasks and investments related to preparing for production. In this case, prices are calculated on the basis of *non-recurring costs*. Prices for units produced in series production are based on *recurring costs*.

Because aerospace contracts commonly span periods of many years, it is standard practice for contracts to stipulate that prices will be escalated annually. The exact terms of the escalation vary, but normally are based on a formula that utilizes published labor and material price indices that apply to the aerospace industry.

Sometimes aerospace customers insist upon reassurance that the seller is offering them the most favorable possible price. A common practice in the industry is to confer status of *most favored customer* on buyers. In theory, this is a guarantee by the seller that the buyer is receiving a price that is at least as low as any price offered to other customers. Some government customers are legally required to obtain contractual assurance that they will be given most favored customer status. This status is accompanied by a promise that, if the product is sold at a lower price to any other customer, the most favored customer will receive a refund equal to the price difference.

A typical most favored customer clause might read:

Supplier warrants that it will not charge Buyer more for any goods or services, or any item thereof, than it charges its best customers under comparable conditions. Supplier will refund to Buyer promptly upon demand any amounts paid by Buyer which reflect a breach by Supplier of the immediately preceding sentence.

In fact, pricing of most aerospace contracts is so complex that indirect discounts can easily be offered to individual buyers without violating the terms of most favored customer guarantees committed to other customers. In pricing negotiations, catalogue prices of basic aircraft are often maintained, and discounts are often buried in pricing of options, training, spare parts, technical support, and so on.

The broader subject of pricing is discussed in detail in Chapter 3 of this book.

Financing or Leasing Arrangements

Sometimes the customer will request that the seller offer terms for leasing or financing. Generally, financial arrangements involve the participation of specialized third-party financial institutions, although large aerospace manufacturers often have in-house financial subsidiaries that offer sales financing. If the sale qualifies for export financing, the manufacturer generally works with the buyer to complete applications for government loan guarantees.

Airworthiness Requirements

In the case of civil aircraft or aerospace equipment, the purchase contract will stipulate that the deliverable item be accompanied by airworthiness certificates that allow the item to be legally utilized in the geographical region of the buyer. If the item is not already covered by airworthiness certificates, the seller will be required to obtain them by a specific date. Because the buyer will be unable to use the equipment unless the certificates are forthcoming, contractual penalties for failure to provide certification are severe.

Program Master Schedule

Every contract specifies commitment dates for deliveries or for completion of other important milestones. In addition to delivery of end items, the customer is likely to insist upon schedule commitments from the seller for critical events such as completion of engineering design, completion of testing, certification by airworthiness authorities, completion of training, delivery of documentation, and so on.

In the case of sophisticated government customers such as the US Department of Defense, contractual schedules sometimes become voluminous documents with literally thousands of milestones to which the seller becomes committed. For conventional arms-length sales of commercial aircraft, however, the schedule is a comparatively simple document that stipulates a limited number of essential events.

Often master schedules commit the buyer as well as the seller to perform tasks. In order for the seller to fulfill his commitments, he is sometimes dependent upon timely completion of commitments by the buyer. These commitments might include providing buyer-furnished material (such as engines or avionics, or aircraft interior furnishings), detailed definition of technical requirements, or making pilots or technicians available to attend scheduled training classes.

Payment Schedules

Practices concerning payment schedules vary widely. For military aerospace contracts with government customers, progress payments are standard. Sometimes these payments are simply three or four lump sums of a certain percentage of contract value, paid at specified times between contract signature and aircraft delivery. US Department of Defense practice is to pay, at frequent fixed intervals, a fixed percentage of labor and material costs incurred by the contractor. Remaining unreimbursed costs and profits are then paid upon aircraft delivery.

Practices are more diverse for civil aircraft. Sometimes the entire payment for aircraft is made upon delivery, which burdens the manufacturer with financing the entire value of work-in-process. Sometimes, financing arrangements are written so that manufacturers are paid incremental stages-of-completion payments by third-party financial institutions.

General Terms and Conditions

In addition to the specific contractual clauses that define what the seller will provide to the buyer, the contract also stipulates general conditions that apply to the agreement between the two parties. Often this section is standard 'boilerplate' language intended to eliminate potential ambiguities and misunderstandings. Terms and conditions, known within the industry as *T's & C's*, are subject to negotiations between the parties, but often major buyers such as governments are required by law to impose specific terms. In these cases, the seller is essentially presented with a take-it-or-leave-it situation.

Terms and conditions are generally in standardized language, but they vary according to the nature of the contract and the product involved. International contracts, for example, have different T's & C's than domestic contracts; T's and C's for government contracts are different than for civil contracts; service contracts have different terms than hardware contracts; and so on. Typical terms and conditions sections for a standard aerospace contract might consist of the following titles:

- Acceptance
- Packing, marking, shipping
- Invoicing
- Most favored customer
- Delivery
- Inspection

- Proprietary information
- Patent infringement indemnity
- Confidentiality
- Flow down
- Changes
- Suspension of work
- Default
- Termination for convenience
- Warranties
- Indemnification
- Tools and materials
- Design work
- Liabilities
- Insurance
- Progress reporting
- Order of precedence
- Dispute resolution
- Force majeure
- Labor disputes
- Government contracts
- Assignment and subcontracting
- Waiver and severability
- Choice of law
- Integration and merger
- Certifications
- Performance guarantees and liquidated damages

Each of these individual sections is likely to have evolved over years of business experience. Although contractual language of individual companies may be different, the actual intent is often very similar. Each of the T's & C's could be a fertile subject for exhaustive legal discussions and debate. Following is brief commentary on a few of the T's and C's that are most likely to be the subject of differences of opinion during the negotiating process.

Contract Changes

Because of the complexity and long period of performance of major aerospace contracts, changes to the contract are almost inevitable. Although any contract can be amended through mutually agreed changes negotiated by the parties, urgent circumstances often require that changes to the contract be effected immediately. In a case of discovery of a design flaw, for example, the buyer may want to unilaterally order the seller to implement design changes immediately. The changes clause in the T's & C's defines how these contract modifications will be handled. Common practice is for the buyer to have the right to issue a *contract change notice*, or *CCN*, that directs the seller to make a change. Later, the two parties meet to negotiate the cost impact of the change, and jointly sign a *change order*, or *CO*, which is a formal change to the contract and to the relevant pricing.

Flow-downs of Contractual Terms and Conditions

Particularly in the case of large official entities such as national governments, the prime contract between the buyer and the seller will include diverse terms and conditions based upon national legal requirements. In the United States, for example, the US Government normally includes contractual language that requires contractors to give preferential treatment to minority-owned firms, to implement Equal Employment Opportunity programs, to avoid buying materials from certain proscribed countries, to observe security controls, and so on. The prime contractor, in turn, is required to 'flow-down' these terms to all lower tier subcontractors that will perform work on the program, and this flow-down requirement is formalized in the prime contract. This flow-down language is customarily included in the 'assignments and subcontracting' section.

Warranties

The contract should include a very specific definition of warrantee coverage. The language describes what is covered under warranty, what is not covered, and how warranty claims should be submitted by the buyer and honored by the seller.

Disclaimers of Liability

Because of the spectacular potential for aircraft accidents to cause devastation, the seller generally attempts to limit his liability in the case of damage or loss of life caused by his product. Obvious examples of potential liability are lawsuits resulting from deaths attributable to technical failure of the aircraft.

National laws impose varying degrees of potential liability on aircraft manufacturers. In the United States, for example, manufacturers of military equipment are generally not liable for deaths or damage resulting from failure of their equipment, whereas manufacturers of civil aircraft are exposed.

Regardless of legal limitations on liability, aircraft manufacturers will normally try to include contractual language that will provide maximum protection against liability, particularly against incidental damages.

Performance Guarantees and Liquidated Damages

The customer's purchase decision will be heavily influenced by the manufacturer's promises of how their products will perform. Consequently, the customer will want contractual assurances that the seller's data is accurate. It is common practice for the seller to guarantee critical performance criteria, and to agree to pay penalties if the criteria are not met in service.

For commercial customers, projected profitability of planned routes has a direct relationship with aircraft performance. Airlines rely upon manufacturers' promises that aircraft will fly a specified distance, at a specified speed, with a specified cargo load, consuming a specified fuel volume, at a specified reliability rate. If the aircraft fails to meet any of these performance parameters, operator profitability will suffer, so the buyer will seek contractual guarantees at the time of aircraft purchase.

Liquidated damages are generally payments in cash to the customer, payable if the aircraft fails to meet performance parameters. Formulas for calculating the amount of liquidated damages are subject to negotiation, but the damages are normally intended to reimburse the customer fully for loss of profits caused by failure of the seller's product to perform as promised. In some cases liquidated damages are intended to be partially punitive in nature, and are set at levels that exceed the operator's projected losses.

In some contracts, final customer payments are not due until the aircraft in service has demonstrated that it can meet the specified performance parameters. Under these circumstances, failure to perform can result in permanent withholding of payment of an amount specified by the liquidated damages formula. Other provisions for assuring payment of eventual liquidated damages include establishing escrow accounts, or requirements that the seller obtain a third-party performance bond that is not released until an impartial arbiter determines that the performance guarantees have been met.

A very public example of financial penalties imposed upon a prime contractor resulted from late deliveries of Airbus A380s to initial launch customers. The launch customers, including Singapore Airlines, Qantas, Emirates, and others, had developed elaborate business plans that were heavily dependent upon introduction of the very large new aircraft. These plans were thrown into disarray when, in late 2004, Airbus announced that deliveries would not begin in 2006 as originally scheduled. Airbus negotiated individual financial settlements with the airlines affected by the projected delivery delays of approximately six months. Details of the settlements were not publicly disclosed, but the parties concerned commented that the settlement values ran into millions of dollars.

Performance guarantees are equally important to military customers, whose ability to perform missions will be compromised if their aircraft have insufficient range, payload, speed, reliability, or lethality. Because it is sometimes not feasible to demonstrate military performance under war conditions, military customers typically establish narrowly defined performance reviews in which specified performance characteristics of aircraft or equipment are measured. In case of shortfalls in these reviews, the manufacturer is required to make design changes to fix the problem or is subject to dissuasive liquidated damages.

Often military procurement contracts are written so that the customer makes progress payments as design and manufacturing work advances. Sometimes progress payments are specifically tied to satisfactory demonstration of aircraft performance at progressive milestone reviews. In this case, failure to perform can result in withholding of payments.

PART 4
The Governmental and Administrative Framework

Chapter 16

The Broader Administrative and Regulatory Context of Aerospace Marketing

By its very nature, the aerospace industry invites intensive oversight by government: its products have a direct impact on public safety; its military segment is of vital interest to national defense and international diplomatic relations; national governments often are shareholders in the industry; the industry is a large employer of highly trained workers; and the financial scale of the business invites malfeasance and corruption.

Government involvement in aerospace is too broad a subject to be explored in detail in this book. Some areas of government involvement, such as measures to control corruption, are of particular interest to marketers, but have been widely discussed elsewhere and are not examined here. Because of space limitations, this chapter limits itself to briefly exploring the nature of government oversight and regulation of the aerospace industry as it affects export controls and airworthiness institutions and practices.

Export Controls

Throughout the modern era, governments and their citizens have wrestled with the issue of control of exports of military equipment. On one side of the issue, manufacturers of equipment generally want to sell their products to the broadest possible market, and therefore do not support rigorous controls on exports. On the other side, many diplomats and concerned citizens recognize that armaments provide power to their owners, and believe that governments should prevent domestically produced armaments from being furnished to regimes that will misuse them.

Modern aircraft are particularly potent instruments of military power, and are often the focus of international debates concerning government control over exports.

An obvious problem facing efforts to regulate exports is that, because multiple sources exist for most types of aircraft and other armaments, controls imposed upon a small group of exporters will be ineffective unless similar controls are imposed by other exporters of similar material.

In recent years there has been a major movement by most industrialized nations, the principal suppliers of military aircraft and other armaments, to band together to prevent exports of military equipment to countries that might misuse it. In a noble effort, these producer countries have agreed on moral standards for armament exports, and have fashioned international treaties that formally govern their behavior.

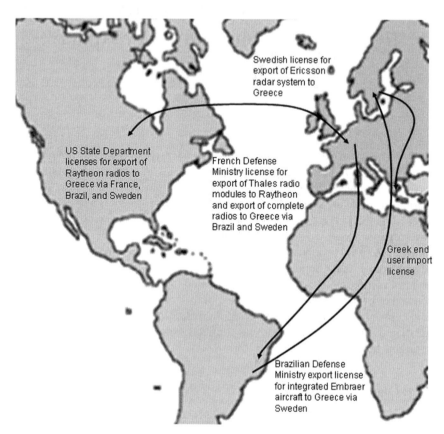

Figure 16.1 Export licenses for a cooperative international program
Note: Export licenses have always added administrative complexities, but international cooperative programs such as Thales' proposal for the Greek Airborne Early Warning system are particularly daunting. The program involved Swedish radars, French electronic modules, American radios, and Brazilian airframes.

Noteworthy among these international agreements is the E C Common Regime for Export of Dual Use Material and Technology, described later in this chapter, which regulates all members of the European Community under a common standard.

Of broader scope, but less specific, is the Wassenaar Arrangement, an ambitious undertaking that attempts to codify international standards for military exports, to standardize national laws regulating these exports, and to share information among member countries concerning their efforts to implement the terms of the Arrangement.

The Wassenaar Arrangement

The Wassenaar Arrangement, the first global multilateral agreement on export controls for conventional weapons and sensitive dual-use goods and technologies, received final approval by 33 co-founding countries in July 1996 and began operations in September 1996.

The significance of the Wassenaar Arrangement is monumental, in that it represents the first worldwide effort by major weapons-producing nations to unite to establish a common policy for control of military exports. In fact, national rivalries, business interests, and conflicting national diplomatic objectives often prevent the member companies from maintaining common policy. Nevertheless, Wassenaar remains an essential symbolic step towards establishing effective worldwide control of armaments and military technology.

Wassenaar was designed to promote transparency, exchanges of information, and greater responsibility in transfers of conventional arms and dual-use goods and technologies. It complements and reinforces the existing regimes for non-proliferation of weapons of mass destruction and their delivery systems, by focusing on control of transfers of armaments and sensitive dual-use goods and technologies where the risks are judged greatest. The arrangement is also intended to enhance cooperation to prevent the acquisition of armaments and sensitive dual-use items for military end-uses, if the situation in a region or the behavior of a state causes concern to the participating states.

The participating states seek through their national policies to ensure that transfers of arms and dual-use goods and technologies do not contribute to the development or enhancement of military capabilities that undermine international and regional security and stability. The Arrangement does not intend to impede legitimate civil transactions and is not directed against any state or group of states. All measures undertaken with respect to the Arrangement are in accordance with member countries' national legislation and policies.

Wassenaar countries are expected to maintain effective export controls for the items on the agreed lists, which are reviewed periodically to take into account technological developments and political factors.

Membership in the Wassenaar Arrangement is open on a global and non-discriminatory basis to prospective adherents that comply with the agreed criteria. To be admitted, a state must be an exporter of arms or industrial equipment; maintain non-proliferation policies and appropriate national policies, including adherence to relevant non-proliferation regimes and treaties; and maintain fully effective export controls.

The participating states of the Wassenaar Arrangement are: Argentina, Australia, Austria, Belgium, Bulgaria, Canada, the Czech Republic, Denmark, Finland, France, Germany, Greece, Hungary, Ireland, Italy, Japan, Luxembourg, the Netherlands, New Zealand, Norway, Poland, Portugal, the Republic of Korea, Romania, the Russian Federation, Slovakia, Spain, Sweden, Switzerland, Turkey, Ukraine, the United Kingdom and the United States.

United States Export Control

The Arms Export Control Act (AECA) is the cornerstone of US munitions export control law. This statute is implemented by the International Traffic in Arms Regulations (ITAR). All persons or entities that engage in the manufacture, export, or brokering of defense articles and services must be registered with the US Government. The ITAR sets out the requirements for licenses or other authorizations for specific exports of defense articles and services. The AECA requires the State Department to provide an annual and quarterly report of export authorizations to Congress. Certain proposed export approvals and reports of unauthorized re-transfers also require congressional notification. Within the Department of State, the agency responsible for management of military export controls is the *Office of Defense Trade Controls*, or *DTC*.

The Export Administration Act of 1979, as amended, authorizes the Department of Commerce, in consultation with other appropriate agencies, to regulate the export or re-export of US-origin dual-use goods, software, and technology. The Department of Commerce implements this authority through the Export Administration Regulations (EAR). In addition to export controls agreed in the multilateral regimes, the Department of Commerce also imposes certain export and re-export controls for national security, foreign policy, and other reasons, most notably against countries designated by the US Secretary of State as state sponsors of international terrorism, as well as certain countries, entities and individuals subject to domestic unilateral or UN sanctions. Additionally, the Department of Commerce administers and enforces regulations that prohibit certain trade and transactions with certain countries, entities, and individuals by US persons or from the United States under the Trading with the Enemy Act and the International Emergency Economic Powers Act. The entity within the Commerce Department with authority for control of exports of commercial goods, services, and data is the Bureau of Export Administration, or BXA.

Various other US agencies have licensing authority for sensitive exports of a specialized nature. Exports related to nuclear technology are controlled by the Nuclear Regulatory Commission, with reports to the Departments of Energy and Commerce. Any exports that are the subject of official US Government embargoes and sanctions are controlled by the Department of the Treasury.

US control lists correspond directly with the lists maintained by the various multinational non-proliferation regimes, but are augmented by unilateral controls deemed necessary by the US Government to ensure national security and foreign policy imperatives. The three major lists of controlled items are the Commerce Control List (CCL), the United States Munitions List (USML), and the Nuclear Regulatory Commission Controls (NRCC).

Common European Community Export Control Policy

As part of the movement by the member states of the European Community towards economic and political integration, the EC has progressively instituted a body of policies that have greatly reduced differences and incompatibilities between national policies of the individual members pertaining to controls of exports of military and dual use material, services, and technology.

Standardization of export control policy has particularly been effected as a result of three particular initiatives involving the EC membership:

- EC Common Regime for Export of Dual Use Material and Technology
- The Wassenaar Arrangement
- European Union Code of Conduct for Arms Exports.

EC Common Regime for Export of Dual Use Material and Technology   Under the terms of the Treaty of Rome, the fundamental document that is the basis for the European Union, member states retain control over their own national defense, including control over exports of military equipment. However, the member states agree that the EU should have regulatory control over dual-use material and technology. 'Dual-use items' are goods and technology developed for civilian uses, but which can be used for military applications, or to produce weapons.

The European dual-use Regulation n°1334/2000 setting up a Community regime for the control of exports of dual-use items and technology was adopted by the Council on 22 June 2000. This regulation was an update of a series of earlier versions of export control rules.

The major innovation with the new regulation was the creation of the Community General Export Authorization, which liberalized most of the trade with close trading partners and created a level playing field for EU exporters. For ten specific countries of destination, export controls were greatly relaxed in order to reduce unnecessary administrative obstacles to trade. The ten countries on the preferential list were: Australia, Canada, the Czech Republic, Hungary, Japan, New Zealand, Norway, Poland, Switzerland, and the USA. The Community General Export Authorisation applied to nearly all goods that could be traded freely in intra-Community trade.

As for intra-Community trade, the new regulation harmonized the list of dual-use items that were so sensitive that they needed an authorization to circulate within the EU. It was focused on most sensitive items in the ballistic, nuclear and chemical fields. Encryption was largely liberalized in order to facilitate the development of the European computer and software industries.

The last innovation was the introduction of controls of intangible transfers of technology for exports outside the European Community. The new regulations defined technology transfer via fax, telephone, and electronic media transmission, and dealt with control of technical assistance related to certain military end-uses, including oral transfers.

EU bureaucrats were given authority to introduce changes to the Council Regulation in order to update the lists of items to be controlled by the EU. The EU was also empowered to participate in and enhance information exchanges and administrative cooperation with licensing authorities of member states. A representative of the European Commission was designated to chair the Coordination Group responsible for establishing best practices among national licensing authorities.

The Wassenaar Arrangement   The countries of the European Union have acted to incorporate the terms of the Wassenaar Arrangement, described above, into binding regulations of the Union.

European Union Code of Conduct for Arms Exports   The individual countries of the European Union control arms exports by means of their own unique legislation covering the subject. However, the EU member states exchange information on all issues relating to conventional arms exports, ranging from customs rules in force and control of the arms trade in third countries to the member states' policies with regard to specific countries or regions. One of the first steps in this coordination of arms export policy among the member states was the adoption of the Luxembourg and Lisbon Common Criteria in 1991 and 1992. In 1997, Great Britain and France proposed that the members of the European Union draft an EU Code of Conduct for Arms Exports. This Code was adopted by the 15 foreign affairs ministers in the form of a Council Declaration on 8 June 1998.

The Code of Conduct defines a list of criteria that all member states agree to observe. In principal, the national legislation of each of the member states has been revised to ensure compliance with the criteria, which define principles of responsible behavior for international arms exports.

In addition to the EC Common Regime for export controls, the individual nations continue, at least for the time being, to regulate national exports that may have military application. German export control laws are administered by the Federal Office of Economics and Export Control, known as *BAFA*, an acronym for *Bundesamt fur Wirtschaft und Ausfuhrkontrolle*. In the United Kingdom, licenses to export arms and other goods controlled for strategic reasons, including many types of aircraft, are issued by the Secretary of State for Trade & Industry acting through the *Export Control Organisation*, or *ECO*. All relevant individual license applications are circulated by the Department of Trade and Industry (DTI) to other government departments whose responsibilities involve controls of certain materials and technologies. In France, normal procedure for issuance of licenses is that approval is given by the Minister of Defense, acting on behalf of the Prime Minister, upon advice from the Interministerial Commission for the Study of Military Equipment Exports, known as *CIEEMG* (*Commission Interministérielle pour l'Étude des Exportations de Matériels de Guerre*). However, in cases where the Prime Minister authorizes it, the Minister of Defense can deliver the authorization of prior consent directly, without consultation with the CIEEMG.

National Airworthiness Institutions and Practices

To protect its citizens from the inherent dangers of flying machines, almost every nation has a national airworthiness authority, known generically as a *civil airworthiness authority*, or *CAA* (not to be confused with the UK's Civil Aviation Authority, which is the airworthiness authority for that country), that regulates matters involving air safety. In most countries, regulation of civil aviation safety consists primarily of controlling five critical aspects of aircraft and their operation:

- Design of aircraft, airborne equipment, and ground-based equipment affecting flight safety
- Conditions of manufacture and test of aircraft and equipment
- Standards of maintenance of aircraft and equipment
- Standards of operation of aircraft and equipment
- Control of air traffic.

Airworthiness considerations are a subject of constant attention in the civil aerospace market. The aircraft marketer needs a basic understanding of how the airworthiness system works and how it affects the aerospace business.

Historically, airworthiness standards have been imposed by national laws that varied from one country to the next, creating an international web of inconsistent and often incompatible regulations. In recent decades the major aerospace nations have undertaken initiatives to harmonize their airworthiness rules, and the countries of the European Community have established an international agency empowered to manage airworthiness for most of Western Europe. However, the process of standardization is far from complete, and sales of aircraft across international borders generally entail complex regulatory issues that must be dealt with.

Table 16.1 National civil airworthiness authorities

Country	National Civil Airworthiness Authority
United States	Federal Aviation Administration
France	Direction Générale de l'Aviation Civile
Germany	Luftfahrt-Bundesamt
United Kingdom	Civil Aviation Authority
Japan	Japan Civil Aviation Bureau
Russia	State Civil Aviation Authority of Russia
China	Civil Aviation Administration of China
India	Directorate General of Civil Aviation
Australia	Civil Aviation Authority – Australia
European Community	Joint Aviation Authorities, EASA

Note: Virtually every modern country has a national civil airworthiness authority, and their responsibilities are remarkably similar.

The Type Certificate

The *type certificate*, or *TC*, is the official document, issued by a national airworthiness authority, that attests that the design of an aircraft or item of equipment complies with the standards of the authority. The airworthiness standards themselves are stipulated in voluminous technical references that regulate every aspect of aircraft design, much as building codes regulate design of ground-based office buildings and residences. In the United States, FAA technical standards are contained in the Federal Airworthiness Regulations, or FAR. Different volumes of the FAR pertain to different types of aircraft. FAR part 29, for example, controls large transport helicopters. FAR part 25 applies to large fixed wing transport airliners. Other national CAAs maintain their own airworthiness standards.

Airworthiness standards are fundamental to aircraft design. Consequently, when aerospace manufacturers develop concepts for new aircraft that they intend to design and manufacture, the design engineers and the airworthiness authorities begin collaboration from the outset of the project. This process of collaboration continues until the aircraft has been manufactured and tested and the type certificate has been issued. In peculiar aerospace industry parlance, an aircraft that receives a type certification is said to be 'certificated'.

The process of obtaining type certification for aircraft or equipment is complex, detail-oriented, and time-consuming. From the point of view of the marketer, however, the good news is that responsibility for managing the certification process is normally assigned to the program manager and the engineering department. But the marketer must never lose awareness of the reality that any civil aircraft or piece of airborne equipment, delivered almost anywhere in the world, must be accompanied by a type certificate recognized by local authorities.

Therein lies another complication. Aerospace products are widely exported and imported. Government airworthiness authorities have historically been national authorities. Standards and regulations have varied from one country to the next. How does the industry deal with the issues involved with aircraft crossing national frontiers?

One way of dealing with the problem would be for each national airworthiness authority to individually perform re-certification for every type of aircraft, prior to allowing the aircraft to operate in the national airspace. Although this is obviously an unsatisfactory solution because of the time and resources required to perform redundant type certifications in each country, it has in the past been a normal practice. The FAA procedure for issuing type certification is to require the applicant to prove complete compliance with Federal Airworthiness Regulations. Almost always, any aircraft that is proposed for international export has a type certificate from the airworthiness authority in the manufacturer's home country. The FAA process for certifying imported aircraft allows the applicant to use the home-country certification process to show compliance with some FAR requirements. In the case of differences between requirements of the home-country CAA and the FAA, the applicant is required to demonstrate to the FAA that the equipment to be imported does indeed meet the additional requirements of the FAA. This is a laborious and time-consuming process that essentially requires the aircraft to be re-certified. As a result of these obvious problems, national airworthiness standards in most of the world have converged over the years. Until 1990, the obvious major exceptions to this historical convergence were the countries of the former Soviet Bloc, who since the end of the Cold War have been making rapid progress to re-write their national airworthiness standards to be compatible with those of the rest of the world.

The most prevalent modern solution to reconciling national airworthiness standards is the concept of reciprocal agreements, also known as *bilateral agreements*, between national governments. Bilateral agreements between national airworthiness authorities result from painstaking efforts by the authorities to harmonize their standards, and to confirm that the verification processes in both countries are satisfactory to both parties. Implementation of such standardization demands a major investment of time and resources, but when it is complete, the airworthiness authorities in the two countries agree to accept each other's type certificates. The export-import process is greatly simplified.

This movement towards internationalization of airworthiness standards has gathered enormous momentum in recent years. Within Europe, the *Joint Aviation Authorities*, or *JAA*, has been a very visible symbol of this movement.

The JAA is an associated body of the *European Civil Aviation Conference*, or *ECAC*, which represents the civil aviation regulatory authorities of the European governments who have agreed to cooperate in developing and implementing common safety regulatory standards and procedures. The JAA has also placed much emphasis on harmonizing the JAA regulations with those of the USA. The JAA was created in 1990, when the founding members signed the 'JAA Arrangements' in Cyprus. The founding members were Austria, Belgium, Cyprus, Denmark, Finland, France, Germany, Greece, Hungary, Iceland, Ireland, Italy, Luxembourg, Malta, Monaco, the Netherlands, Norway, Poland, Portugal, Spain, Sweden, Switzerland, Turkey, and the United Kingdom. Membership has continually grown since 1990.

The signatory countries have implemented the terms of the JAA Arrangements, and national airworthiness authorities in the member countries now issue type certifications based upon technical verification, testing, and investigation performed by the JAA.

Building upon the success of the JAA, the European transport ministers agreed in June 2001 to create the *European Aviation Safety Agency*, or *EASA*, which will become a true pan-national European equivalent of the FAA for certification matters. The agency was formally created in 2003. EASA effectively takes over responsibility for many important functions of the national airworthiness agencies of all of the European Union countries. It will take some years for the agency to become fully operational, but eventually it will significantly simplify the way aircraft and their systems are certified, replacing today's diverse national processes with a common system and a single certificate. EASA will make access to external markets easier by ensuring agreements can be swiftly reached on harmonization and the mutual recognition of certificates. It will also strengthen the free movement of commonly qualified engineers within the EU.

At the same time that the JAA has been harmonizing standards in Europe, the FAA has been working to reconcile American standards with Europe, Asia, and the rest of the world. To this end, the FAA has formalized numerous international bilateral agreements. The harmonization efforts of the JAA have greatly facilitated this process.

Summary of Products Eligible for US Import
Under Bilateral Agreements Between FAA and International Airworthiness Authorities
(as of October 2000)

BILATERAL COUNTRIES (Revised 2000)	Aircraft	New Replacement/Modification parts For Exported Aircraft	Aircraft Engines	New Replacement/Modification Parts for Exported Engines	Propellers	New Replacement/Modification Parts for Exported Propellers	Appliances	New Replacement/Modification Parts for Exported Appliances	Conformity Inspection			Third Country Provisions	Maintenance	Agreement Date	See Reference Notes Number
									Materials	Parts	Subassemblies				
Argentina	X	X	X	X	X	X	X	X	X	X	X			1991	2
Australia	X	X	X	X	X	X	X	X	X	X	X	X		1975	1, 2, 3
Austria	X	X	X	X	X	X								1959	
Belgium	X	X	X	X	X	X	X	X	X	X	X	X		1973	1, 2
Brazil	X	X	X	X	X	X	X	X	X	X	X	X		1976	1, 2
Canada	X	X	X	X	X	X	X	X	X	X	X	X	X	1984 2000	1, 2, 15
China	X	X					X		X	X	X			1991, 1995	2, 4
Czech Republic	X	X	X	X	X	X	X	X						1970	
Denmark	X	X	X	X	X	X	X	X	X	X	X	X		1982	2
Finland	X	X					X	X						1974	5
France	X	X	X	X	X	X	X	X	X	X	X	X	X	1973 1999	1, 2, 14
Germany	X	X	X	X	X	X	X	X	X	X	X	X	X	1997 1999	1, 2, 13
Indonesia														1992	6
Israel	X	X	X	X	X	X	X	X	X	X	X			1968, 1974	2
Italy	X	X	X	X	X	X	X	X	X	X	X	X		1973	1, 2
Japan	X	X	X	X	X	X	X	X	X	X	X	X		1977	1, 2
Malaysia	X	X					X		X	X	X			1997	2, 7
Netherlands	X	X	X	X	X	X	X	X	X	X	X	X		1974	1, 2
New Zealand	X	X					X	X	X	X	X			1970, 1979	2, 8
Norway	X	X					X	X						1957, 1978	
Poland	X	X	X	X	X	X	X	X	X	X	X	X		1976, 1980	2, 9
Romania	X	X												1976	10
Russia	X	X							X	X	X			1998	2, 11
Singapore							X	X	X	X	X	X		1981	1, 2, 12
South Africa	X	X	X	X	X	X	X	X	X	X	X			1955, 1984	2
Spain	X	X					X	X						1978	
Sweden	X	X	X	X	X	X	X	X	X	X	X	X		1973	1, 2
Switzerland	X	X	X	X	X	X	X	X	X	X	X			1977	2
United Kingdom	X	X	X	X	X	X	X	X	X	X	X	X		1972	1, 2

Figure 16.2 FAA bilateral agreements

Note: The extent of FAA bilateral agreements with national CAAs continues to grow.

Exporting and Importing Aircraft and Equipment

The actual mechanics of exporting an aircraft vary from country to country, but most of the major aerospace manufacturing countries require a document called an *export airworthiness approval* before a civil aircraft or major piece of aerospace equipment can be exported. In the case of the USA, an export airworthiness approval is issued by the FAA for aircraft, engines, propellers, appliances, and other major items being exported. Prior to issuance of an export airworthiness approval, a determination is made that these items conform to their FAA-approved design, are in a condition for safe operation, and meet all special requirements established by the importing country's civil airworthiness authority.

Note that, in the United States, civil aircraft and major equipment are not normally exportable unless they are certified by the FAA and the FAA determines that they are certifiable in their country of destination. This practice, which also prevails in most other major aerospace-producing countries, obviously is a key consideration of international aerospace marketers. Particularly when potential customers are located in countries that are not parties to any of the major multi-national certification agreements, and do not have bilateral agreements with the FAA or JAA, it may be problematic to obtain an export certificate. Fortunately, as airworthiness standards and management practices become progressively standardized, this problem has become uncommon except for customers in a few backward countries.

Most countries are signatories to The Convention on International Recognition of Rights in Aircraft, known as the 'Mortgage Convention', which defines procedures for de-registration of aircraft in one country and re-registration in another. Before an imported aircraft can be registered in the United States, for example, the FAA must receive written notification from the government of the former country of registry, confirming that the aircraft's registry in the original country has been cancelled. Under the terms of the Mortgage Convention, the government agencies must confirm that the exported aircraft has no outstanding financial liens against it before the written notification of de-registration is sent. In the case of aircraft to be exported, the home airworthiness authority will be requested to send confirmation of de-registration to the airworthiness authority in the receiving country. The confirmation will contain all known information concerning ownership and financial encumbrances against the aircraft.

Airworthiness Control of Military Aircraft

Civil airworthiness authorities, as their names infer, have responsibility for matters involving civil aircraft. Military aircraft are generally not included in their responsibilities. Standards for designing and maintaining military aircraft are customarily the responsibility of the military owners. In the United States, for example, US military aircraft and engine parts are certified under the provisions of Air Force Policy Directive 62-6 as 'public aircraft'. AFPD 62-6 designates the Single Manager (SM) for each aircraft as the airworthiness certification official and establishes the Airworthiness Certification Criteria Control Board (AC3B). The SM sets the technical specifications for each separate program, which drives the system program engineering offices, the OEMs, part manufacturers, and repair facilities.

The special needs of commercial and military aerospace dictate some degree of difference between civil and military certification processes. However, the existence of parallel standards often requires that MRO operations have completely separate facilities for civil and commercial activities, with the obvious cost penalties and redundancies that such an arrangement implies. Labor costs and efficiency of mechanics are negatively affected by the proliferation of different technical standards. Commercial mechanics are generally required to be certified by the civil airworthiness authorities, whereas mechanics working on military aircraft are subject to different qualification requirements.

The International Civil Aviation Organization (ICAO)

In concert with the national and regional airworthiness authorities, *ICAO* is the principal international organization with the mission of coordinating the activities of the national authorities. ICAO, whose activities extend well beyond the narrowly defined subject of airworthiness, is chartered with responsibility for the following aims and objectives related to the development of the principles and techniques of international air navigation and to fostering planning and development of international air transport:

- Ensure the safe and orderly growth of international civil aviation throughout the world
- Encourage the arts of aircraft design and operation for peaceful purposes
- Encourage the development of airways, airports and air navigation facilities for international civil aviation
- Meet the needs of the peoples of the world for safe, regular, efficient and economical air transport
- Prevent economic waste caused by unreasonable competition
- Ensure that the rights of contracting states are fully respected and that every contracting state has a fair opportunity to operate international airlines
- Avoid discrimination between contracting states
- Promote safety of flight in international air navigation
- Promote generally the development of all aspects of international civil aeronautics.

ICAO is a specialized agency of the United Nations, created with the signing in Chicago, on 7 December 1944, of the *Convention on International Civil Aviation,* which is universally referred to as the *Chicago Convention.* ICAO is the permanent body charged with the administration of the principles laid out in the convention.

The 96 articles of the Chicago Convention establish the privileges and restrictions of all contracting states and provide for the adoption of International Standards and Recommended Practices (SARPs) regulating international air transport. The convention accepted the principle that every state has complete and exclusive sovereignty over the airspace above its territory, and provided that no scheduled international air service may operate over or into the territory of a contracting state without its previous consent.

Standards and practices established by ICAO have no legal force until they are formally adopted by national governments. Incorporation of ICAO's recommendations is strictly voluntary on the part of member states. However, ICAO's exceptional international credibility and moral force, combined with the interest of the members in maintaining international standards of behavior, have the result that the organization's recommendations are almost always incorporated into local regulations.

ICAO's activities are relevant to marketers because the body's rulings bearing on aircraft operations often direct aircraft design and sometimes establish technical factors that put competitors to relative advantage or disadvantage. ICAO is, for example, the primary international arbiter for noise standards governing civil aircraft. Because all aircraft have different noise characteristics, relatively minor differences in noise standards can have major impact upon the ability of specific aircraft to comply. ICAO technical staff and engineers from the aerospace manufacturers work closely during the process of writing standards, to ensure that the standards accomplish their objectives without imposing unfair arbitrary terms.

Chapter 17

What Lies Ahead in the Aerospace Marketplace?

Over the century of its existence, the aerospace industry has been characterized by constant and rapid change, affecting its technology, products, and business structure. We can safely assume that the industry and the aviation marketplace will continue to evolve in the future, and that marketing professionals will be compelled to adapt to new circumstances. Yet, in spite of these changes, we can expect that many of the most recognizable characteristics of the industry will endure.

What will be the nature of the future aerospace industry and marketplace?

Aerospace and defense technology will meld into a single industry

Although the defense industry will always include low-tech products such as boots, tents, and rifle bullets, the value of future defense products will increasingly be in the domain of aerospace-derived technologies. Military and civil aircraft will increasingly share production and design methods, materials technologies, propulsion technologies, and electronics. Ground military forces will rely on miniature unmanned aerospace vehicles, digital communications, and aerospace-derived sensors and targeting systems. Naval forces will operate ships powered by aerospace-derived turbine engines, equipped with advanced radars, and will launch fixed-wing aircraft, helicopters, and missiles. All military service branches will be integrated into communications and control networks developed by the aerospace industry. Virtually all significant aerospace firms will have direct or indirect involvement in the defense industry. In recognition of the blurring of distinctions between the two industries, stock market analysts have begun to refer to the combined industry as Aerospace & Defense. This combined identity will be an earmark of the aerospace industry of the twenty-first century.

Consolidation of the aerospace industry will continue

An irresistible trend in the international aerospace industry will be that market forces and economic realities that have driven the consolidation of the industry since the end of World War II will continue until a few aerospace prime contractors remain to dominate the industry. Complex technologies will continue to raise the investment levels required to introduce new aircraft, with the result that only very large corporations with access to extraordinary investment funds will be able to bring new aircraft to market. In its end state, the market consolidation will probably be characterized by two major manufacturers in the United States, one in Europe, one in Russia, and one in China.

This highly concentrated industry will have noticeable differences from today's industry, but also recognizable similarities:

- *Niche producers will continue to survive and prosper in smaller market segments outside the focus of the giant aerospace prime contractors.* Embraer and Bombardier may survive as makers of regional jets, CAE may continue to dominate the market for flight simulators, and leaders of the avionics and airborne electronics segment will continue to exist independently.

- *Most aerospace market segments will become increasingly oligopolistic in nature.* As defined by economists, oligopolistic markets are characterized by a small number of large and powerful sellers who do not have true monopoly power, but who have sufficient market power to influence pricing. Reflecting the future oligopolistic nature of the industry, the dominant firms will attempt to use their market power to influence market forces to maximize profits. Firms will attempt to avoid cut-throat competition in pricing and new product development. However, major customers, particularly leasing firms, will use their own market power on the buying side to ensure that competition among sellers remains aggressive. Experienced buyers will play sellers against one another to force price competition, and development of new products and technologies will be encouraged as customers perform technical evaluations of products and reward suppliers of superior products.

- *Competitors' new product offerings in mature markets will tend to be similar.* The oligopolists will tend to match each other's product lines. Because oligopolists already control major market shares and face entrenched competitors, it is extremely difficult for them to achieve major increases in market share. Consequently, large investments in new product offerings will entail high financial risks but will be unlikely to yield major increases in market share. The safest strategy for oligopolistic competitors such as transport aircraft producers will be to make new-product investments at levels that will enable them to make incremental improvements to existing products, assuring technological parity or slight superiority vis-à-vis competitors.

- *New programs will increasingly entail international risk-sharing partners and international coproduction.* Faced with ever-higher investment requirements for the launch of new products, prime contractors will recruit other major firms to share design, development, and manufacturing tasks, and to provide investment funding for their workshare.

- *Aerospace firms will become increasingly international in terms of ownership and market involvement.* The economic and market forces causing industry consolidation do not stop at international frontiers, and neither will the consolidation process. Europe has demonstrated a business model for establishing true multinational aerospace giants, and similar models will emerge elsewhere as firms chase resources and markets internationally. BAE Systems will continue to acquire American subsidiaries to gain access to US markets, Boeing will acquire and develop Asian units, and EADS will expand its manufacturing presence in the United States and in Asia.

Aerospace technical standards, government regulation, and operating practices will follow a trend of increasing international standardization

As the aerospace and aviation industries have become increasingly internationalized since the end of World War II, the diverse and haphazard body of domestic aerospace technical norms and practices has proceeded inexorably towards international standardization. The process is far from complete, but will continue to advance as part of the indispensable infrastructure of the global industry.

At the end of World War II, virtually every individual aerospace manufacturing country had its own peculiar set of technical standards pertaining to aerospace design and manufacturing. As international cooperation expanded in the aftermath of the war, the American MILSPEC system became a commonly used de facto standard throughout Europe. Later, formal institutions were created by governments and industry for the express purpose of establishing standardized international technical norms. In the technical domain, these international standards continue to grow and enter common use. Likewise, national regulations and practices for airworthiness certification are evolving from a fragmented collection of distinct national standards to a single international concept for airworthiness practices. The European nations have accomplished the admirable task of establishing a Europe-wide airworthiness authority known as the *European Aviation Safety Agency*, or *EASA*, which issues aircraft certification for all member countries. At the same time, EASA and the American Federal Aviation Administration have standardized most of their certification requirements, to the extent that aircraft type certifications issued by one of the agencies is customarily followed within a few days by issuance of a similar certification by the counterpart agency on the other side of the Atlantic. This standardization will continue to spread throughout the world as international coordination and cooperation in aerospace matters continues to expand.

E-business will grow in transactions involving commodity equipment and hardware

As consistent international technical standards are increasingly embraced by the industry worldwide, standard material, hardware and equipment will be commonly bought and sold in electronic commodity markets. Several large and well-organized virtual markets for aerospace commodities already exist and are used by many of the major aerospace companies, which frequently make direct on-line procurements from qualified suppliers. These e-business transactions will grow in value and importance, but will not expand significantly beyond lower-tier markets for commodity items.

Aerospace business practices will become increasingly standardized internationally, and business managers will become increasingly professionalized

In concert with the broader movement towards internationalization of the aerospace industry and standardization of technical norms, business practices and management techniques will become progressively standardized. International buyers and sellers worldwide will tend to use similar contracting practices, legal terms and conditions, financing arrangements, and practices for conducting competitive selections. To facilitate participation by international competitors, national governments and individual airlines will structure their purchasing programs in ways completely familiar to international sellers. The basic framework of requests for proposal, proposal formats, pro forma contracts, payment schedules, and terms and conditions will tend to become highly similar. The fundamental business culture of the industry will progressively become standardized, making it easier for suppliers to cooperate among themselves, and facilitating business transactions between buyers and sellers.

As aerospace business practices become increasingly uniform, specific management disciplines within the industry will become more codified, and professionals working within specialties such as marketing will be expected to operate competently within the framework of procedural requirements. The marketing culture will still accommodate imagination and personal flair, but will conform to a well-defined body of procedural norms and common paradigms.

Military aerospace will continue to be dominated by the United States

Since the end of World War II, the national defense budget of the United States has by far surpassed other industrialized nations, and has significantly exceeded the aggregate defense expenditures of all European countries. Much of the American defense budget is allocated directly to the aerospace sector for development of new aircraft, airborne equipment, and military space systems. In the absence of comparable European government defense budgets, European industry will face an enduring structural disadvantage that will prevent it from competing on an equal footing with its American competitors, who will receive preferential treatment as a result of protectionist US Government procurement policies. Although European governments will continue to maintain a basic defense aerospace capability in order to avoid total reliance on the United States, the European aerospace sector will be a secondary presence in international defense markets.

However, European participation in the American defense market will increase as European aerospace firms acquire ownership of smaller American defense firms and team with American partners on programs that involve licensed American production of European designs.

In the long term, China will emerge as a military counterweight to the United States. The Chinese Government clearly has the ambition to return China to its historical position as a world power, and has designated military aerospace as a key sector to be developed to acquire political power. Assuming that Chinese economic development continues without drastic upheavals or disruptions, the Chinese Government will continue to fund development of a national military aerospace design and manufacturing capability, and will, following the American model, buy large numbers of military aircraft from domestic industry. China has already demonstrated its intention to use this expanding defense industrial capability as a tool to expand its international political influence. Increasingly, China will offer its military aerospace products to markets where American suppliers are not implanted, often in third-world markets where customers do not require the sophistication and cost of American equipment, or are prohibited by the American Government from buying American equipment.

International ownership of defense firms across national borders will entail export-control complications that will require innovative management techniques, structures, and processes

International acquisitions of aerospace firms involved in defense and space will require further development of innovative management structures to enable foreign managers and shareholders to exercise business control over their foreign subsidiaries without giving the foreign stakeholders access to restricted technology that cannot be legally released to non-citizens. In early European acquisitions of American defense firms, for example, European senior management has experimented with creating local management boards of senior American managers or directors whose citizenship legally allows their exposure to sensitive information. These local American management boards have typically reviewed technical and business data and have made business recommendations to the parent European boards at the home company. Arrangements of this sort, intended to permit effective management without violating national export control laws, will become increasingly prevalent internationally.

Asia will become an increasingly important center of aerospace demand and supply

The focus of the market for aerospace products, which historically has overwhelmingly been Europe and North America, will broaden to include Asia. Asia's geographical size, population density, burgeoning economic power, and international political tensions will create fertile circumstances for rapid growth in civil and military aerospace markets. The aerospace industry, aware of Asia's increased importance as a market, will shift its marketing emphasis accordingly. Western aerospace firms will increasingly develop industrial alliances with Asian partners to better gain market entry.

China will continue its national emphasis on development of the aerospace industry, and will eventually emerge as a major pole of civil and military aerospace design and manufacturing. Europe and the United States will continue to cooperate industrially with China, but will recognize China as a formidable future competitor, and will become increasingly reluctant to share critical technology as China advances. Japan will continue to maintain a significant civil aerospace industry, and for the foreseeable future will adhere to their policy of developing alliances with American industry rather than Europeans. Early in the twenty-first century Japan will renounce its post-war policy of prohibition of exports of military equipment, and will become progressively involved with the United States in cooperative development and manufacture of military aerospace products for export.

Aerospace companies will attempt to derive increased profits from their core competencies

As they seek areas of growth, major aerospace firms will broaden their product offerings related to their core competencies, and will increasingly offer diversified turn-key programs including aircraft financing, training, logistics support, leasing, re-purchase, flight services, and so on. Large-scale involvement by the major manufacturers in maintenance, repair, and overhaul business will be particularly visible. At the same time, the companies will outsource business activities, such as fabrication of detailed parts, that are not core competencies and can be performed by subcontractors at lower cost.

Aerospace managers recognize that they can most effectively add value to their products, and thereby maximize profits, when their companies engage in business activities that directly utilize their core competency, which consists of detailed knowledge of how to build, sell, maintain, and operate aerospace products. The companies will search for new areas of growth and diversification in which these core competencies give them a competitive advantage over other players.

Costs of developing new products will continue to rise

As succeeding generations of new aerospace products become increasingly complex, development costs will rise. Because of these prohibitive development costs, intervals between introductions of aerospace products will tend to increase, although critical products derived from rapidly developing new technologies, such as unmanned aerospace vehicles, will continue to be introduced as prototypes in rapid succession. New models of more conventional products such as commercial transports and military fighters will be introduced less frequently and will remain in service longer. This longer service life will offer increased business opportunities to the maintenance, overhaul, and repair industry segment.

Value of the airframe itself will continue to diminish in comparison to major systems such as engines, avionics, and integration

Most of the increased value of new aircraft models will derive from equipment, subsystems, and integration, whereas the value of the airframe itself will remain relatively constant. The prime contractors will continue to retain control over the design process, but will outsource much manufacturing work other than final assembly. More importantly, the prime contractors will be in control of the increasingly important systems integration process, which will place them in a position to control the overall design and manufacturing processes, to add special value, and to extract commensurate profits.

Integration of European firms will be increasingly based upon business factors rather than politics, and government ownership will continue to decline

European politicians will continue to protect their national employment in EADS, Airbus, Thales, MBDA, and other European aerospace entities vigilantly, but the entities will in the future be managed more like conventional profit-making firms, and less like instruments of political patronage. Senior management will increasingly be appointed on the basis of merit rather than nationality or political connections, and selection of manufacturing sites will be based upon technical and business parameters rather than upon political compromise.

The American system of export control will be problematic

The United States Government will continue to struggle to establish an export control regime that enables efficient cooperation with its international allies. The existing system will improve, but problems will remain. The persistent conflict will remain between the American desire to protect indigenously developed technology, with the competitive advantages that it entails, and the desire to sell advanced products to friendly nations and allies and to gain access to the indigenously developed technology and financial resources of those international friends. At best, the American system for granting export licenses will be slow, conservative, and unpredictable. However, the system will be open to appeal by aerospace exporters who are denied licenses, and political lobbying will generally enable companies to eventually obtain reasonable authorizations to export defense products.

National governments in Europe, Asia, and the Americas will continue to subsidize their domestic aerospace industries

In spite of efforts by the World Trade Organization and other free-trade conventions, governments will continue to support their own national champions in the aerospace industry, using approaches tailored to their national circumstances. Europe will provide launch aid to Airbus, the United States will award rich defense contracts to Boeing and Lockheed, China will ensure that international manufacturing work is placed at Xian, Shengyan, Shanghai, and Harbin, and the governments of Brazil and Canada will provide financial support for Embraer and Bombardier. Competitors will continue to protest that direct and indirect subsidies violate international agreements.

Government customers will insist upon offset programs and other forms of industrial participation

The overwhelming majority of big international defense sales will include customer requirements that local firms participate in industrial work related to the procurement. Customer insistence on industrial participation will also become commonplace in large civil aircraft sales to countries such as China and Japan, where the governments have historically maintained linkage between airline purchases and the well-being of the national aerospace industries. Future offset programs will progressively involve local firms as integral partners, often involving risk-sharing participation, rather than as arm's-length subcontractors.

Aerospace products will continue to change rapidly as new technologies become available. However, radical changes in airliner design are unlikely

Over the first 60 years of the aerospace industry, the shape and technological nature of passenger transports changed radically, from wooden biplanes, to unpressurized metal-skinned monoplanes, to intercontinental multi-reciprocating-engine airliners, to high-altitude, multi-engined, swept-wing jets. However, since the introduction of these earliest civil jet transports in the post-war era, personified by the British Comet and the Boeing 707, the fundamental design formula for commercial airliners has changed comparatively little. Today's transports have more efficient engines, digital cockpits, refined aerodynamics, and advanced structural materials, but in most respects they remain very similar to their antecedents introduced in the 1950s. Physical and economic factors dictate that today's civil aircraft shapes and layouts will remain standard for the foreseeable future. Although technology is readily available to produce radical supersonic shapes and enormous blended-wing-to-fuselage bulk carriers, economic factors and consumer preferences seem to indicate that future civil transport aircraft will overwhelmingly operate in the high subsonic speed domain at altitudes less than 45,000 feet, and will have today's standard swept wing and tail layout. The design concept will continue to be refined and improved, but will remain recognizable to today's passengers.

In military aerospace, electronics, communications, navigations, and rotorcraft, however, the story will be profoundly different, as new technologies continue to emerge, mature, and manifest themselves as new products or significant changes to existing products:

- Unmanned aerospace vehicles, or UAVs, will grow into a major segment of defense aerospace, and will eventually find a place in civil aerospace.
- Satellite communications will grow, but at a rate less than the unrealistic forecasts of the 1990s. The market segments for satellite manufacture and launch will benefit, and satellite-related technologies such as GPS, satellite communications, and television transmission will exploit the technology and continue to expand into new applications.

- Helicopters will become safer and more comfortable, and will benefit from improved air traffic control regimes that will enable them to better apply their capabilities to fly directly from point to point.
- Tiltrotors, the hybrid of fixed-wing turboprops and conventional rotary-wing helicopters, will overcome lingering technical obstacles and will find broad application, initially in military service, but soon thereafter in civil applications.
- Mini jets will rapidly emerge as an important new market segment at the market overlap of general aviation and business jets. The small new jets will find acceptance by affluent private owners, air taxi services, corporations, and fractional ownership enterprises.
- Integration of systems will expand continuously into every segment of the aerospace market, and the value of the software component of products will increase proportionally. Capabilities for high-bandwidth data transmission, accurate sensors, high-throughput processors, mass data storage, digitization of data, and standardized data busses will enable full integration of systems in which all nodes communicate with each other, report meaningful information, and permit action.
- Self test and diagnosis of systems will continue to expand as one of the many tangible benefits of systems integration, as on-board diagnosis systems enable aircraft to detect and identify equipment failures or incipient problems, automatically report specific required maintenance action, and in some cases adjust aircraft operation to minimize adverse impact of the failure until it is fixed. Positive implications for cost, effectiveness, and rapidity of aircraft maintenance will be enormous.
- New materials will continue to be developed and introduced into aerospace products, resulting in lower weights, increased durability, and improved damage tolerance. In civil aerospace, where cost is generally a more sensitive consideration than for military applications, manufacturers will aggressively develop means to lower production costs through the use of new materials.
- Engines and avionics will continue their long-term trends towards greater reliability and longer service life, as better designs, improved materials, closer tolerances in the manufacturing process, and improved sensors and software are incorporated into products.

Low-cost overseas competitors will continue to grow in the Maintenance, Repair, and Overhaul (MRO) segment

Airlines under constant financial pressures will increasingly search for ways to reduce maintenance costs by out-sourcing. As qualified repair centers continue to emerge in Asia, aircraft owners will consider these competitors as they evaluate financial alternatives, and will send their aircraft offshore for heavy maintenance if a compelling financial motivation exists.

Innovative financing methods will evolve to address changing circumstances

As tax laws, customer financial circumstances, and world economic conditions change, financial institutions and aircraft sellers will find creative new ways to finance aircraft under terms advantageous to the customer. Today's financial instruments will become obsolete as the market adapts to tomorrow's circumstances.

Off-balance-sheet ownership will become increasingly common

As the cost of ownership of aircraft rises, and as innovative financing and leasing options enable operators to have access to aircraft without actually owning them, operators will increasingly choose to forego ownership. Customers of all sorts, particularly airlines but also government customers for military aircraft, will increasingly choose to use aircraft that they do not own, and which do not appear on their balance sheets. Titles to aircraft will increasingly repose with leasing companies, financial institutions, fractional ownership corporations, or with financing arms of the aircraft manufacturers themselves.

An important secondary consequence of this separation of ownership and operation will be increasing concentration of buying power on the demand side of the market. As a counterbalance to the concentrated oligopolistic selling power of the small number of sellers, vast buying power will repose with a small number of leasing companies and financial institutions, who will exploit their power to negotiate favorable pricing and terms from the sellers.

The colorful historical entrepreneurial tradition of the aerospace industry will be replaced by bottom-line emphasis

At the dawn of the twenty-first century, virtually all of the prior century's aerospace entrepreneurs have been replaced by professional managers strictly accountable to boards of directors that expect unfailing focus on bottom-line results. Gone are the days in which a Donald Douglas, a Howard Hughes, or a Henri Zeigler could draw on his personal force of character and belief in a concept to bring an aircraft to market In the modern era of multi-billion-dollar aircraft development costs and skeptical financial analysts, all aircraft launch decisions will be the result of consensus approvals by committee.

Quantitative analysis in the selling process will expand

Sophisticated buyers will increasingly utilize quantitative methods and operational analysis to arrive at purchasing decisions, and sellers will vie to provide analysis and data to support their products. International buyers will embrace concepts such as life-cycle costing, and will utilize intricate quantitative models to consider a wide range of variables having an effect upon cost-effectiveness or profitability of competing products over their hypothetical periods of ownership. Personal relationships between buyers and sellers will remain important as an essential conduit of information between the parties, but the buyer will require hard analytical data to support his ultimate purchase decision, and will be expected to present the data to his board of directors or senior government officials as he justifies and supports his decision. Gone are the days of seat-of-the-pants judgments by purchasing executives based upon personal biases, intuition, and friendships with old cronies.

Uncontrollable exogenous factors will continue to affect markets

The aerospace industry will continue to experience major impact from external factors such as wars, terrorism, fuel prices, availability of airport slots, and international political relationships. These factors will have the consequence of accentuating the inherently cyclical nature of the aerospace business.

Corruption will remain a reality

Increased international vigilance and scrutiny at all levels, supported by international conventions and national laws, will reduce the extent of blatant corruption in the industry. However, the opportunities and potential rewards for corrupt activity will remain irresistible to some elements within both buyer and seller communities. The values of aerospace contracts will always be large enough to tempt customer decision-makers in government and industry to sell their influence, and the financial incentives and competitive pressures for sellers will remain enormous. Increased attention and visibility will reduce the extent of corruption, but it will remain an unfortunate characteristic of the industry for the foreseeable future.

Change will occur, and the next generation of aerospace managers, like every generation before them, will experience the adventure of awesome new technology, business challenges, and fascinating international relationships with world-changing implications. No doubt some of the readers of this humble book will be the leaders of that new generation of the aerospace industry. The author, who will be observing you from his rocking chair, sincerely wishes you good luck and Godspeed.

Havre de Grace, Maryland
August 2006

Index